SS

‖‖‖‖‖‖‖‖‖‖‖‖‖‖‖‖‖‖‖
D1414552

STUDIES IN HISTORY, ECONOMICS AND
PUBLIC LAW

Edited by the
FACULTY OF POLITICAL SCIENCE
OF COLUMBIA UNIVERSITY

Number 555

RELATIONS BETWEEN THE FEDERAL AND STATE COURTS

BY

MITCHELL WENDELL

RELATIONS
BETWEEN THE FEDERAL
AND STATE COURTS

BY

MITCHELL WENDELL

AMS PRESS
NEW YORK

COLUMBIA UNIVERSITY
STUDIES IN THE
SOCIAL SCIENCES

555

The Series was formerly known as *Studies in History,
Economics and Public Law.*

Reprinted with the permission of Columbia University Press
From the edition of 1949, New York
First AMS EDITION published 1968
Manufactured in the United States of America

H
31
.C7
#555
1968

Library of Congress Catalogue Card Number: 68-58637

AMS PRESS, INC.
New York, N.Y. 10003

PREFACE

I<small>T</small> is a commonplace that American federalism has a large judicial ingredient. The Constitution itself is a legal document and the publicity given to landmark decisions of the Supreme Court interpreting some of the more familiar provisions such as the Commerce Clause, the Implied Powers Clause, and the Tenth Amendment has brought the realization that judicial decision often sets the pattern for national and state action. But the fact that the celebrated constitutional cases have ultimately been fought out in the United States Supreme Court has fostered the seldom spoken although pervasive belief that the primary contribution of the judiciary to our federalism has been made via the interpretation of basic constitutional principles in the Supreme Court. This highest tribunal in our federal judiciary has undoubtedly exerted a primary influence on the character of our federal system by its historic interpretations of the key clauses in the Constitution but it should also be remembered that the United States Supreme Court is only one tribunal among many and that both lower federal courts and state courts contribute significantly to the operation of our federal system. They also interpret the Constitution and in addition, they perform the painstaking tasks necessary to the day by day adjustment of federal-state judicial relations.

In reality the task of both federal and state judiciaries is twofold: 1. The delimiting of the respective range of federal and state power, and 2. The division of judicial jurisdiction between Nation and States. Of course, both of these tasks are performed within a framework provided by the Constitution and legislative enactments, but the brunt of the labor still falls on the courts themselves. The first of the above mentioned judicial activities is, for reasons already indicated, fairly well understood. However, the public significance of the second task is little understood. The people who know most about the functioning of the federal and state judiciaries and the re-

5

lations between these court systems are the lawyers. They have been led to study the organization and jurisdiction of federal and state courts because it is necessary for them to do so if they are to serve the needs of their clients. However, the researches of the legal profession seldom treat judicial federalism in such a way as to bring out its governmental significance. Their interests lie in another direction and their inquiries are shaped by the needs of private practitioners of the law. Most political scientists, on the other hand, are not familiar with the more technical aspects of the law and so have been led to assume that the bulk of the litigation in the lower federal courts and in the state courts has little or nothing to teach us about the nature and operation of our federal system. It is in the hope of shedding some light on this neglected phase of our judicial federalism that the present study has been made.

We in the United States can derive obvious advantages from a more thorough understanding of our federalism for the simple reason that it is our own governmental system and a closer knowledge of its character should lead to an even more efficient use of our present institutions. But conditions in the world today disclose even more far-reaching purposes for an examination into the operation of American federalism. The recently created Dominion of India, for example, is at present faced with the necessity of building a stable government that will take account of the manifold traditions and political desires of her people. The experience with national-local adjustment in this country may consequently be of value to this new government in planning its future. It may also be noted that the Dutch have declared their intention of reorganizing their empire along federal lines. Should the disturbed situation in Indonesia eventually be resolved by resort to federation, American experience, along with that in other federal countries, would be of value there too.

Indeed, the history of the ill fated League of Nations and the present strivings of the world community in the United

Nations evidence a growing awareness that comprehensive international organization is necessary if all peoples are to live at peace. But these strivings also indicate that if cooperation on a global scale is ever to become effective, it must be achieved through a powerful yet flexible international structure that will permit the widely divergent views and aspirations of the world's peoples to find their places within a single governmental framework. It is probably too much to hope that world government will become a reality in the near future. But if ever it is to come, federalism may provide an answer to the need for flexibility and compromise.

I am indebted to many persons without whose generous assistance and guidance this book could not have been written. Among those to whom I wish to say a special word of thanks for their contributions to the present work are Professor Arthur W. Macmahon of Columbia University under whose general guidance the book was written and whose painstaking criticism of the entire manuscript has been invaluable to me; Professors Elliot E. Cheatham, Herbert Wechsler, and Noel T. Dowling who read and criticized various portions of the manuscript in rough draft and who have also been kind enough to give me the benefit of their opinions of the completed work; and Professors John D. Millett and Henry S. Commager, who have also read and criticized the completed manuscript. I also owe a special vote of thanks to my parents who suffered through many tedious hours of correction and retyping of the manuscript in each of its several stages of preparation.

CONTENTS

PART I

Introduction

PART II

Access to the Federal Courts

PART III

Swift v. Tyson: An Experiment in Nation-wide Uniformity

PART IV

Erie v. Tompkins: A More Modest Uniformity

PART I. INTRODUCTION

CHAPTER I

A DUAL SYSTEM OF COURTS AND LAW ENFORCEMENT

"... it is manifest that during the time men live without a common Power they are in that condition which is called Warre." [1]

" The final Cause, End, or Design of men, ... in the introduction of that restraint upon themselves, (in which we see them live in Commonwealths,) is the foresight of their own preservation, and of a more contented life thereby; that is to say, of getting themselves out from that miserable condition of Warre, which is necessarily consequent to the natural Passions of men, when there is no visible Power to keep them in awe, and tie them by fear of punishment to the performance of their Covenants, and observation of those Laws of Nature ..." [2]

These remarks of Thomas Hobbes were obviously authored in a bygone age. Archaic spelling and punctuation put the modern reader on notice that he is not examining contemporary material; but even more important, the substance of these passages belongs to a political philosophy of former times.

1 Hobbes, " *The Leviathan* " (Waller ed., 1904), p. 83.

2 *Ibid.*, p. 115.

Present day writers are not in the habit of explaining social and political phenomena in terms of Natural Law and even those ideologists who assert that human beings are basically evil do not describe government as a contractual arrangement.

Despite the centuries between Hobbes' time and our own, his writing can be of more than historical interest. It can remind us of something that is just as true today as it was in the seventeenth century: namely that a primary purpose of government is the preservation of public order. The work done by our judiciaries is directed to this end. In the days when the courts were virtually the only agencies of law enforcement, a discerning observer had less difficulty in appreciating the governmental interest in all lawsuits. But today the tremendously expanded content of the law, its specialized character, and our growing preoccupation with law enforcement by administrative processes have made it progressively more difficult to understand the close relation between the routine work of the courts and the totality of government. Nonetheless, such a relation does exist, and it is as significant today as it ever was.

Government employs many instruments useful in promoting the public order. Some of these instruments, notably police forces, are clearly intended to serve this purpose. The governmental character of their activities is manifest because they furnish elementary protection against outbreaks of violence. Other agencies of government also promote public order, but their methods are more subtle and the effects of their work less obvious. These agencies do not apprehend criminals or keep people from driving on the wrong side of the road, their concern is rather with the economic and social fabric of national life. By regulating some aspect of community living, they attempt to obviate confusion, to provide orderly patterns of human intercourse, and to produce a politically stable society in which individuals may know what their rights and duties are and, possessing such knowledge, be induced or coerced into acting as reliable members of society.

PUBLIC SIGNIFICANCE OF LITIGATION

All of the work done by our courts is of governmental significance. One might suppose that public support and operation of judicial systems would be conclusive evidence of a general awareness of this fact, but such is not the case. Despite universal acceptance of the traditional doctrine that holds the Judiciary to be one of the three great departments of Government, most people appear to believe that much of the litigation flowing through our courts is strictly private in nature and consequently of no concern to the community at large. There are two factors that have played a leading part in fostering this misunderstanding of the judicial process. They are:

1. The intricacy of the law which makes it difficult or impossible for untrained observers to follow legal proceedings.

2. The tendency to regard the practice of law as a private business.

These obstacles to widespread understanding of the judicial function are at a minimum when courts are administering the criminal law. Of course, the intricacies of criminal procedure make it impossible for the general public to follow every detail of this type of litigation but such complete knowledge does not seem to be necessary to an appreciation of the public significance of the enforcement of our criminal laws. It is apparent that whatever the mechanics of the judicial process may be, the outcome is a determination of innocence or guilt. An understanding of this objective of judicial action does not depend on specialized legal knowledge. In fact the governmental nature of enforcement processes is well attested to by the appearance of the State itself as plaintiff. It is recognized that such government initiative is necessary because murder, rape, arson, burglary, etc. present imminent danger to the public safety.

Government agencies also appear as litigants in a large number of civil suits. In many instances the reason for public initiative is similar to that which motivates government participation in criminal prosecution: namely, the stopping of anti-social conduct. It sometimes happens that such a goal may best be achieved by the use of civil rather than criminal remedies. For example, the Anti-Trust Division of the Federal Department of Justice seems to be much more interested in securing injunctions than in making violators of the Sherman Act and companion statutes submit to fine or imprisonment. This preference for the civil remedy rests on the belief that in the anti-trust field court orders directing future compliance with the law are more effective in combating monopoly than punishment for past offenses.

In other types of litigation, Government appears in a capacity similar to that of a private suitor. A state has contracted for the purchase of office equipment and a dispute relating to the meaning of the agreement arises. A pedestrian slips on an icy street and sues the city. Identical cases in contract or tort occur between private individuals daily and when Government appears as a party in these types of litigation its interests in them are little different from those of private suitors.

It is generally assumed that the vast stream of litigation to which no government agency is a party is of no public interest. The role of our courts as umpires rather than as combatants in legal proceedings does much to encourage such an assumption. If someone breaks a contract or commits a tort, our courts initiate no action. From this inactivity it is possible to infer that violations of non-criminal laws are of no public concern, but this is certainly untrue. The stability of our entire economic system would be placed in serious jeopardy and perhaps be completely destroyed if businessmen were unable to rely on the performance of the multitude of agreements which define the rights and responsibilities existing within our economic structure. Persons who have suffered injury to themselves or to their property also rely upon judicial settlement of their grievances as the proven substitute for self help and violence. Yet in the face of continual violation of contract and tort law, no government agency initiates remedial action—

Why? An example of our legal system in operation may suggest the answer.

A wholesale grocer refuses to deliver food stuffs to retailer Jones in accordance with the terms of a contract made between them. The wholesaler's refusal is a violation of law. In a legal system organized differently from our own, it is conceivable that some public agency similar to a police force or a district attorney's office would watch for contract breakers and see to their prosecution. But we assume that no organ of government is likely to find out about such violations of law as speedily or as surely as Jones who is certain to feel the effect of his wholesaler's conduct. Experience has taught us that we can rely on Jones to bring his grievance to court and so place the law breaker in the public eye. Moreover, since society is more interested in seeing that Jones is compensated for any loss he may have suffered than in sending the wholesaler to prison, it is feasible to rely on private initiative in bringing such violations of law to light and to rely on the self interest of private persons to finance the prosecution.

Law enforcement by ordinary lawsuit necessarily permits private individuals considerable leeway in specific cases. Every prospective plaintiff must decide whether he will call the machinery of public justice into operation and, in any given case, he may choose to overlook the violation of law. As a result, the precise order and nature of the business in our courts is largely fortuitous. In matters of common law the elaboration of principles is haphazard, and where the meaning of a statute is in doubt, it is often difficult to know when an authoritative judicial interpretation will be forthcoming. But even though private litigation provides an administration of justice without unified direction from a single government agency, the character and substance of non criminal law enforcement remain in governmental hands. To cite only a few examples:

1. A person who is injured by a negligently driven automobile may not receive compensation for his injury if his

carelessness in crossing the street against the light contributed to the accident. This is not a rule made by private citizens but is law emanating from our legislatures and courts.

2. A person who owes a sum of money will be forced to pay his creditor if the latter resorts to a court of law. In issuing its judgment the judicial branch of government is giving effect to public policy as declared in statutes and common law.

3. If two men bet with one another regarding the outcome of of a horse-race and the loser subsequently refuses to pay, the winner may not prevail upon a court to render judgment for the amount of the debt. The wager may be in the form of a valid contract, but the courts will not enforce gambling contracts because such agreements are against public policy.

INCREASING JUDICIAL BUSINESS

There was a time when the private lawsuit provided virtually the only vehicle for the enforcement of non criminal law. During the latter part of the nineteenth century, however, federal and state governments began a much closer supervision of the economy than had formerly been practiced. It seemed probable that regulatory programs would not succeed unless specialized governmental organizations were empowered to take the initiative in their enforcement. As a result new agencies, many of them administrative in character, came to hold an important place in the process of government. But even where the need for better coordinated policy execution has dictated the use of newer law enforcement technicques, the private suit is still retained as an additional tool for the administration of non-criminal law. The Anti-Trust Division of the Federal Department of Justice is charged with the enforcement of the Sherman Act and allied statutes. Yet federal law also provides that persons injured by the violation of the anti-trust laws may sue the violator and recover treble damages.[3]

3 38 Stat. 731 (1914).

During World War II, the Emergency Price Control Act was administered by the Office of Price Administration, but this law also provided for the bringing of private suits for treble damages.[4] The Fair Labor Standards Act is enforced by the Wages and Hours Division of the Department of Labor. Nevertheless, this statute also provides that persons who do not receive the minimum compensation to which the law entitles them may sue their employers and obtain back wages plus penalties.[5] An obvious purpose of these inducements to the use of private suits is to encourage enforcement of these laws without need for burdening the newer enforcement agencies.

The growth of these new enforcement techniques was accompanied by a steady increase in the regular judicial establishments. Regulation agencies have themselves contributed to the business of the courts because administrative rulings are often subject to judicial review and also because administrative agencies often initiate suits designed to punish violators of the law or to force compliance with statutes and administrative orders. But even more important has been the growth of litigation in the vast areas of the law wherein the private lawsuit remains the primary means of law enforcement. In the early days of our Republic, the members of the United States Supreme Court functioned as lower court judges in addition to discharging their appellate duties. By the 1880s the Supreme Court, its members relieved of all lower court duties, was three years in arrears in its work.[6] Today this tremendous burden has been partly lifted from the shoulders of our nine highest judges, but only by the creation of Circuit Courts of Appeals and by giving the Supreme Court drastic powers to curtail the exercise of its own jurisdiction through almost

4 Emergency Price Control Act, Sec. 205(e), 56 Stat. 23 (1942) as amended 58 Stat. 640 (1944).

5 Fair Labor Standards Act, Sec. 16(b), 52 Stat. 1060 (1938).

6 Taft, *Possible and Needed Reforms in the Administration of Justice in the Federal Courts*, 8 ABAJ 601, 602 (1922).

ruthless use of its authority to deny petitions for certiorari. State court systems have also grown apace. Most obvious, of course, has been the increase from thirteen judicial systems in the original states to the forty-eight made necessary by the present number of states. However, this has not been the full measure of the increase. As population has grown, and the flood of business traceable to an ever more intense economic activity throughout the country has increased the load to be carried by our local courts, the judiciaries in each of our states have expanded their personnel and organization in much the same manner as the federal courts.

The expansion of our federal and state judiciaries has aggravated a number of defects in our court systems and has created difficulties unknown to the less burdened judiciaries of former times. Many of these problems center about the need for procedural reform within a single judicial system; such matters will receive only collateral attention here. An entire set of problems, however, are traceable to the nature of our federal system, and it is these which will be of direct concern to us in this study.

A Dual Judiciary

From the very beginning of government under the Constitution we have had complete sets of federal and state courts. Perhaps the need to establish a strong national government, the desire of the states to retain as much of their independence as possible, and our theory of a tripartite separation of powers have made this duality in our judicial system a logical development. If it is proper for both federal and state governments to have their own legislatures and executives, it would seem equally proper for these governments to have separate judicial departments. In this way both federal and state governments can make their own laws, enforce and interpret them. Each government thereby gives the appearance of possessing a complete organization, of being an independent sovereignty. Nevertheless, the adoption of federalism did not make a dual system of courts inevitable. Brazil whose judicial system once resembled that of the United States has abolished all lower federal courts with the exception of those in the Federal District and in the Territories.[7] Venezuela has gone to the opposite extreme and completely nationalized the administration of justice.[8] And the Weimar Constitution adopted by Germany in 1919, although permitting the enlargement of a federal judiciary, envisaged law enforcement as primarily a function of the states.[9]

Even our own Federal Constitution does not make the establishment of an extensive national judiciary a necessity. Article III provides that " The Judicial Power of the United States, shall be vested in one Supreme Court, and in such inferior Courts as the Congress may from time to time ordain and establish. . . ." [10] This language does not compel the establishment of any federal tribunals in addition to the Supreme Court. Accordingly, it is conceivable—although, to be sure, not likely—that Congress might abolish the United States District Courts, the Circuit Courts of Appeals, and the special tribunals which it has created. That would leave us with a system which, at least in formal outline, would resemble the Brazilian.

But whatever their uses in other federal systems may be, plans to make the judicial department of either federal or state government auxiliary in character and to center the judicial function in one part of our federal system have never gained recognition in the United States. In this country the federal government and each of the states has a complete system of

7 Riesenfeld and Hazard, *Federal Courts in Foreign Systems*, 13 Law and Contemp. Problems 29, 48 (1948).

8 *Ibid.*, p. 54.

9 Article 19, Sec. 1 of the Weimar Constitution of 1919 supplies the basis for the development of federal courts. However, the administration of justice in the Weimar Republic was primarily a function of the states. Oppenheimer, *The Constitution of the German Republic* (1923), p. 166.

10 U. S. Constit., Art. III.

courts including trial and appellate tribunals. Yet our various court systems cannot be as independent of one another as they would be if each of them belonged to a separate foreign country. Even though the United States is organized as a federalism, it is a single nation and the various units within the federal structure must coordinate their activities so as to produce a sound and congruous administration of the law. In order to accomplish this result, the total labor of government is divided between the nation and the states. Each government is responsible for the tasks alloted to it. In the judicial field, the Constitution and laws of Congress enacted pursuant thereto mark out the jurisdiction of federal courts. The states retain judicial power in all fields not pre-empted by the federal government.

This division of labor is for the same general purpose as the entire division of power between nation and states. Certain problems are primarily of local concern and federalism holds that it is best to let local governments handle them. Other problems are of national scope, and these should be within the province of a central government. As a matter of theory, this principle appears simple enough, but if it is to be successfully applied, some way must be found to decide what is of predominantly local character and what constitutes a national problem. Even in countries organized along unitary lines, the requirements of practical administration make it necessary for central governments to decide how much authority may be delegated to localities. But in a federalism the formal division of powers between two levels of government makes the problem more acute. Moreover, it appears that no matter how skillful the architects of a federal system may be, there is bound to be an area where state and national power meet and where conflicts between the two must be resolved.

American experience contains ample proof that this border area is an extensive one. Students of government know that in the constitutional field a number of crucial problems never seem to be completely solved. The line between interstate and intrastate commerce is an ever shifting one; the need for balancing the legitimate taxing power of the states against the federal commerce power is continuous, and the task of finding some way for the police power to operate in the face of many infringing national powers is constant. Points of possible friction between the parts of our federal system appear to be almost infinite.

It is perhaps less well understood but abundantly true that actual or potential conflicts between federal and state interests exist in virtually all sectors of the law. Admiralty is supposed to be a federal preserve, but do the states lose all interest in the enforcement of their mechanic's lien laws just because the property in dispute happens to be a vessel? Only state courts exercise jurisdiction in probate, but can a federal court assume jurisdiction if the United States claims property which is due to pass to private persons under the terms of a will? Federal courts have exclusive jurisdiction in bankruptcy; does this mean that commercial rights created by state law cannot be protected merely because someone is bankrupt? An imposing list of such questions can be asked. However, in order to illustrate one aspect of the problems raised by our dual judicial system, it may be in order to summarize an actual case.

Several years ago an Omaha radio station changed hands. One of the old owners believed that the sale had been accompanied by fraud and brought suit for the station's return. A Nebraska court found that there had been fraud as claimed and ordered the defendants to do " all things necessary " to restore the radio station properties to their former owners.[11] The rendering of such a decree seemed to be clearly within the province of Nebraska courts. The applicable law of fraud was Nebraska law. The law governing transfers of property within the state was Nebraska law. But the properties here involved were those of a radio station, and among them was a

11 *Johnson* v. *Radio Station WOW*, 144 Neb. 406, 13 NW2d 556 (1944).

broadcasting license issued by the Federal Communications Commission. On appeal to the United States Supreme Court, that tribunal held that the transfer of the license was a matter of federal interest and that the execution of the Nebraska decree must be stayed in order to give the FCC an opportunity to decide who should receive the license.[12] As everyone concerned recognized, this was a crucial question because transmitters, microphones, leases of station facilities, and all other equipment were of no use without the permit to broadcast. When it received the mandate of the United States Supreme Court, the highest court of Nebraska announced that the federal tribunal had misunderstood the nature of the case. In its view there was no matter of federal concern. This was a simple case involving only the transfer of property—routine business for state courts to handle without interference from the Federal Judiciary. Consequently, the Nebraska court decided to treat the opinion of the Federal Supreme Court as merely advisory and proceeded to order enforcement of its original judgment.[13] Obviously, federal and state views of this matter were contradictory. How should the controversy have been resolved?

The successful operation of a federal system requires coordinated action by the central and local governments. Where it is possible to consign an activity to the sole care of either nation or states, the decision as to which government shall discharge the task must be an appropriate one arrived at through the use of recognizable standards for the determination of proper spheres of action. Where it seems best for nation and states to operate concurrently, care must be taken lest the actions of each government conflict with those of other governments within the federal structure. Federal-state coordination is as important in the judicial field as it is in other

12 *Johnson* v. *Radio Station WOW*, 326 US 120 (1945).

13 *Johnson* v. *Radio Station WOW*, 146 Neb. 429, 19 NW2d 853 (1946) commented on in 9 Detroit L. J. 106 (1946).

areas of government. The administration of justice is the function of all courts, but our judiciaries cannot accomplish their assigned tasks unless they are sure of the extent of their jurisdiction and of the ways in which they are to exercise it. Moreover, the people who rely on the courts for the protection of their rights must know which judicial system—state or federal—is equipped to hear each grievance as it arises and to make a generalized law come alive by applying it to specific situations.

CHAPTER II

BUILDING RESPECT FOR THE FEDERAL COURTS

In 1789 our federal system was new and untried; there was little assurance that it would prove to be a workable plan of government. Despite the attempts of Hamilton and Madison to discover historic and contemporary examples of federally organized countries,[1] the plain fact was that the Constitution outlined a system of national-local relationships quite different from anything then known in governmental experience. Would it be possible to keep the states and the national government in balance so that they could operate together with a minimum of friction? That was the all important question.

The ability of the states to maintain their virility and power, although it has become a question of some seriousness today, was not then open to genuine doubt. Even in 1789 the original thirteen states had long histories behind them. They had existed as colonies for a century and a half or more and as virtually independent states since the Revolution. The people were already accustomed to think of Massachusetts, New York or Virginia as the governments to which they owed allegiance; state patriotism and obedience to state laws were an established fact. It might be challenged, as indeed it was in Shays' Rebellion, but the legal power of a state to put down insurrection was undoubted. The strength of the Federal Government on the other hand was not so obvious. It had been granted a number of powers not possessed by the preceding Confederation, but the ability of the national government to bring these powers into practical operation was still to be demonstrated. The Constitution had been adopted by a narrow margin and only after the bitterest of struggles. The numerous opponents of a strong

1 See Hamilton and Madison, *The Federalist*, Nos. 18, 19, 20.

central government were far from reconciled and their willingness to submit to the new system was open to doubt.

It is apparent that in 1787-1788 a majority of the politically powerful people in the country were in sympathy with a strong national government; for had this not been so, the Constitution would never have been adopted. However, this support of the federal government did not come from any desire for a vigorous regime which would pre-empt all power and leave the states with little freedom of action. The Constitution was rather a reaction against the unfortunate conditions prevailing under the Articles of Confederation. Somehow there had to be an end to chaos, and if the federal government devised by the Constitution promised to accomplish this purpose, it was worth a try. But once the new national government was established and began to address itself to the specific problems of the day, would the central authority be able to hold its own in the battle for power with the states? It might be that men who had seen a general need for effective national government would begin to make exceptions when asked to decide on specific issues.

If Congress and the President had always refrained from using the federal power when its exercise was likely to incur displeasure in the states, there would have been little danger of collision with local interests. But the federal government did not always decide in favor of inaction in matters that might offend the states, and when such controversial issues arose, the problem became one of the authority of the national government and the capacity for defiance by the states. This situation was aggravated during the early years of the Republic by the fact that the national government was in the hands of the Federalists while many of the state governments were dominated by Jeffersonians. Of course, Jefferson and his party came to national power in 1801, but the appointive federal judiciary continued under the control of hold-over Federalists for some years. As a result there was increased opportunity for strife in the field of judicial federal-state relations.

In the final analysis, whether federal law would be obeyed in the states depended on the extent of national power. This fact becomes plain when we remember that it was force that overcame the Whiskey Rebellion of 1794, the Nullification Movement in South Carolina, and the attempt at Secession of 1861-1865.

The three branches of the central government were not in equal control of instruments useful in the coercion of the states. Congress had the power to raise tax revenues by direct contact with the citizenry. The President was Commander-in-Chief of the military establishment and could order it to enforce national policy. But the federal courts had neither the purse nor arms at their disposal.[2] How, then, were they to get unpopular judgments obeyed? Unless the national executive and legislature, both of which were in the hands of the rival Jeffersonians, could be persuaded to assist the courts, and indeed even where such help was forthcoming, the principal insurance of obedience to the mandates of federal courts was necessarily the respect which the national judiciary could command.

In the decades immediately following the adoption of the Constitution, the federal judiciary was still untried. Under the Articles of Confederation, the only semblance of a national court system was to be found in a single tribunal charged with the duty of hearing appeals in prize cases;[3] there was nothing more. During the early years under the Constitution, there had not yet been time for a national judiciary to win the esteem of the states and the people. Indeed, some idea of the prestige

2 See Warren, *The Supreme Court and Sovereign States* (1924), pp. 78-79.

3 Articles of Confederation, Art. IX. In addition to authorizing the creation of a prize court, this Article also provided for trial of piracies by a court of the national government. But in practice, jurisdiction over piracy cases was actually exercised by state courts. Frank, *Historical Bases of the Federal Judicial System*, 13 Law and Contemp. Problems 1, 8 (1948). A cumbersome procedure of the settlement of boundary disputes among the states was also provided, but this machinery did not contemplate the creation of a regularly functioning court.

of the federal bench may be had from the fact that one of the original appointees to the Supreme Court, John Rutledge of South Carolina, resigned his office in order to accept the Chief Justiceship of his home state on the ground that the latter position was a post of greater importance.[4] In this same connection it may also be noted that Chief Justice Oliver Ellsworth left the Supreme Court in 1800 disgusted with the impotence of that tribunal.[5]

POTENTIAL AND ACTUAL JURISDICTION OF FEDERAL COURTS

The Constitution was generous in its grant of judicial power to the United States. The extent of this grant is to be measured by the scope of the potential jurisdiction permitted federal courts as described in Article III of the Constitution. This potential jurisdiction may be both original and appellate and encompasses a multitude of situations to which the judicial power may be addressed. The original jurisdiction of the Supreme Court is reserved for a limited number of special situations, the most important among them, if we take its effect on the operation of the federal system as our criterion, being the suit by one state against another state, or between the United States and a state. Indeed, the mere suggestion that the sovereign states were to be amenable to federal legal process was of considerable significance in establishing the potential political importance of the Supreme Court. Much wider, however, was the scope of the appellate jurisdiction permitted to the nation's highest tribunal. This jurisdiction was of two kinds: (1) that depending on the character of the parties to a litigation, and (2) that depending on the subject matter of a dispute. Suits between citizens of different states, which may be prosecuted in the federal courts without regard to their subject matter, form the most familiar examples of

4 Warren, *The Supreme Court in United States History* (1922), pp. 56-57.
5 *Ibid.*

the first type. Suits arising under the Constitution and federal laws are the most common examples of the second type.

In describing the national judicial power as it was to be in actual practice, the Constitution was not nearly so helpful. Here, as in other phases of our federal structure, Constitutional provisions provide an indispensable prelude to an understanding of the operation of the governmental machinery. But our fundamental law mentions only one tribunal by name: the Supreme Court of the United States. Whether there were to be any inferior federal courts and wherein their duties might consist, were matters left to the discretion of Congress.[6] That body would clearly have remained within the bounds of its authority had it decided to leave all judicial activity not originally placed within the province of the Supreme Court to the state judiciaries. Undoubtedly, this would have worked a practical limitation on the exercise of federal power more severe than we have known at any time in our history since 1789.

STATE GOVERNORS AND LEGISLATURES vs. FEDERAL COURTS

However, the First Congress did not propose to give the states quite this degree of freedom. It passed a Judiciary Act[7] creating a system of lower federal courts and conferring jurisdiction over suits between citizens of different states (diversity jurisdiction) upon them. Strangely enough, the power to determine cases and controversies arising under the Constitution and laws of the United States was not conferred upon the inferior national courts in 1789, and, indeed, remained in the primary possession of state judiciaries until 1875.[8] Even in this instance, however, it could be said that the federal interest was protected by the right to appeal to the Supreme Court.

The first test of the power of the Supreme Court in an area of political interest to the states came in 1792. In the next year,

6 U. S. Constit., Art. III, Sec. 1. "The Judicial Power of the United States, shall be vested in one Supreme Court, and such inferior Courts as the Congress may from time to time ordain and establish..."

7 1 Stat. 73 (1789).

8 18 Stat. 470 (1875).

the case of *Chisholm* v. *Georgia*[9] was decided by the Supreme Court. This was a suit by a South Carolinean against the State of Georgia, brought in a federal court without the State's consent. Article III, Section 2 of the Constitution specifically provided that the Supreme Court shall have jurisdiction of suits between a state and citizens of another state but Georgia still contended that as a sovereign, it could not be sued without its consent. Accordingly, the Governor and Attorney-General, who had been duly served with legal process, steadfastly refused to appear. Nevertheless, the Supreme Court proceeded to render judgment for the South Carolinean.

States' rights sentiment throughout the country was sufficiently strong to make the Chisholm Case a politically explosive one even if the only question had been one of federal jurisdiction. There was, however, an additional element in the case that intensified the bitterness evoked by the suit. It so happened that the claim being pressed by the South Carolinean was in reality that of a British creditor and had accrued in a period covered by the Georgia expropriation law. This was one of many statutes passed by the states during and soon after the Revolutionary War absolving debtors from any liability to British creditors. These laws enjoyed strong popular favor both because they relieved many Americans from unwelcome obligations, and because anti-British sentiment was widespread. Of course, the Treaty of Peace of 1783 had provided for the payment of debts owing to British creditors but this provision of the Treaty was also unpopular. Two points in the Chisholm Decision stood out, and neither of them was calculated to increase affection for the federal judiciary. The first observation to be made was that the Supreme Court had decided in favor of its power to compel a state to appear before a federal court; the second was that the decision had protected the rights of foreign creditors against American debtors.

9 2 Dall. 419 (1793).

The reaction to the Chisholm Case was immediate and drastic; the Eleventh Amendment to the Constitution was adopted. This constitutional provision is brief and speaks for itself:

" The Judicial power of the United States shall not be construed to extend to any suit in law or equity, commenced or prosecuted against one of the United States by Citizens of another State, or by Citizens or Subjects of any Foreign State."

This amendment of 1795 made a suit like that arising out of the Chisholm Episode impossible. A politically significant portion of the jurisdiction of the Supreme Court was withdrawn and, to this extent, the national judicial power was diminished. Open defiance of the federal judiciary by the states was averted, but this was achieved by eliminating the federal power. If the next decade or so was relatively free of clashes between the federal judiciary and the states, it was not because of any rapidly growing sentiment of national solidarity and allegiance to the central government. During this period, the theory that a state might nullify an act of Congress if it believed the legislation to be contrary to the Constitution gained its celebrated expression in the Virginia and Kentucky Resolutions.[10] This was also the time of the notorious Pickering Conspiracy [11] which demonstrated the looseness of the bonds holding the New England States to the Union. If these events did not produce open strife between the national judiciary and the judicial arms of the state governments, it was only because

10 For text see: 1 Commager, *Documents of American History* (4th ed., 1948), p. 178.

11 In 1804 Senator Timothy Pickering and a number of other Federalists laid plans for the secession of the northern states. However, the opposition of Hamilton to any action which would break up the Union and the disgrace of Aaron Burr, led to the abandonment of the project. See Prentiss, *Timothy Pickering As Leader of New England Federalism, 1800-1815* (1934), pp. 23-35. For a comprehensive account of this period see 2 Adams, *History of the United States During the Administrations of Thomas Jefferson and James Madison* (1909).

no cases involving controversial issues of states rights reached the Supreme Court at this time. But sooner or later, the smouldering political disturbances of the day were bound to find their mirror in legal controversy.

This time Pennsylvania was the storm center and land speculation was at the root of the trouble. In 1792 the Pennsylvania legislature had passed an act providing for the sale of public lands in small parcels.[12] The purpose of the enactment had been to encourage small farmers to settle the frontier areas in the western part of the state. In order to make it more likely that settlement would actually accompany the purchase of these homestead lots, the legislature had further provided that in order to perfect title to the tracts purchased under the act, the owners would have to work and improve the land for a period of years immediately following purchase.

This precaution, however, did not stop the speculators from acquiring much of the land. Working through its agents, the Holland Company bought 464,800 acres.[13] The Company's purpose was, of course, to resell its holdings to small farmers at advanced prices. In order to accomplish this project, the Company did procure some settlers; but due to the size, remoteness, and unstable conditions prevailing in the territory surrounding its tracts, was unable to meet the requirements of the law in anywhere near full measure.

Because of the virgin character of the territory, it was not customary for sales under the act to be evidenced by the type of deed familiar in real estate transactions of the present day. Purchasers obtained certificates from the state land office entitling them to claim a parcel of land anywhere in the area of the unsettled country provided only that no legitimate claimant had preceded the holder of such a certificate. As the Holland Company had failed to improve much of its land, it was only

12 An Act for the sale of the vacant lands within this Commonwealth (April 3, 1792), 3 Cranch 1.

13 See *Huidekoper's Lessee* v. *Douglass,* 3 Cranch 1, 12 (1805).

natural that holders of these general grants from the state should have settled upon the untenanted sections of the countryside claimed by the Company. The inevitable result of these conditions was dispute concerning the true ownership of these tracts.

In 1805 just such a case came before the Supreme Court of the United States.[14] In form the action was between Huidecoper's Lessee, (holder by virtue of the Holland Company's alleged title), and Douglass, (a settler on the land who founded his claim upon one of the land office's certificates). The aim of the suit was to force Douglass from the land, which could be done only if the Company's title was superior to the defendant's.

In order to excuse its failure to make the requisite settlement on the land, the Holland Company argued that Indian wars had made actual occupancy of the tracts impossible immediately after the receipt of its grants from the state and that under the terms of the Pennsylvania legislation, the Company was not required to effectuate the contemplated settlement when a cessation of hostilities made occupancy of the land feasible. This construction of the statute was contested by the defendant, was not definitely settled by the lower federal court, and so came to the Supreme Court for final disposition.

Chief Justice Marshall, speaking for a unanimous Court, upheld the Holland Company. In so doing, he accepted a dubious construction of the Pennsylvania law.[15] But even more

14 *Huidekoper's Lessee* v. *Douglass*, 3 Cranch 1 (1805).

15 The Pennsylvania statute reads in part as follows: Sec. IX. "And be it further enacted by the authority aforesaid, that no warrant or survey, to be issued or made in pursuance of this Act, for lands lying north and west of the rivers Ohio and Alleghany, and Conewango Creek, shall vest any title in or to the lands therein mentioned, unless the grantee has, prior to the date of such warrant, made, or caused to be made, or shall, within the space of two years next after the date of the same, make, or cause to be made, an actual settlement thereon, by clearing, fencing and cultivating, at least two acres for every hundred acres contained in one survey, erecting thereon a messuage for the habitation of man, and residing, or causing a family to

serious than this was the rough treatment accorded to the interest of the State of Pennsylvania. Because of the vital effect of this decision on its land policy, the Commonwealth had an obvious stake in the case. The presence of the Commonwealth's Attorney General as counsel for the defense gave some indication of the state's concern and, in fact, the Court actually referred to Pennsylvania's interest in the outcome, although it did so only in passing.[16] In its handling of the case, however, the Court treated the suit as a controversy solely between two private parties and proceeded to render judgment for one of them: the Holland Company.

The decision stirred up a hornet's nest in Pennsylvania. The state legislature proceeded to pass a resolution in defiance of the Supreme Court.[17] This enactment declared that the Commonwealth was the real defendant in the case, and that the Supreme Court's decision in *Huidekoper's Lessee* v. *Douglass* was void because rendered without jurisdiction. For, it will be remembered, the Eleventh Amendment to the Constitution deprived the federal courts of jurisdiction over suits between a state and citizens of another state. Although Governor McKean was as hostile to the national judiciary as most Pennsylvania Jeffersonians, he vetoed this enactment because he did not wish to provoke an open clash with the federal government. So the decision of the Supreme Court stood, and its acceptance must be counted as a victory for the national judicial power. But for the moment, it also served to intensify the antipathy toward the federal courts felt in the states.

---

reside thereon, for the space of five years next following his first settlement of the same, if he or she shall so long live; ..."

The Court interpreted this section to mean that title to lands vested upon the fulfillment of one of the described conditions: either settlement or residence, despite the statute's use of the conjunction "and" which would seem to indicate that the vesting of title should not occur until the satisfaction of both requirements. 3 Cranch 1, 65-66.

16 3 Cranch 1, 69.

17 1 Warren, *The Supreme Court in United States History* (1922), p. 369.

The Holland Company Case was only the first of three serious disputes between Pennsylvania and the federal judiciary. The second of them arose out of the attempt of the United States to apply a priority statute giving the federal government a preferred claim to funds also claimed by the Commonwealth. In this instance, as in the earlier case, the federal power won.[18] The third dispute had a long history and, because it came closest to settlement by violence, is worth a special word of comment.

In the days before the adoption of the Constitution, when the country was still living under the Articles of Confedertion, the old national Prize Court had rendered a decision in favor of a certain Gideon Olmstead. This sea captain had been engaged in privateering activity and was awarded the proceeds from the sale of a prize. But the Commonwealth of Pennsylvania also claimed the money, and since its treasurer had the funds in his possession, proceeded to ignore the judgment of the national court. Under the Articles of Confederation, there was no way to procure national enforcement of the court's judgment, and so Olmstead was forced to sleep on his rights. Indeed, he appears to have slept much longer than necessary; for it was 1803 before he applied to a federal court in Pennsylvania for a mandamus designed to compel the Commonwealth to honor the old decision. Judge Peters of the Federal Circuit Court recognized the justice of Olmstead's claim but, because of the explosive political situation, declined to give any actual assistance. A few more years intervened and finally, in 1809, the case reached the stage of decision by the Supreme Court.[19]

Judge Peters was ordered to issue the mandamus, and a United States Marshall proceeded to secure its enforcement against the estate of the Commonwealth's treasurer. At this

---

18 *United States* v. *Nicholls*, 4 Yeates 251 (1805) ; *Miller* v. *Nicholls* 4 Wheat. 311 (1819).

19 *United States* v. *Judge Peters*, 5 Cranch 115 (1809).

point, the Government of Pennsylvania took a hand. Its legislature had passed a law directing the executresses of the late state treasurer to retain possession of the disputed funds,[20] and in order to see that this was done, the Governor ordered the Commonwealth's militia to protect the two women from the federal authorities.

For a short time the armed forces of a state were actively engaged in opposing the enforcement of federal justice. The national courts, having no military establishment at their disposal, had to wait upon any support which the President of the United States saw fit to render. Of course, the President's duty to co-operate with a co-ordinate department of his own Government was clear. But the Chief Executive was Madison, and the judiciary under Chief Justice Marshall was still considered a Federalist stronghold. The political passions of the times were intense; the nation was young; and the effectiveness of the National Government in a time of crisis was still open to some question. Nevertheless, Madison intimated that he would support the federal judiciary.[21] In the face of this threat from the National Government, Pennsylvania decided that discretion was the better part of valor and withdrew its militia, thereby permitting the execution of the federal judgment. General Bright, who had led the Pennsylvania militia, was tried and sentenced by a federal court for his part in the episode. Although President Madison soon pardoned him, the triumph of the federal courts was no less complete. It had met a show of force and come off the victor.

State Courts vs. The Federal Supreme Court

These earliest struggles over the national judicial power were between the federal courts on one side and the state legislatures and governors on the other. But if state courts did not immediately become parties to the fray, it was not because

20 Act of April 2, 1803. See 5 Cranch 133-134.

21 11th Cong., 2nd Sess., 2269-2290 (June 11, 1809).

they had no interest in and no opinions concerning the merits of the controversy. State judges were as partisan in their attachment to Federalist or Republican views as their colleagues in the more avowedly political departments of government, and a clash between rival judicial powers awaited only the unfolding of an appropriate incident. Such an occasion might well have arisen during attempts to enforce the highly controversial Alien and Sedition Laws of 1798. A number of editors were tried under these laws, and in handing down its decision in a suit connected with one of these events, the Pennsylvania Supreme Court said:

" The government of the United States forms a part of the government of each state; its jurisdiction extends to the providing for the common defence against exterior injuries, and violence, the regulation of commerce, and other matters specially enumerated in the constitution; all other powers remain in the individual states, comprehending the interior and other concerns; these combined, form one complete government. Should there be any defect in this form of government, or any collision occur, it cannot be remedied by the sole act of the Congress, or of a State; the people must be resorted to for enlargement or modification. If a State should differ with the United States about the construction of them, there is no common umpire but the people, who should adjust the affair by making amendments in the constitutional way, or suffer from the defect. In such a case the constitution of the United States is federal; it is a league or treaty made by the individual States, as one party, and all the States, as another party. When two nations differ about the meaning of any clause, sentence, or word in a treaty, neither has an exclusive right to decide it; they endeavour to adjust the matter by negotiation, but if it cannot be thus accomplished, each has a right to retain its own interpretation, until a reference be had to the mediation of other nations, an arbitration, or the fate of war. There is no provision in the constitution, that in such a case the Judges of the Supreme Court of the United States shall control and be conclusive: neither can the Congress by a law confer that power." [22]

These views were clearly contrary to those soon to become familiar doctrine in the Federal Supreme Court and would surely have been contradicted at once had the case been taken from the Pennsylvania courts to the Federal Tribunal. But the case was not appealed, and that put a temporary end to the matter. The First Congress had also taken it for granted that the United States Supreme Court might constitutionally review cases from state courts where federal rights were called in question and had provided for the granting of writs of error to accomplish this end. [23]

During the early years under the Constitution, the writ of error was used a number of times without arousing any ill feeling in the states. [24] It was apparently accepted as a matter of course by both state and national judicial systems and seemed to be on its way to becoming an important but routine part of our judicial federalism. But shortly after the Supreme Court had successfully weathered its difficulties with the Commonwealth of Pennsylvania, it became embroiled in a bitter dispute with the courts of Virginia.

As land was the chief source of wealth in early nineteenth century America, it is not surprising that the origin of the trouble should once more have been a dispute over land titles. The case was the now famous *Martin* v. *Hunter's Lessee*, [25] and although the parties interested in it were constantly in the courts for a period of a quarter of a century, the essential elements of the dispute may be briefly stated.

When Virginia was still a Royal Colony, the King had granted a large estate to Lord Fairfax. His heir and successor

22 *Respublica* v. *Cobbet*, 3 Dall. 467, 473-474 (1798).

23 1 Stat. 73, 85 (1789).

24 1 Warren, *The Supreme Court in United States History* (Rev. ed., 1947), p. 443.

25 1 Wheat. 304 (1816).

died in Virginia in 1781 after having lived there all his life. By the terms of the Fairfax will, the Virginia estate was supposed to pass to Denny Martin, a nephew who had been born in England and who had lived there since birth. However, state legislation passed during and soon after the Revolution expropriated the holdings of Tories and British aliens, made it impossible for British aliens to inherit real estate within the Commonwealth, and created a land office empowered to regrant the land affected by this legislation. By 1791, the Commonwealth had regranted some of the acreage belonging to the former Fairfax Estate, and in that year, a prolonged chain of litigation began among the various claimants under the Fairfax will and the holders of grants from the land office. One of these suits was *Martin* v. *Hunter's Lessee* which reached the highest court of Virginia in 1810. It was there decided that, because of the Virginia statutes, the Martin claim was invalid.[26] A writ of error to the United States Supreme Court was allowed as a matter of course by the Virginia Supreme Court, and the former tribunal rendered its decision in 1813.[27] The Court, led by Mr. Justice Story, reversed the judgment of the Virginia Court pointing out that certain provisions of the Treaty of Peace with England and of the Jay Treaty must, in this instance, be considered, and that by virtue of these treaty provisions, the Martin claim was good.

The case was then returned to the Virginia Supreme Court so that the mandate of the Federal Supreme Court might be carried out. The Virginia judges, however, refused to do this and declared that the original allowance of the writ of error had been a mistake. In explaining this decision, Judge Cabell of the Virginia Court wrote:

" The constitution of the United States contemplates the independence of both governments, and regards the residuary

---

26 *Hunter* v. *Fairfax's Devisee*, 1 Munford (Va. 1810) 218.

27 *Fairfax's Devisee* v. *Hunter's Lessee*, 7 Cranch 603 (1813).

sovereignty of the states, as not less inviolable, than the delegated sovereignty of the United States. It must have been foreseen that controversies would sometimes arise as to the boundaries of the two jurisdictions. Yet the constitution has provided no umpire, had erected no tribunal by which they shall be settled. The omission proceeded, probably from the belief, that such a tribunal would produce evils greater than those of the occasional collisions which it would be designed to remedy. Be this as it may, to give to the general government or any of its departments, a direct and controlling operation upon the state departments, as such, would be to change at once, the whole character of our system. The independence of the state authorities would be extinguished, and a superiority, unknown to the constitution would be created, which would, sooner or later terminate in an entire consolidation of the states into one complete national sovereignty." [28]

The result of Virginia's defiance was that *Martin* v. *Hunter's Lessee* was argued a second time in the Federal Supreme Court. On this occasion, it was no longer a question of the merits of the Martin claim; the dispute now revolved about the power of the Federal Supreme Court to compel obedience to its mandate. Counsel for the defendant argued that since the Virginia Supreme Court now refused to allow a writ of error, the United States Supreme Court did not have the record of the case before it and so lacked jurisdiction.[29] This argument was brushed aside and, in 1816, Story delivered the Court's second opinion in the case.[30] This opinion is a classic essay on the judicial power of the United States. Indeed, in some respects it is even bolder in its assertion of national power than sound doctrine will support.[31]

28 *Hunter* v. *Martin; Devisee of Fairfax*, 4 Munford (Va. 1813), 1, 9.

29 *Martin* v. *Hunter's Lessee*, 1 Wheat. 304, 315 (1816).

30 *Martin* v. *Hunter's Lessee*, 1 Wheat. 304 (1816).

31 Story said in part: "If, then, it is a duty of Congress to vest the judicial power of the United States, it is a duty to vest the *whole judicial*

Story recognized the explosive character of the situation and attempted to soothe necessarily ruffled state pride by using diplomatic language. He began his opinion by saying:

" The questions involved in this judgment are of great importance and delicacy. Perhaps it is not too much to affirm, that, upon their right decision, rest some of the most solid principles which have hitherto been supposed to sustain and protect the constitution itself. The great respectability, too, of the court whose decisions we are called upon to review, and the entire deference which we entertain for the learning and ability of that court, add much to the difficulty of the task which has unwelcomely fallen upon us. It is, however, a source of consolation, that we have had the assistance of most able and learned arguments to aid our inquiries; and that the opinion which is now to be pronounced has been weighed with every solicitude to come to a correct result, and matured after solemn deliberation."[32]

But Story and his colleagues cherished no illusions concerning the likelihood of gaining obedience from the Virginia Supreme Court. In order to reduce the danger of another rebuff as much as possible, the case was now returned to the lower court in Virginia where it had first been heard.[33] This unorthodox procedure appears to have succeeded in accomplishing its purpose, and the episode was at an end.

The frequent clashes of federal and state land policies is abundantly mirrored in the early volumes of the United States Reports. In a constitutional history of the United States, pub-

---

power. The language if imperative as to one part is imperative as to all. If it were otherwise, this anomaly would exist, that Congress might successively refuse to vest the jurisdiction in any one class of cases enumerated in the constitution; and thereby defeat the jurisdiction as to all; for the constitution has not singled out any class on which Congress are bound to act in preference to others." However, it has been held that Congress even has the power to remove cases from the jurisdiction of the Supreme Court. Ex Parte McCardle, 7 Wall. 50 (1870).

32 1 Wheat. 304, 324.

33 1 Wheat. 304, 362.

lished in 1912, Gustavus Myers attributes this steady insistence of the Supreme Court on the rights of large landowners to a well conceived and sinister plot on the part of judges to advance their own personal fortunes. He reminds us that John Marshall had bought a portion of the Martin interest and so was financially concerned in the outcome of *Martin* v. *Hunter's Lessee*. Of course, Marshall did not participate in the consideration of this case, but for Myers this was merely a detail in the scheme. Other justices were also interested in real estate transactions whose courses had been or would be affected by decisions of the Supreme Court,[34] and Marshall's colleagues were merely doing for him what he had already done for them in previous suits.

There does not seem to be any solid basis for Myers' charges. It is, of course, true that Marshall and his colleagues who practiced law before coming to the bench had made a great deal of money out of real estate practice. But there is no evidence that this fact was a conscious determinant in shaping their decisions. However, it is now generally recognized that the Constitution was the handiwork of the wealthier classes in the country [35] and that the justices of the Supreme Court during this period shared the outlook of these same economic classes. But despite the fact that this pattern of judicial action was formed out of the conviction that it was morally right and legally sound, the small farmers and frontiersmen of the nation were none the less incensed. As their voices were to be heard more loudly at the seats of state government than at Washington, it is only natural that the store of ill will should explode into controversy between national and local judicial systems. The outcome of the battle was, nevertheless, a signal victory for federal judicial power. The ability of the Supreme Court to enforce respect for its judgment had been demonstrated.

34 Myers, *History of the Supreme Court of the United States* (1912), pp. 228-282.

35 See generally, Beard, *An Economic Interpretation of the Constitution of the United States* (1913).

This does not mean that after 1816 everyone was willing to admit that the mandates of the Supreme Court were to be afforded unconditional obedience. Nor does it mean that successful attempts to subvert the federal judicial authority have not been occasionally made. But some examination of these incidences, even though they have been isolated, sheds interesting light on their nature.

Unusual Nature of State Defiance After 1816

It was a decade and a half after *Martin* v. *Hunter's Lessee* before the authority of the Supreme Court was again questioned. The State of Georgia had enacted a law forbidding whites to settle in the Indian Country unless they had first obtained the permission of the state. This legislation grew out of the strained relations between whites and Indians within the state, the increasing pressure from the state government to deprive the Cherokee Nation of its lands, and the fear that the work of missionaries in educating the Indians might put an obstacle in the way of these plans. Nevertheless, two white missionaries went into the Indian Country, were seized by the Georgia authorities, and convicted in a criminal prosecution. In connection with the same incident, a Cherokee Indian was also seized and tried: this despite the fact that by treaty with the federal government, the Cherokee Nation was supposed to have jurisdiction over its own citizens and to administer criminal justice independently of the State of Georgia. When the two cases involving the missionaries and the Indian reached the United States Supreme Court, that tribunal decided that all three defendants should be released.[36] This judicial vindication of personal rights, however, was of questionable practical value. A few days before the Supreme Court announced its decisions, Georgia took matters into her own hands and hanged the Indian. The two missionaries remained in prison, and although they were eventually pardoned by the

36 *Butler* v. *State of Georgia*, 6 Pet. 597 (1832); *Worcester* v. *Georgia*, 6 Pet. 515 (1832).

Governor of the State, Georgia steadfastly refused to recognize the right of the Supreme Court to entertain appeals from state courts under Section 25 of the Judiciary Act of 1789. Indeed, the Georgia courts have never disavowed the stand taken in these Cherokee Cases. However, when sufficient time had passed to quiet the state bitterness, the local courts did go so far as to cite *Martin* v. *Hunter's Lessee* with approval.[37] This fact together with the State's acquiescence in the taking of appeals to the Federal Supreme Court apparently demonstrate Georgia's practical acceptance of the jurisdiction of the federal judiciary.

Some twenty years after the Cherokee incident, the Wisconsin courts resurrected the Georgia doctrine. The occasion was provided by an abolitionist editor named Sherman Booth who was arrested for harboring a fugitive slave from Missouri in violation of the Fugitive Slave Act of 1850. The highest court of the State granted Booth's application for a writ of habeas corpus on the ground that the warrant under which the United States marshal had acted when arresting Booth was technically

37 The following is only a partial list of the many state decisions referring to *Martin* v. *Hunter's Lessee*.

One California case holds Sec. 25 of the Judiciary Act of 1789 providing for writs of error to state courts unconstitutional. *Johnson* v. *Gordon*, 4 Ca. 368 (1854). Overruled in *Ferris* v. *Coover*, 11 Ca. 176 (1858).

In Georgia, where the Cherokee Cases indicated resistance to the Supreme Court, similar resistance to attempts at centralization during the life of the Confederacy was voiced. See *Mims and Burditt* v. *Wimberly*, 33 Ga. 587 (1863). Change in view after the Civil War. See *Chancely* v. *Bailey and Cleveland*, 37 Ga. 532 (1868); *City of Atlanta* v. *Stokes*, 175 Ga. 201, 215 (1932).

Approval of *Martin* v. *Hunter's Lessee* has been general, See *Mabry, Giller, and Walker* v. *Herndon*, 8 Ala. 848 (1846); *Carter* v. *Bennett*, 5 Fla. 92, 94 (1853); *Ex Parte* Holman, 28 Ia. 88, 96 (1869); *McCormick* v. *Mayfield*, 27 Ind. 143, 150 (1866); *Fleming* v. *Clark*, 94 Mass. 191, 195 (1866); *Opinion of the Justices*, 118 Me. 544, 547, 107 A 673, 675 (1919); *State* v. *Hoskins*, 77 NC 530, 541 (1877); *George* v. *Concord*, 45 NH 434, 438 (1864); *United States* v. *Lathrop*, 17 Johns (NY 1819) 4, 5, 15. *Severson* v. *H O L C*, 184 Okl. 496, 497, 88 P 2d 344, 346 (1939); *Simpson* v. *Willard*, 14 S C 191, 195 (1880); *Wills* v. *Allison*, 51 Tenn. 385, 391 (1871).

defective.[38] But Booth, whose abolitionist sentiments led him to desire a test of the Fugitive Slave Act, waived any objection which he might have raised to the marshal's authority. When the Federal Supreme Court issued an order for the record in the case,[39] the Wisconsin courts refused to supply it.[40]

Some of the problems raised by the removal of cases from state to federal courts are similar to those connected with review of state decisions by the Federal Supreme Court. In the first instance, it is the plaintiff who determines whether a local or national court is to have jurisdiction of a lawsuit. This is true because it is the plaintiff who decides whether or not there is to be any legal action at all and who, by designating the court in which a summons is to be returned, chooses the court which is to hear a dispute. If a case involves disputed rights of a federal nature, or if the parties to the suit are citizens of different states, Section 25 of the Judiciary Act of 1789 did not forbid the defendant to let a suit brought against him in a state court remain there. If he chose to follow this course, the defendant could still gain federal protection of his rights by taking a writ of error from the highest court of a state to the United States Supreme Court. However, it has never been necessary for a defendant to adopt this method of procedure. Just as a plaintiff may choose to have his federal rights adjudicated by either a state or federal court, so it is generally true that by deciding whether or not to remove a case from a state to a federal court, a defendant may exercise a similar privilege. The same reluctance which sometimes led state judiciaries to struggle against review of their decisions by the Federal Supreme Court also appeared when the question related to the removal of cases.

38 *In re* Booth, 3 Wisc. 1 (1854).

39 See *Ableman* v. *Booth*, 21 How. 506 (1858).

40 See 11 Wisc. 498, 500. The mandate of the Supreme Court was eventually honored. *Ableman* v. *Booth*, 11 Wisc. 498 (1859).

In 1842 the case of *Gordon* v. *Longest* [41] was decided by the Supreme Court. As in the Booth Case of a decade later, the trouble arose out of the slavery issue. The captain of a river boat plying the Ohio was said to have carried a slave from Kentucky to Ohio thus aiding in the Negro's escape. Under a Kentucky law, such conduct made the captain liable for the payment of a monetary penalty. Accordingly, the State brought suit to collect the penalty, and the captain sought to remove the case into a federal court on the ground that he was a citizen of Pennsylvania. The motive for the captain's maneuver is not hard to find; he knew that a Kentucky court would certainly be sympathetic to slaveholders' interests. The federal courts, on the other hand, might not entertain the same views. The Kentucky court was also alive to this possibility and was just as anxious to keep the captain from getting into a federal court where he would no longer be accountable to state administered justice. In order to prevent the defendant's escape into friendlier hands, the Kentucky court refused to permit the case to be removed. It was therefore necessary for the Supreme Court to order the Kentucky tribunal to release the record in the case to the appropriate federal court.

What was the Supreme Court to do when faced with determined opposition from state judiciaries or from other departments of state government? If one attempts to answer this question with the tools of political or juristic theory, the inquiry must be tremendously difficult. Under our federal system, the states are no less sovereign within their alloted domain than is the federal government. How can a state be coerced? The only way would seem to be by resort to military force. This is certainly not the method of peaceful governments, and its use would signal the disintegration of our federalism. Indeed, this was the situation at the time of the Civil War.

The advance of the Supreme Court, and with it the entire federal judiciary, to a position of focal power within our fed-

41 16 Pet. 97 (1842).

eral structure has been accomplished without violence. In some cases, like those involving the Cherokee Nation, it has been necessary for the federal judiciary to look the other way while its decisions were being flouted. But such incidents are rare. They have almost always arisen out of fundamental political cleavages in our national life and so have involved issues which could not be solved by judicial action alone. Had such episodes become more numerous with the passage of time, the United States could not have endured as a single nation. The Civil War would not have been followed by the establishment of a stronger federal union. It could only have been the prelude to eventual disunion or the forerunner of a unitary type of government in which the desire of the states for a measure of autonomy would needs have been sacrificed to internal order.

Luckily, the tensions caused by the slavery and Indian problems have passed as these problems have evaporated or changed their character. *Martin* v. *Hunter's Lessee* was the last serious attempt to rest the complete independence of state judiciaries in matters of federal law on a constitutional base. Its decision, and the acceptance of that decision by all the states, brought the first phase in the relations between federal and state courts to a close. Disagreement and friction between local and national judicial systems were not precluded by *Martin* v. *Hunter's Lessee,* but open warfare was not to be the rule.

PART II

ACCESS TO THE FEDERAL COURTS

INTRODUCTORY NOTE

WE Americans pride ourselves on being law-abiding citizens, and most of us are. Yet there is no denying that standards of good conduct vary somewhat from community to community across the country. One town is known as an example of clean living, while another gains an unwanted notoriety because of a flourishing " red light " district. There are many reasons for this phenomenon, most of them buried in the economic and social fabric of local neighborhoods. But the adequacy of public law enforcement also has something to do with the complexion of a community.

Some police forces are known for their zeal and efficiency; a few are reputed to be riddled with corruption; while some are merely lackadaisical in their attitude toward the performance of their duty. In so far as police methods can deal with either the causes or manifestations of lawlessness, this uneven administration of justice probably goes far to explain observable differences in local communities.

People interested in public order are naturally troubled when poor enforcement officers help to encourage imperfect observance of the law, but all they can do is voice their indignation and hope that an aroused opinion will force a change. A man who is not satisfied with the local constabulary cannot ask the

47

police of another town to guard his house, raid the neighbor-hood pool parlor, or look into the theft of his wife's jewelry. These are matters which he must entrust to the authorities in his immediate vicinity.

The dispensing of civil justice is also subject to uneven ad-ministration. Some judges are more capable than others; some courts are better than others. But even more striking than dif-ferences in judicial personnel is the competition between two sets of courts. With the exception of a few scattered areas (like the District of Columbia) every inch of the Continental United States is served by two judicial systems; one belong-ing to the national government, the other belonging to the state in whose territory it is located.

While it is impossible for the private citizen to call upon the police force of his own liking, it is often feasible for him to select the judicial system, state or federal, to which he will resort for the protection of his legal rights. Within the bounds set by the judicial codes of his state and of the United States, it is the private litigant who decides which court is to hear his grievance. If a person is a plaintiff, he makes this choice by commencing his action in a tribunal belonging to the judicial system of his choosing. If he is a defendant, he exercises a similar discretion when he moves to have a federal court dis-miss a case for want of jurisdiction, or when he petitions for the removal of a case from a state to a federal court.

If a litigant anticipates no difference in the way that national and local judiciaries will proceed with his case, the choice will be a random one and of no particular importance to either himself or the public. But there have been, and doubtless still are, situations where the very outcome of his case may depend on whether the suitor entrusts his rights to a state or a na-tional court. Whenever this circumstance presents itself, the private litigant is encouraged to make use of technicalities in the law in order to present his grievance to a tribunal which will better suit his needs than those of his opponent.

While litigants pursue their immediate objectives, courts and legislatures must see that the public interest is not compromised. They must devise and administer rules designed to make sure that wherever possible questions of local law and policy are determined in local courts and that questions of national law and policy are decided in federal courts. As the state courts are always available for the determination of questions of local law and are frequently available for the litigation of federal questions as well, the procedural aspect of the relation between state and federal judiciaries resolves itself into an exploration of the circumstances under which a litigant may be heard in a federal court. The current phase of our study is addressed to this problem.

CHAPTER III

JURISDICTION BASED ON A FEDERAL QUESTION

It is only natural to expect that national power should extend to areas of federal concern. The national legislature and executive formulate and administer policy in those fields entrusted to the federal government by the Constitution, and it is not surprising that the federal judiciary should do likewise within the sphere of judicial affairs. What is a cause of some curiosity is the fact that until 1875, cases arising under penal statutes excepted, the lower federal courts had no jurisdiction of federal questions, and litigants wishing to assert rights conferred upon them by the Constitution or laws of the United States were usually forced to rely upon state courts with appeal to the Supreme Court by writ of error as their only recourse to federal authority. Why Congress failed for so long to give lower federal courts power to interpret federal law while authorizing them to decide diversity of citizenship cases is a perplexing question. There has been some speculation on the matter, but the plain fact is that the records of the first Congress, and indeed of all subsequent Congresses up to and including that of 1875, contain virtually no discussion of the reasons for conferring jurisdiction on the federal courts in one instance and refusing it in the other.[1] However, it is clear that in 1875 Congress did empower inferior federal tribunals to take jurisdiction of cases arising under the Constitution and laws of the United States[2] and that this jurisdiction has been freely exercised ever since.

In the majority of cases, the interpretation and enforcement of federal law by national courts occasion no collision with

1 See Chadbourn and Levin, *Original Jurisdiction of Federal Questions*, 90 U. of Pa. L. Rev. 639 (1942).

2 18 Stat. 470 (1875).

the political or judicial interests of the states. But the border-line between federal and state power is often obscure, and when cases fall within this area of doubt, friction is likely to develop.

DOES NATIONAL INCORPORATION RAISE A FEDERAL QUESTION

The first case to bring this truth sharply into focus was *Osborn* v. *Bank of the United States* [3] which reached the Supreme Court while Marshall was still Chief Justice, and the opinion was by his hand. This was a suit for an injunction wherein the decision of a state court would normally have been final. But the Bank sought and obtained review by the Supreme Court of the United States on the ground that it had been incorporated by an act of Congress. The act, so it was claimed, was a *law of the United States* and entitled the Bank to invoke federal jurisdiction whenever it became involved in a lawsuit.

Although Marshall's view was literally correct, it may be doubted that its effect was precisely what the framers of the Constitution had intended. Special acts of a legislature, whether federal or state, incorporating business enterprises are seldom mirrors of national interest and policy in the same sense as public laws, and it is probable that compelling a nationally chartered corporation to play by the same rules imposed upon everyone else would not have exposed the Bank to any special disadvantage or frustrated any policy of the federal government. In Marshall's day, however, the mischief resulting from this decision was not great. There were even fewer nationally chartered corporations then than now, and the effect of the sum total of litigation in which such business enterprises became parties could hardly be noticed.

About sixty years after the Osborn Case, something happened which brought the unfortunate possibilities latent in Marshall's decision to the fore. No significant increase in the number of corporations chartered by Congress had taken place,

3 9 Wheat. 738 (1824).

but a few of the railroads which had been built with the assistance of federal land grants did hold national charters. By asserting that their acts of incorporation were "laws of Congress", these companies succeeded in establishing their right to have cases brought against them tried in federal rather than in state courts. The Pacific Railroad Removal Cases,[4] wherein this point was decided in favor of the companies, were ordinary tort actions prosecuted by passengers who had met with injuries while traveling on the railroad's trains, and presented no federal questions other than the federal incorporation, a fact which was not disputed and had no direct relation to any of the litigants' claims. These were suits normally tried in state courts and, the legal technicality to the contrary notwithstanding, there seemed to be no consideration of genuine policy for their removal from state jurisdiction. Moreover, the fact that the first beneficiaries of this expanded federal power should be the railroads, utilities which had already incurred the special wrath of many state legislatures, helped to magnify popular resentment against this exercise of federal jurisdiction.

In the years which followed, national courts showed no inclination to restrict the rule of the Pacific Removal Cases. But Congress saw the mischief caused by so wide an extension of the decision in the Osborn Case and eventually made it impossible for a corporation with a national charter to bring cases into federal courts solely because it had been incorporated by Congress[5] instead of by a state.

FEDERAL AND STATE LAW INTERTWINED

More perplexing problems of policy are presented by cases in which substantial questions of both state and federal law

4 115 US 1 (1885).

5 Sec. 12, Act of February 13, 1925: "That no district court shall have jurisdiction of any action or suit by or against any corporation upon the ground that it was incorporated by or under an Act of Congress: Provided, that this section shall not apply to any suit, action, or proceeding brought by or against a corporation incorporated by or under an Act of Congress wherein the Government of the United States is the owner of more than one-half of its capital stock." 43 Stat. 941, 28 USC # 42 (1927).

are to be found intermingled. Such cases arise in virtually all of the areas where national and state power meet, but they have appeared with more than common frequency in the public utility field. The continuous stream of litigation has afforded the national courts an unparalleled opportunity for an exploration into the intricacies of this kind of federal jurisdiction. Consequently, it is appropriate to use this type of litigation to illustrate the general problems involved.

With the exception of the Interstate Commerce Commission and Federal Power Commission, public bodies charged with the supervision of utility rates have been state agencies. This is why the electric company, gasworks, or intrastate railroad —to mention only a few of the more familiar utilities—has complained of state action whenever it has thought that its rates were set at too low a figure. These disputes between local public service commissions and the companies they seek to regulate often come into the courts for settlement. Whether the tribunal is to be federal or state is of considerable interest to private litigants and governmental agencies alike.

The laws providing for public approval of rates have been state statutes. It follows that questions relating to their interpretation, or to the action of administrative boards taken pursuant to these laws, are matters of local law to be decided by local judiciaries. But in their battles to obtain what they consider equitable rates, the utilities have not been compelled to rely entirely on the hope of favorable court interpretation of local statutes. Their standard complaint has been that rates allowed by public service commissions are too low to permit a fair return on invested capital. This, so the argument runs, is tantamount to confiscation of the company's property and is a violation of the Due Process Clause of the Fourteenth Amendment to the Federal Constitution. The justice of this contention presents a federal question in every case where it is made and makes it possible for the federal courts to take jurisdiction whenever the utility wishes to have its case tried in a federal rather than in a state court.[6]

6 For a general discussion of public utility regulation and the federal courts see: Lilienthal, *The Federal Courts and State Regulation of Public Utilities*, 43 Harv. L. Rev. 379 (1930).

If the utility desires to abandon its claims under the Fourteenth Amendment and place all of its reliance on a favorable interpretation of the state statute, it will be forced to resort to a local court for the trial and decision of its case. If, on the other hand, it wishes to press its contention that the state regulation offends the Constitution, the company may make this argument in either a state or national court. The latter will have jurisdiction because of the federal question presented by the alleged violation of the Fourteenth Amendment, while the former can hear the suit because neither the Removal Act of 1875 nor any other act of Congress has forbidden state judiciaries to entertain questions arising under the Federal Constitution.

It would be unfair to compel a public utility to abandon one of its two legitimate grounds for relief at the very beginning of a litigation. Questions of law are often intricate, and it frequently happens that not even a well informed lawyer can predict how a court will decide a close question. Moreover, the task of our judicial system is the securing of a maximum degree of justice for all suitors, and this could not be done if litigants were obstructed in their efforts to bring material factors in their cases to the attention of the courts. Nor would it be proper to force a utility into a state court in order that it might present its claims under the Federal Constitution. Since most cases never reach the United States Supreme Court, it would hardly be realistic to contend that the hope of eventual review by that tribunal provides a satisfactory substitute for a hearing before the lower federal courts. Consequently, such a limited use of the federal jurisdiction would inevitably act as a severe restriction of federal authority in matters pertaining to national law.

However, a utility's right to full protection of its interests is not unqualified. The public interest must be safeguarded no less than private rights; and it is probably true that the activities of the federal courts have made local rate regulation more difficult. Congress saw the desirability of traveling as far toward these two divergent objectives as possible when it passed the Johnson Act.[7] This statute provides that no district court shall enjoin the enforcement of a rate order emanating from any state administrative board or commission if state law affords the private company a fair hearing after due notice and if the utility can have a " plain, speedy, and efficient " remedy for its grievance under state law. By the terms of this legislatively declared policy, the utility is to be denied access to the national courts whenever its case can be disposed of by the decision of questions of local law. While the Johnson Act thereby restricts the virtually unfettered choice of forum previously exercised by the private litigant, it certainly does not bar utilities from the federal courts. Wherever state law or practice does not measure up to the standards embodied in the Federal act, the national courts may function as freely as before. Moreover, the Supreme Court has sought to give the private company the benefit of the doubt whenever possible. For example, it has been held that where the state law involved had not yet been interpreted by the state courts, or where the question of local law was a close one, the local remedy is not " plain, speedy, and efficient ", and the jurisdiction of a federal tribunal is not impaired.[8] In addition, it would seem that unless the state courts are in the habit of enjoining the application of a rate order pending conclusive determination as to its validity, the federal judiciary may also act.[9] As this has not been the practice in many states, the necessary result of such a doctrine is to restore much of the federal jurisdiction which the Johnson Act seeks to withdraw unless the states are willing to change their laws so as to make it possible for utilities to avoid compliance with new rate orders while they are being tested in the courts.

7 48 Stat. 775 (1934), 28 USC # 41(1).

8 *Driscoll* v. *Edison Co.*, 307 US 104 (1939) ; *Mountain States Power Co.* v. *Public Service Commission of Montana*, 299 US 167 (1936).

9 Platt, *The Johnson Act and Utility Rate Making in Ohio*, 6 O. St. L. J. 268, 284 (1940).

It should be noted, however, that a strict interpretation of the Johnson Act has not prevented the federal courts from fostering the use of state courts in cases where a decision might rest on the determination of alternative questions—one of them state, the other federal—or, where the preliminary decision of a question of state law may make the reaching of a substantial question of federal law unnecessary. The case that announced this doctrine of "equitable abstention" was *Railroad Commission* v. *Pullman Co.*[10] In the words of Mr. Justice Frankfurter who wrote the Supreme Court's opinion, the facts and problems in the case were as follows:

"In those sections of Texas where the local passenger traffic is slight, trains carry but one sleeping car. These trains, unlike trains having two or more sleepers, are without a Pullman conductor; the sleeper is in charge of a porter who is subject to the train conductor's control. As is well known, porters on Pullmans are colored and conductors are white. Addressing itself to this situation, the Texas Railroad Commission after due hearing ordered that 'no sleeping car shall be operated on any line of railroad in the State of Texas ... unless such cars are continuously in the charge of an employee ... having the rank and position of Pullman conductor.' Thereupon, the Pullman Company and the railroads affected brought this action in a federal district court to enjoin the Commission's order. Pullman porters were permitted to intervene as complainants, and Pullman conductors entered the litigation in support of the order. The Pullman Company and the railroads assailed the order as unauthorized by Texas law as well as violative of the Equal Protection, the Due Process and the Commerce Clauses of the Constitution. The intervening porters adopted these objections but mainly objected to the order as a discrimination against Negroes in violation of the Fourteenth Amendment.

"The complaint of the Pullman porters undoubtedly ten-

10 312 US 496 (1941).

dered a substantial constitutional issue. It is more than substantial. It touches a sensitive area of social policy upon which the federal courts ought not to enter unless no alternative to its adjudication is open. Such constitutional adjudication plainly can be avoided if a definitive ruling on the state issue would terminate the controversy. It is therefore our duty to turn to a consideration of questions under Texas law.

" The Commission found justification for its order in a Texas statute which we quote in the margin." (The statute deals with discrimination by transportation utilities but this is done in a context of provision for rate fixing.) " It is common ground that if the order is within the Commission's authority its subject matter must be included in the Commission's power to prevent ' unjust discrimination . . . and to prevent any and all other abuses' in the conduct of railroads. Whether arrangements pertaining to the staffs of Pullman cars are covered by the Texas concept of ' discrimination ' is far from clear. What practices of the railroads may be deemed to be ' abuses' subject to the Commission's correction is equally doubtful. Reading the Texas statutes and the Texas decisions as outsiders without special competence in Texas law, we would have little confidence in our independent judgment regarding the application of that law to the present situation." [11]

The Court's approach to the problem was clear. If the meaning of the word "discrimination" in the Texas statute was not sufficiently broad to cover discrimination against Negroes as well as discrimination in the charging of rates, the order of the Railroad Commission would fall because not supported by state law. Such a result would make it unnecessary to consider the constitutional questions. But the meaning of the Texas law was a matter appropriate for the decision of the state courts. Accordingly, the Supreme Court remanded the case to the District Court with instructions to retain jurisdic-

11 312 US 496, 498—499.

tion of the suit pending the institution and determination of appropriate proceedings in the Texas courts.

The Supreme Court came to a similar result in Chicago v. Fieldcrest Dairies [12] where the two questions involved were, 1. The conformity to a state statute of a city ordinance banning the distribution of milk in paper containers, and 2. The possible conflict between the ordinance and the Due Process Clause of the Fourteenth Amendment. The Fieldcrest Case is of particular interest because it specifically notes that the Dairy was a Michigan corporation and one would suppose that a decision of the case on the merits could have been justified because there was diversity of citizenship. Nevertheless, the Supreme Court preferred to see an adjudication of the ordinance's validity under state law in the Illinois courts.

That the doctrine of "equitable abstention" is connected with the Johnson Act only in the sense that both represent a desire to see adjudication in state courts wherever possible, is abundantly clear from both the Pullman and Fieldcrest Cases. Although the former was a public utility case, it did not concern a disputed rate order, and the latter is not a utility case at all.

A further point to be made in connection with the Pullman and Fieldcrest Cases relates to their effectiveness in discouraging proceedings in the federal courts. It is to be noted that the federal courts did not dismiss these cases. Instead, they were continued on the district court dockets pending proceedings in the state courts. Presumably this maintenance of federal jurisdiction was to permit of a resumption of proceedings in the federal courts when the state questions had been determined. Since the litigation of the questions of state law might involve appeals to the local appellate courts before they were finally decided, litigants who are compelled to make use of the state judiciary machinery as a preliminary to proceedings in the federal courts may indeed wonder whether it is not

12 316 US 168 (1942).

less cumbersome to litigate both state and federal questions in the local courts and accept possible, although by no means certain, review in the United States Supreme Court as the extent of their appeal to federally administered justice.

However, the technique used in the Pullman and Fieldcrest cases can be used only when resolution of the state law question is clearly seen to be a complete alternative to the decision of the federal question.

In all other instances it continues to be necessary that suitors who invoke judicial protection for rights founded partly on state and partly on federal grounds, be permitted to resort to federal courts when they choose to do so. Although this practice is just from the point of view of the private litigant, it raises a delicate problem in the relation of national and state governments. It makes it inevitable that important questions of state law and state policy be decided by federal tribunals. A recognition of this fact is essential to an understanding of the judicial aspect of our federalism; for it gives true color to the problem which our courts and legislatures must solve. The goal is not the complete and unrelenting separation of national and state questions; that is impossible. Rather, the objective must be to see that cases which are both national and local in significance are decided by the judicial branch of whatever government has the predominant interest in their decision. In some instances, this is a federal tribunal; in others it is a state court. Each judicial system can be trusted to deal properly with those phases of a case which concern its own law. The challenge comes when the court is called upon to exercise self-restraint in handling the law of another jurisdiction.

The national judiciary, and particularly the Supreme Court, has the paramount responsibility in achieving this delicate balance between the interests of Nation and States. The extent of the national judicial power is set by the United States Constitution and by acts of Congress. These are part of our federal law, and as a consequence, the Federal Supreme

Court is the ultimate authority on the meaning to be given legislative limitations of federal jurisdiction.

Litigants cannot be expected to be of any help in this work. Their attention is centered on the winning of the case in hand, and general principles are of interest to them only in so far as they can be used to gain a victory or to the extent that they must be explained away in order to forestall defeat. If a controversy relates exclusively to matters of local law, and the parties to it are all citizens of the same state, it is obvious that local courts will be used. If, on the other hand, the questions involved are clearly matters of federal law, it is equally obvious that a national court can take jurisdiction. But when there is the slightest hint that elements of both federal and state laws are present, suitors are likely to seek the tribunal which gives them a real or fancied advantage. Throughout much of our history,[13] differences in substantive rules of law were often determinative. But these were not the only considerations that a litigant had to weigh. A public utility, for example, usually preferred to contest the ruling of a public service commission in a federal court for procedural reasons. As David E. Lilienthal has pointed out, the federal court would normally permit the company to charge a disputed rate during the period of litigation, whereas a state court usually insisted on the observance of the commission's order until it was finally determined in the judicial proceeding that the commission was in the wrong.[14]

In order to keep litigants from disturbing the balance between state and national judicial systems, the Supreme Court of the United States has evolved a number of rules. The purpose of all of them is the same: to ferret out those cases which can be decided by state courts on the basis of local law and to prevent partisan suitors from bringing them before national tribunals. As one might expect, some of these rules are better

13 See Chapters VI-VIII, *infra*.

14 Lilienthal, *op. cit., supra* note 6, pp. 415-420.

than others. Nor is it an accident that the most mechanical of them should be the least satisfactory.

FINDING A FEDERAL QUESTION: THE MECHANICAL TEST

Something over half a century ago, it was decided that a case could not be brought into a national court because of the presence of a federal question unless the right to be protected appeared in the plaintiff's original statement of his cause of action.[15] The route which led the Supreme Court to this conclusion was paved with an expensive brand of legal logic. It commenced with the observation that the statute giving the federal courts jurisdiction over cases involving federal questions follows the words of the Constitution: the District Courts shall have jurisdiction of cases and controversies " arising under this Constitution, the laws of the United States, and treaties made ... under their authority ".[16] The important word in this phrase is *arising;* for, said the Court, a case *arises* when someone has a grievance, or, to employ the legal terminology, a cause of action. A cause of action, it will be noted, belongs to a plaintiff and has already arisen by the time the defendant is served with a summons. It follows that any federal question in the case must be found in the plaintiff's statement of his cause of action. If it cannot be discovered there, it does not exist and the case is not an appropriate one for decision by the federal courts.

This rule works well enough in many cases. If a Negro complains that he is denied a ballot because of his color, this violation of the Fifteenth Amendment will certainly appear in his orignal statement of his cause of action. If a plaintiff wishes to obtain an injunction against infringement of his patent, he will surely detail the alleged violation of the federal patent law in the original statement of his case. In these and similar instances where the plaintiff's rights are expressly con-

15 *Tennessee* v. *Union & Planters' Bank*, 152 US 454 (1894).

16 U. S. Constit., Art. III, Sec. 2.

ferred upon him by federal law, it is reasonable enough to assume that if a federal question is not presented by the complaint, it is not likely to be uncovered at a later stage of the litigation.

But the very case which decided that the only place where one may look for a federal question is in the plaintiff's complaint illustrates the weakness of the rule. Tennessee sought to collect taxes from the Union & Planters' Bank under a general statute of the state. The plaintiff's case could be very simply put. All that was necessary was to set forth the provisions of the tax law, point out that the bank was in existence, and allege the failure of the bank to pay the tax. From these facts, one would hardly suspect that federal law could have even a remote bearing on the case. The statute involved was an act of Tennessee; the bank was in Tennessee; its failure to pay was a breach of Tennessee law. Indeed, this is what the Supreme Court's decision said; for it was held that a federal question must appear in the complaint if a federal court is to take jurisdiction.

But Tennessee's statement of her case, although perfectly sufficient to meet the technical requirements of pleading, did not tell the whole story. The bank did not claim that it had paid the tax, or that under Tennessee law it was not required to do so. Instead, it contended that, by the terms of its charter, it was exempt from the tax and that if the state statute was construed so as to apply to the bank, it would violate the clause of the Federal Constitution forbidding a state to impair the obligations of a contract. This defense obviously raised a federal question. Its decision necessitated an interpretation of the Constitution and there cannot be any doubt that a federal court was an appropriate tribunal to make such an interpretation in the first instance. But in the view of the Supreme Court, this was not so because the defendant, and not the plaintiff, was the party claiming rights under federal law.

This decision has never been overruled. Its effect is certainly to keep many cases in local courts which would otherwise receive consideration by the federal judiciary. If the rightful preserve of state judicial authority has all too frequently been invaded by the national courts, this test for a federal question has undoubtedly helped to redress the balance, but we may wonder whether it has done so in such a way as to effectuate the basic policies for which our federal system stands. It is hard to see why the rights of defendants under federal law are any less worthy of the attention of national courts than those of plaintiffs. Yet the effect of the rule is to permit resort to federal authority by one party while denying it to the other.

The only consideration of policy that can be urged in favor of the Planters' Bank Rule is that, were a defendant permitted to remove a case from a state court because of the presence of a federal question not raised by the complaint, questions of state law presented in the plaintiff's original statement of his case would inevitably be decided by the federal courts. As there is no way to obtain review of a federal court decision in the state courts, the loss of state jurisdiction over the local aspects of the litigation could not be remedied. On the other hand, defendants who now fail to gain access to the federal courts in the first instance have at least some chance of ultimate appeal to federal authority by way of review in the United States Supreme Court. However, such relief from the rigors of the Planters' Bank Rule is of practical value in relatively few cases. The overwhelming majority of suits are settled in the lower courts and in these instances, an initial resort to the local courts determines the forum of final disposition. Moreover, appeal to the Supreme Court is costly in both time and money and so is out of the question in many of the cases where it might otherwise be used to lessen the hardships of the Planters' Bank Rule.

One may argue that if the results flowing from the Planters' Bank Rule are bad on grounds of policy, the fault lies with the Constitution. The words " arising under " appear in Article III, Section 2 and if the necessary result of their use is to limit federal question jurisdiction to rights set forth in a plaintiff's original statement of his case, the only way to secure equal treatment for a defendant's rights is by Constitutional amendment. However, this does not seem to be a practical solution because the problem is a technical one and does not lend itself to wide popular understanding. Accordingly, it is doubtful that anyone could stimulate sufficient interest in the problem to gain the extraordinary majorities needed to pass a constitutional amendment. Nor is the evil of *Tennessee* v. *Union & Planters' Bank* especially irksome to an active class or special interest in our society. Its mischief travels at random throughout the borderland between national and state judicial power, visiting first one litigant and then another, but never playing favorites. The defendant who is disadvantaged today may find himself a favored plaintiff tomorrow. Many of the cases which come within the rule have defendants who suffer from it, but the harm is never systematic and seldom obvious.

Congress may be able to supply the impetus needed for a change. It has been intimated that a revision of the Judicial Code more sweeping than the one recently completed may be in order. Such a revision might include the repeal of the general statute permitting trial of all causes of action arising under the Constitution and federal laws and a complete reliance on a series of special statutes conferring or withholding federal jurisdiction over cases involving the enforcement of particular federally created rights.[17] In the unlikely event that Congress should decide upon a substantial contraction of the jurisdiction of the United States District Courts, the complete substitution of special statutes for the all inclusive pro-

17 Professor Herbert Wechsler has indicated that such a solution might be desirable. *Cf.* Wechsler, *Federal Jurisdiction and the Revision of the Judicial Code*, 13 Law and Contemp. Problems 216 (1948). However, the special statutes generally provide for federal jurisdiction over "actions" to enforce rights created by the statute. This raises the old difficulty because an "action" is brought by a plaintiff.

vision embodied in the Act of 1875 would have the advantage
of inducing a careful examination of the real necessity for federal jurisdiction in each of the many classes of case to which
it presently applies. But such a solution of the problem raised
by the Planters' Bank Rule would have to surmount the same
constitutional obstacles as the proposal made below. If Congress can improve the present situation, it is submitted that
the following proposal provides a much simpler way to establish equality of protection for the rights of plaintiffs and defendants.

It will be remembered that a legislative declaration to the
effect that national incorporation is not of itself sufficient to
raise a federal question succeeded in removing the effects of
the decision in the Osborn Case. The Judiciary Act delimiting
the jurisdiction of the inferior federal courts reproduces a portion of the language to be found in Article III, Section 2 including the phrase " arising under the Constitution and laws of
the United States ". Congress might define the words " arising
under " as they appear in the jurisdictional statute to include
claims of federal right raised by all parties to a suit. Such legislative action, however, would not be as certain of success as the
statutory nullification of the Osborn Rule because the power
of Congress to reduce the federal jurisdiction is well established,[18] whereas its power to expand the federal jurisdiction
must be exercised subject to constitutional limitations on the
judicial power of the United States. If it were so inclined the
Supreme Court could sustain a broad Congressional redefi-
nition on the ground that the decision in the Planters' Bank
Case rested on an interpretation of the Judiciary Act and not
of the Constitution. However, such a distinction would indicate a real change of doctrine because the words " arising
under " are used no differently in the Judiciary Act than in the
Constitution itself. Indeed, were it convinced of the inappro-
priateness of the present rule, the Supreme Court might be able

18 *Ex Parte McCardle*, 7 Wall. 506 (1869).

to reach the desired result by the normal process of judicial change. A Supreme Court which has worked such wonders in defining and redefining terms like " interstate commerce " and " due process " need hardly hesitate to expand the test for a federal question so that it may apply to both sides in a suit. This could be the more easily done because such a change would not violate any policy embodied in the Constitution. The reasoning of the majority opinion in the Planters' Bank Case to the contrary notwithstanding, it is not likely that the framers of the Constitution believed that the interest of the federal judiciary in a case was dependent upon so extraneous a factor as the role of the party claiming the protection of national authority.

FINDING A FEDERAL QUESTION: SUBSTANTIVE TESTS

A number of other tests which are used in conjunction with the rule of the Planters' Bank Case are much better suited to the accomplishment of their purpose and might well be used as the sole standards by which to measure the presence of a federal question. They are: 1. That a proposed construction of the Constitution or of a federal law will lead to one result in a particular case, whereas another construction would lead to a different outcome; [19] 2. The question of federal law must be an essential element in the case;[20] 3. The question of federal law must actually be disputed by the parties to a litigation.[21]

There may be minor differences between these rules. But it is submitted that they are all statements of the same basic proposition: that the controversy must really concern a matter of federal law if the case is to be a proper one for the exercise of jurisdiction by a federal court.

The number of cases wherein national tribunals have been asked to decide whether the federal interest in them is substan-

19 *Carson* v. *Dunham*, 121 US 421 (1887).

20 *Starin* v. *New York*, 115 US 248 (1885).

21 *Gully* v. *First National Bank in Meridian*, 299 US 109 (1936) ; *Gold-Washing Co.* v. *Keyes*, 96 US 199 (1877).

tial enough to warrant their decision by a federal rather than by a state court is very large. Indeed, each of the rules just set forth is relied upon in a long line of reported judicial opinions. For our purposes, it will not be necessary to examine many of them. However, it will be helpful to refer to a few of the more important cases in order to gain some idea of what the Supreme Court has done when confronted with actual problems of conflict between state and national interests as presented by private litigation.

The plaintiff in *Barney* v. *City of New York* [22] appears to have had a genuine grievance. He was the owner of property in the general vicinity of the excavations being made for the New York subway system. It was Barney's contention that the engineers directing the tunneling operations had strayed from the route authorized by state law and were building their tunnel along a course which, if pursued, would damage his property. Accordingly, he brought suit for an injunction to stop the construction along the unauthorized route. He pressed two propositions upon the courts: 1. The tunnel was being built in such a way as to violate the state statute authorizing construction of a subway, and 2. Continued prosecution of the work would result in injury to his real estate, and consequently in a taking of his property without due process of law. On the basis of this claimed violation of the Fourteenth Amendment, Barney contended that his case presented a federal question and should be adjudged by a federal court.

Had the Supreme Court been anxious to extend federal jurisdiction as far as the bounds of argumentation would permit, it could certainly have accepted Barney's assertion that he was seeking protection of a constitutional right. But the Court preferred to evaluate the relative importance of the contentions made under federal and state law. Its analysis pointed out that the substance of Barney's complaint was that certain state officers, or their representatives, were violating state statutes pre-

22 193 US 430 (1904).

scribing the route to be taken by a subway. The denial of due process, if it existed at all, was caused solely by the infraction of state law. The proper way to obtain relief from a violation of state law was a suit in a state court. The case could be completely and satisfactorily disposed of by the decision of a question of local law. It followed that the state courts were the appropriate tribunals before which the case should come.

A leading case of more recent date also demonstrates the Supreme Court's intention that the jurisdiction of local judiciaries be protected wherever possible. *Gully* v. *First National Bank in Meridan* [23] was a suit by the Treasurer of Mississippi to collect certain taxes owed by an insolvent national bank. By contract, the defendant had assumed all of the liabilities of the bank, and it was this liability which the State wished to enforce. In an unsuccessful attempt to introduce an ingredient of federal law into the case so that it might be adjudged by a federal court, the First National Bank in Meridan claimed that as its predecessor, like itself, was a national bank, Mississippi would have been powerless to lay the tax except for an act of Congress consenting to local taxation of national banks. Mr. Justice Cardozo, speaking for the Court, pointed out that neither side in the litigation questioned the existence of the act of Congress or its applicability to the case in hand. While it was perfectly true that Mississippi would have had no case at all if Congress had not consented to state taxation of national banks, the dispute concerned the defendant's liability under a Mississippi contract and should be settled by the courts of the State. Cardozo made a number of cogent observations on the conduct of the national courts in handling federal questions. At one point he said: " Looking backward we can see that the early cases were less exacting than the recent ones in respect of some of these conditions .... Partly under the influence of statutes disclosing a new legislative policy, partly under the influence of more liberal decisions, the

23 *Supra* note 21.

probable course of the trial, the real substance of the controversy has taken on a new significance." [24]

This disposition on the part of the Supreme Court to view federal question jurisdiction as a practical problem in the relation between national and state judiciaries instead of as a technical exercise in pleading is most hopeful. It is probable that the approach which has produced the less mechanical rules for the testing of a federal question can do all that is necessary to keep cases which really belong in local courts from being brought before national tribunals on spurious claims of federal right. This is not to say that all cases which are ultimately disposed of on grounds of local law can be kept out of the federal courts. It is a well recognized fact that many legal disputes are complex, and in these more difficult cases, it is not always possible to evaluate the relative importance of national and local questions at the outset.

From the viewpoint of political theory, even these litigations do not present insuperable obstacles to the separate treatment of federal and state questions. For it would be possible to return a case to the state courts whenever it became apparent that the final decision was to be on a point of local law. This might even be done if the case had already passed through trial and intermediate appeal and was docketed in the Supreme Court. But the practical administration of justice would surely be compromised were this plan to be followed. Legal proceedings already consume extended periods of time and impose heavy financial burdens on suitors. They have a right to expect that once they have fought a case through its initial stages, they will not be compelled to start all over again in another forum.

Assuming that the federal courts have done their best to protect local jurisdiction, the remaining question is how they may dispose of such questions of local law as do come before them. Until a decade ago, this was a serious problem because of the disposition of the national judiciary to consider itself free to decide many matters of local law without reference to state decisions. But now that the policy of *Erie* v. *Tompkins*[25] appears to be firmly rooted in our jurisprudence, there is much less cause for concern. For we have the assurance that even where a national court is called upon to decide a local question, it will follow the same precedents observed by state tribunals and will, except in cases where the law is unsettled, always arrive at the same result that would have been reached had the case been adjudged by a state court.

25 See Chapters IX-XI, *infra*.

CHAPTER IV

DIVERSITY OF CITIZENSHIP

THE meaning of diversity of citizenship is basically simple. The relevant portion of Article III, Section 2 of the Constitution says: "The judicial power shall extend...to controversies between citizens of different states,..." In terms of an example, this constitutional provision means that if you are a citizen of New Jersey and I am a citizen of New York, a federal court has jurisdiction in a suit between us. But if we are both citizens of New Jersey, neither of us may gain entry into a national court on this ground.

This rule is clear enough so long as a single individual (plaintiff) faces a single individual (defendant). However, when the two opposing sides in a litigation do not conform to this simple pattern, the Constitution by itself is an insufficient guide to the law. In *Strawbridge* v. *Curtiss*,[1] decided long before the rule of *Swift* v. *Tyson* made the forum in which a case was to be heard so important a factor in determining the substantive law to be applied, there were two plaintiffs arrayed against two defendants. Both plaintiffs and one of the defendants were citizens of Massachusetts, while the second defendant was a citizen of Vermont. In dismissing the suit for want of jurisdiction, Chief Justice Marshall said that he understood the constitutional provision and the act of Congress passed pursuant thereto to mean that a federal court could not obtain jurisdiction on the ground of diversity of citizenship unless each of the plaintiffs in a litigation could show that his citizenship was different than that of each defendant. Marshall's one page opinion gives no reason for this limitation of the diversity jurisdiction beyond the Court's faith in its correctness, nor does it appear that any could have been given. The framers of the Constitution and the authors of the Judiciary Act of 1789

1 3 Cranch 267 (1806).

seem to have overlooked the problem presented by *Strawbridge* v. *Curtiss* and to have made no special provision for its solution. As a matter of logic, the arguments for and against Marshall's position are of equal weight. On the one hand, it can be said that the decision prevented the Massachusetts plaintiffs from bringing a fellow citizen before a federal tribunal: something which they could not have done if he were sued alone. On the other hand, it is just as true that the plaintiffs were denied their right to have their controversy with the resident of Vermont adjudicated in a national court merely because his interest happened to be linked to those of a Massachusetts citizen. Nor would an opposite holding have removed the injustice, for it is obvious that where there was a controversy over the appropriate forum, at least one of the defendants must have been prejudiced no matter which court, state or federal, took jurisdiction. However, as a matter of policy, the decision, which has been consistently followed down to the present day,[2] was fortunate because it put at least one obstacle in the way of suitors who wished to pervert justice by taking undue advantage of the differences in substantive law enforced by state and national judiciaries. But the Strawbridge Rule was not designed as a complete cure for the excessive use of federal diversity jurisdiction, nor can it be employed for that purpose. Lawyers have found a number of ways to create diversity of citizenship solely in order to permit a resort to the federal courts. One of them, the raising of a colorable federal question, has already been discussed. Others in common use have been: 1. Pretended assignments. 2. The improper joinder of parties, and 3. The establishment of a fake domicile.

1. Pretended Assignments

Where a suit was to be brought on a contract or other written instrument, a plaintiff who wished to come into federal

2 *Indianapolis* v. *Chase National Bank, Trustee,* 314 US 63 (1941); *McComb* v. *McCormack,* 159 F. 2d 219 (CCA 5th, 1947).

rather than a state court but was prevented from doing so because he was a resident of the same state as the prospective defendant was naturally anxious to remove the bar which circumstances had put in his way. Obviously, he could not ask his adversary to oblige him by moving to another state, and it might be inconvenient for him to pull up stakes just so that he could claim the necessary diversity of citizenship. But if people do not always find it easy to move about, the same is not true of legal claims. These can often be transferred from one person to another with little difficulty. What, then, could be simpler for the person desiring to bring suit in the federal court than to transfer his claim to a non resident and let the latter bring the suit? Of course, Congress was not blind to this attractive device and has sought to prevent its use ever since 1789. From that date until the present, there has been a statute declaring that a suit is not maintainable on a claim which has been assigned unless such a suit could have been maintained before the assignment.[3] However, the effectiveness of this legislation depends upon the ability of the courts to distinguish between bona fide transfers and improper ones. This is often difficult and there is room for more than a suspicion that many of the culprits are not detected and succeed in accomplishing their purpose.

2. IMPROPER JOINDER OF PARTIES

As we have already discovered from our brief allusion to *Strawbridge* v. *Curtiss,* the presence of more than one individual on either side of a litigation may affect the ability of the parties to claim diversity of citizenship. In such situations, an attempt is sometimes made to remove the difficulty by making a person who would normally be a plaintiff appear as a defendant, or vice versa. The rules relating to the proper and improper joinder of parties are of considerable importance to lawyers, but as they are highly technical and have no direct

3 1 Stat. 73, 76 (1789).

relation to the merits of a particular dispute, they will not be considered here.[4]

3. FAKE DOMICILE

State citizenship is more easily acquired or changed than national citizenship. The latter requires naturalization by a court of competent jurisdiction after a prolonged waiting period; the former can be accomplished simply by a change of residence. For it is usually true that a citizen of the United States is also a citizen of the state in which he lives.

A person who is prevented from litigating in a federal court because his prospective adversary enjoys a common citizenship with him may create the diversity necessary to establish federal jurisdiction merely by moving into another state. This maneuver is unlike either the assignment of a claim or the improper joinder of parties in that it is not the subject of Congressional prohibition and can be done openly without fear of defeat by a watchful court. Of course, this method of creating diversity has formidable disadvantages. Whereas the two previously mentioned devices are purely mechanical and require little effort or inconvenience, a change in one's residence is not likely to be accomplished without some change in a person's way of life. Family ties may have to be broken or another means of livelihood may have to be found in the new location. These practical difficulties insure against the widespread migration of suitors who wish to invoke the aid of federal rather than of state authority. In a very few cases, the fabulous reward to be had from a successful litigation in a national court and the certainty of defeat in the local courts may have induced persons to go to extremes, and in such instances the wrong worked on the victim by the material size of the judgment taken against him is a matter of no small concern. From the standpoint of general policy, however, it

---

4 For the rules relating to joinder of parties see Dobie, *Handbook of Federal Jurisdiction and Procedure* (1928), pp. 213-220; 4 *Moore's Federal Practice* (1942), chs. XIX-XX.

can be said that these miscarriages of justice are too infrequent to be serious.

If it is too much to expect people to upset their entire lives merely in the hope of capitalizing on an idiosyncracy of our judicial federalism, it is only natural that many attempts to accomplish the same result by less drastic means should be made. In consequence, many lawyers have become adept at inventing devices which have permitted such of their clients as were so disposed to satisfy the conditions for federal jurisdiction without undue inconvenience to themselves. Several rules of law have made the success of some of these attempts possible.

The opening words of the Fourteenth Amendment to the Constitution make it clear that a definition of the word " residence " is of key importance in determining state citizenship.[5] If the test were to be the same one used to ascertain eligibility for voting, the chance of establishing federal jurisdiction by a feigned changed in residence would be small indeed, because the length of time involved would raise all of the difficulties just discussed. But the enterprising litigant can achieve his purpose by meeting a much less stringent requirement, for it seems to be true that residence, for jurisdictional purposes, is synonymous with domicile.[6]

There are two essential elements in the concept of domicile. A person must be physically present in the place where he establishes it and, concurrently with this presence, he must intend to make the place his home for an indefinite time.[7] The first of these elements affords little opportunity for chicanery: a man is or has been within the state which he claims as his

5 "All persons born or naturalized in the United States, and subject to the jurisdiction thereof, are citizens of the United States and of the State wherein they reside."

6 *Bjornquist* v. *Boston & A. R. Co.*, 250 F 929 (CCA 1st, 1918); *Hiramatsu* v. *Phillips*, 50 F. Supp. 167 (DC Cal. 1943); Note, 42 Mich. L. Rev. 321, 322 (1944).

7 Goodrich, *On Conflict of Laws*, p. 37 (1938).

domicile, or he has not been there. The matter of intention, however, is more nebulous. It is a condition of the mind, and knowledge of it must come largely from what we are told. If Mr. Jones tells you that he intends to live in Tennessee, we would be hard put to it to prove that he is really thinking something else. Should he desire to fool us, the chances are good that he can do so. Of course, we may be able to draw certain conclusions from his behavior. If Mr. Jones merely takes an automobile ride to Nashville and returns to his old home immediately, we can probably show that his intention is other than what he says it is. However, should he rent a room in Nashville, it is a little more difficult to be sure that he is trying to fool us. And if Jones is determined to make it appear that he is thinking of making Nashville his home, he can do any number of things that will indicate this fact short of moving all his baggage and breaking all his ties with his old community. Nor does the law require that he go to great lengths in order to satisfy " doubting Thomases " that his intention is what he says it is. To understand this, one need only remember that non residents are constantly taking advantage of the brief waiting periods required by Nevada and Florida law to obtain divorces which are perfectly valid in other states.[8] They are able to succeed because they can acquire a formal domicile with ease and abandon it as soon as it has served its purpose without relinquishing the fruits of their deception. It is true that the trouble which a litigant who wishes to create diversity of citizenship must encounter varies with the facts of each case and is affected in some measure by the astuteness of his adversary. But it is also true that it is generally possible to establish diversity without actually making a complete and irrevocable change of residence.

8 Some limitation on what is often considered the abuse of the Nevada waiting period was made in *Williams* v. *North Carolina*, 325 US 226 (1945) where it was held that the courts of another jurisdiction may reopen the question of domicile.

The litigant who takes advantage of these circumstances can succeed in bringing his adversary before the bar of federal justice when the latter might prefer to entrust his rights to the judicial arm of a state government. But this is not the complete task. Most cases require a matter of months for their completion, and some legal proceedings take even longer. Were a litigant required to maintain his pretended domicile during all this time, the inconvenience would be sufficient to discourage all but the hardiest souls. But another principle of law has come to the aid of the enterprising suitor. It has become well established that once the jurisdiction of a federal court has been secured, it is not defeated by a subsequent change in the citizenship of the parties.[9] Nor does it matter that the motive for establishing the residence existing at the time of the commencement of the case was solely that of invoking the jurisdiction of a national court.[10] It is apparent, then, that once the litigant has created a sufficient impression of diversity of citizenship, he may discard his ruse.

USE OF DIVERSITY JURISDICTION BY CORPORATIONS

Corporations have found it especially easy to come into federal courts, but their favorable position in this regard could not have been attained without a reversal of early Supreme Court doctrine. Three years after the decision in *Strawbridge* v. *Curtiss* had made it clear that diversity of citizenship did not exist unless all the plaintiffs in a case were of a citizenship different from that of all of the defendants, the Court had its first opportunity to consider the applications of this rule to corporations. *Bank of United States* v. *Deveaux*[11] concerned

---

9 *Morgan's Heirs* v. *Morgan*, 2 Wheat. 290 (1817) ; *Conolly* v. *Taylor*, 2 Pet. 556 (1829) ; *Boesenberg* v. *Chicago Title & Trust Co.*, 128 F 2d 245 (CCA 7th 1942).

10 *Wheeler* v. *City and County of Denver*, 229 US 342 (1913) ; *City of Chicago* v. *Mills*, 204 US 321 (1907) ; *Sias* v. *Johnson*, 86 F 2d 766 (CCA 6th 1936).

11 5 Cranch 61 (1809).

the application of the diversity principle to a suit by a corporation, and it is notable for Chief Justice Marshall's opinion refusing to recognize the corporation as a single legal entity for purposes of diversity jurisdiction. Instead, he insisted upon an inquiry into the citizenship of the individual members of the corporation. The effect in that case, and in *Commercial & Railroad Bank of Vicksburg* v. *Slocomb* [12] which followed it, was to make it impossible for the litigant corporation to gain admittance to the federal courts. For in each instance, at least one member could be found whose citizenship was the same as that of the adverse party. Had Marshall's rule persisted, its effect must certainly have been to close the national courts to all of the large business enterprises which came to play so dominant a part in our economic life. To realize the truth of this statement, one need only think of a few well known corporations and imagine what their situation would be. General Motors, American Telephone and Telegraph, the Pennsylvania Railroad, United States Steel: these compnaies and others like them have stockholders in every state and could hardly find an opportunity to take advantage of diversity of citizenship in order to litigate in the federal courts.

In the early days, this disability was probably more of an asset than a handicap. Such corporations as were in existence, and there were very few of them, had been chartered by special acts of the state legislatures and granted monopolistic privileges with respect to the construction and operation of public improvements like toll bridges and roads. It is more than likely that these enterprises had nothing to fear in the way of prejudice on the part of a branch of the state government which had already shown favorable partisanship in granting them special privileges. It is more likely that persons who might become parties to a dispute with such a corporation would find themselves disadvantaged in a local court. But if a corporation could not come into a national court as plaintiff,

12 14 Pet. 60 (1840).

it was also true that it could not be forced to appear there as a defendant. Accordingly, a corporation had a greater assurance than other litigants that legal proceedings in which it might become involved would be conducted before a sympathetic tribunal.

However, as the industry and commerce of the nation developed, the corporate form became increasingly common. Its creation no longer depended on special legislation but was achieved by a simple and mechanical process of filing with the Secretary of State. All kinds of enterprises from multi-million dollar railroad companies to neighborhood retail stores availed themselves of this procedure and placed the letters " INC." after their names. The privilege of resorting to this form of business organization was open to all and the fact of its exercise signified nothing with respect to the condition of local sentiment.

In fact, local bitterness against big business in general, and railroad, insurance, and public utility corporations in particular, became widespread in many sections of the South and West. In such circumstances, corporations became increasingly anxious to litigate in federal rather than in state courts: something which they could not easily have done under the rule in the Deveaux Case. But it so happened that some years before this change in popular attitude took place, the Supreme Court had reversed its position. According to the new rule, announced in 1844 and adhered to ever since, a corporation is, for purposes of federal jurisdiction, deemed a citizen of the state in which it is incorporated.[13] This is so regardless of the citizenship of its stockholders. The effect of this doctrine has been to make it even easier for a corporation to gain access to the federal courts than for an individual.

The bit of make-believe which turns every corporation into a legal person has been of great use to the proper functioning of our economic system. It has permitted the law to fasten the

13 *Louisville, Cinn., & C. R. R. Co.* v. *Letson*, 2 How. 497 (1844).

same standards of good conduct on intricate business organizations which it applies to the behavior of individuals: a task which would certainly be difficult if the courts were compelled to think of these business enterprises as collections of office equipment, assorted machines, and anywhere from two or three to several hundred thousand individuals, each connected with the corporation in a different capacity from his neighbor. And what is even more to the point, this personification of a business unit has facilitated that limitation of liability which, after all, is the fundamental reason for the existence of the corporate form. An individual enterprise or partnership is responsible for its obligations to the extent of the business assets and to the limit of the owner's personal fortunes as well. A corporation, because it is a legal person quite separate and distinct from its stockholders, is responsibile for its debts only to the extent that they may be satisfied out of business properties.

But the persuasive analogies which can be drawn between corporate persons and live human beings cannot erase the elementary differences between them. For a human being is a single animate entity while a corporation is only a certificate in the filing cabinet of some Secretary of State.

In matters of diverse citizenship, this fact circumscribes real people much more narrowly than their inanimate legal brothers. It is a simple truth that a man cannot be in Delaware three hundred and sixty five days in the year and simultaneously operate a business whose only activity takes place in the State of California. A mere mortal cannot be in two places at the same time. But a corporation does not labor under this disability. It is, for example, a well known fact that many corporations are chartered in Delaware in order to gain the advantage of its lenient laws, but that their officers and stockholders do not necessarily reside in that state, nor do they ever intend to do any business there.

This ability of corporations to conduct their actual operations in places other than the state of their incorporation is far from being an evil. It gives many business organizations the flexibility which is absolutely necessary to their success. Indeed, in the frequent instances where business activity is interstate in character, the power of a corporation to be present in several states at the same time is an obvious necessity. However, it is none the less true that in this respect corporations enjoy a power not possessed by ordinary human beings who are limited by the realities of physical existence and must confine their activities to one geographic location at a time.

As we have seen, in matters of diversity of citizenship, the Supreme Court long ago attempted to place corporate litigants on the same footing as other persons by deciding that a corporation, like an individual, could have only one native state,—the one in which it has been incorporated.[14] In most cases, this rule has worked admirably. The overwhelming majority of small corporations, and not a few large ones, quite logically carry on all or most of their activities in the state of their incorporation. Such corporations enjoy no jurisdictional advantages over natural persons. However, corporations doing a substantial part of their business outside their home states find it unusually easy to invoke the federal diversity jurisdiction. They are bound to be classified as non citizens in most of the states where they become involved in legal disputes. In addition wherever astute lawyers have sought to bring their client's troubles before federal rather than state authorities, the purely formal test of corporate citizenship has suggested a means of invoking the federal jurisdiction where it would not normally exist.

Here, as in those cases where a natural person has sought to establish diversity of citizenship, success has gone to those who were able to convince the courts that their change of domicile was real and not pretended. With corporations, however, this has been done with less inconvenience than is normally possible for individuals, but this does not mean that every attempt to invoke the jurisdiction of a federal tribunal in this

14 See note 13, *supra*.

way achieves its purpose. Much can be learned from a study of the failures because these are the instances in which the courts have seen most clearly the abuses to which unscrupulous parties often put the letter of the law. The scope of this study does not permit an exhaustive examination of such instances, but two cases are worthy of attention because of the clarity with which they illustrate some of the prevalent practices.

In 1897 the firm of Miller & Lux incorporated in California. Three years later it filed suit against the East Side Canal and Irrigation Company, also a corporation of California, in a state court in order to obtain an injunction against the diversion of the waters of the San Joaquin River. In 1905 this suit was still pending in the California courts, and the owners of Miller & Lux decided that it might be wise to try their fortunes in a federal court. Accordingly, they entered into an agreement in which it was stated that the stockholders believed that their rights would be better protected in the federal courts and that for this reason, among others, they would form a Nevada corporation; transfer all of the California company's property to the new organization, and distribute all of the stock of the Nevada corporation among themselves. Within a few weeks, this plan was executed. The new firm then commenced suit against the Irrigation Company in a federal court, and the California Corporation dismissed its action in the state court. The defendant objected to the jurisdiction of the federal court claiming that the diversity of citizenship upon which it was based had been created for the purpose of removing the original case from state control and that the establishment of the Nevada firm was only a pretense. In 1908 the case reached the Supreme Court of the United States, and Mr. Justice Harlan, delivering the opinion of the Court said:

" If before the institution of this suit the California corporation had distributed among those entitled to it the stock of the Nevada corporation, issued to it as fully paid up stock, and had then ceased to exist or been dissolved, a different question might have been presented. But such is not this case. As the facts were, when this suit was brought the California corporation could at any time, even after this suit was concluded, have required the Nevada corporation, without any new or valuable consideration, to surrender all its interest in the property which it had obtained from the California corporation for the purpose of acquiring a standing in the Circuit Court of the United States." [15]

Justice Harlan continued by pointing out that the Court did not intend to modify the long established rule that a party's motive has nothing to do with his success in invoking the jurisdiction of a federal court. What was made clear was that the change of domicile must be real and not merely feigned. In this view of the matter, it is obvious that Miller & Lux did not fail because the creation of the conditions necessary for success would have placed any additional burdens on the corporation: the Nevada firm could have operated in California just as effectively whether or not the original corporation was formally dissolved. All that prevented Miller & Lux from supplanting the state courts with federal authority was the neglect of a purely mechanical detail—the dissolution of the California company.

The case of *Southern Realty Investment Co.* v. *Walker* [16] received a certain amount of notoriety at the time of its decision because of the unmistakable way in which it demonstrated the perverted use being made of " dummy corporations " in order to evade the law as administered by state courts. Justice Harlan, who wrote the opinion in this case as well as that in the Lux Case, explained the situation with such simplicity and candor that one could hardly do better than to reproduce his words.

15 *Miller & Lux* v. *East Side Canal and Irrigation Co.*, 211 US 293, 304 (1908).

16 211 US 603 (1909).

" There was evidence leading to the conclusion that the Southern Realty Investment Company was brought into existence as a corporation only that its *name* might be used in having controversies that were really between citizens of Georgia determined in the federal rather than in the state court. It did not have, nor was it expected to have, as a corporation, any will of its own or any real interest in the property that stood or was placed in its name. It was completely dominated by the two Georgia attorneys who secured its incorporation under the laws of South Dakota through the agency of a South Dakota lawyer, who, in a letter to one of the Georgia attorneys, claimed that his office had within three years secured nine hundred and eighty-five charters under the laws of that state for non residents, and part of whose business was to ' furnish ' South Dakota incorporators, when necessary. In short, the plaintiff company was and is merely the agent of the Georgia attorneys, who brought it into existence as a corporation that individual citizens of that state might, in their discretion, have the use of its corporate name in order to create cases apparently within the jurisdiction of the Federal court. It had, it is true, a president and a board of directors—all of whom were citizens of Georgia—two of the five directors being the Georgia attorneys, and one being the female stenographer of such attorneys—but the president and a majority of the directors were the holders each of only one share of donated stock and recognized it to be their duty to represent the Georgia attorneys and to obey, as they did obey, their will implicitly. The company, in respect of all its business, was the agent of those attorneys to do their bidding. Its president testified that he did not know for what purpose the company was really organized, or that it had ever done any business except ' as to the bringing of these suits,' or that it had any money. Its place of business in Georgia was in the office of the Georgia attorneys. Its pretended place of business in South Dakota was in what is called a domiciliary office, maintained by the attorney in that state who procured its charter. In the latter office there could have been found, no doubt, a desk and a chair or two, but no business. The company's president never knew of its doing any business in South Dakota. As a corporation the South Realty Investment Company must be deemed a mere sham." [17]

The people behind the Southern Realty Investment Company had run afoul of that portion of the Removal Act of 1875 which directs federal courts to proceed no further with a case if it shall appear that jurisdiction has been conferred upon it by collusion.[18] Indeed, this provision of the statute is the principal safeguard against abuses of jurisdiction based on diversity of citizenship. It is declared to be the policy of Congress and the duty of the national courts to prevent the flowering of schemes designed to oust the states from control over judicial matters legitimately within their proper sphere. As contained in the act of Congress, this is no more than a general indication of the standard which the federal judiciary is to apply. Its amenability to judicial interpretation makes the courts themselves the judge of its use.

Since collusion is the evil against which the national courts have been asked to guard, their views on what does or does not constitute collusion have been of paramount importance in determining the effectiveness of this attempt to safeguard state authority. Clearly, the citizens of Georgia whose activities Justice Harlan described went too far. But what was the nature of their fault? There was nothing wrong with their desire to set up a South Dakota corporation: non residents are every day incorporating enterprises in states other than those in which they intend to do business, and this practice is considered perfectly respectable. Nor was the vice to be found in the fact that a South Dakota corporation chose to sue Georgia citizens in a federal court rather than in the courts of an appropriate state. This was no more than an ordinary use of diversity jurisdiction. What irked the Supreme Court was the

17 211 US 603, 606-607.
18 18 Stat. 470 (1875).

knowledge that this was not really a controversy involving the South Dakota corporation, but that the claims which that firm was pressing were given to it for the sole purpose of defeating the jurisdiction of state courts. The tenuous character of this distinction is easily appreciated when one realizes that the owners of Miller & Lux were no less strangers to Nevada than the Georgians were to South Dakota. Yet their failure to gain federal protection for their claims was in no way traceable to the artificiality of their pretensions to Nevada citizenship.

The reluctance of the federal courts to defeat their own jurisdiction by finding the presence of collusion can be seen from the litigation over Denver's water system.[19] In response to strong popular sentiment at the turn of the century, that community undertook the construction of a municipal water-works. The private utility which was then furnishing the city's water supply recognized the obvious threat to its interests and was anxious to resort to the courts in the hope of stopping the project. For any number of reasons the private company wished to submit to the ministrations of a federal rather than a state court. But how was this to be done? The company and the City of Denver were both " citizens " of Colorado and the state judiciary was the proper agency of government to settle a dispute between them.

A way out of this difficulty was near at hand. All that the company had to do was to consult the local real estate records in order to find some non residents with property in Denver. This was done, and two of the people whose names were obtained were asked if they would have any objection to permitting the use of their names in the legal proceedings which the utility was anxious to bring. They agreed to the plan whose main outlines can be gleaned from a letter sent to one of them by the company's attorney.

19 *Wheeler* v. *City and County of Denver*, 229 US 342 (1913).

" My dear Mrs. Wheeler:

" On yesterday I wired you for permission to bring a suit in your name against some of the city officials for misuse of taxes, and received your reply authorizing me to go ahead. I brought the suit and filed it on yesterday. The suit is to restrain the Water Commissioners of Denver from further expenditures looking toward the purchase of a water plant by the City of Denver. The city is already enjoined in another proceeding in which the Water Company was a party.[20] Since that time the Water Commission has spent $31,000 to hold an election, and about $25,000 for other purposes; and are seeking to compel the city to pay out on warrants about $20,000 more.

" The courts have already held that the amendments to the charter establishing a Water Commission for the purpose of purchasing or building a water plant is unconstitutional and void, and it is our purpose to stop the spending of any more of the people's money in that direction.

" I desire to bring suit in the Federal Court, and therefore had to get permission of a non-resident taxpayer to bring suit, which accounts for my telegraphing you for permission.

" You will not be charged with any expense or costs in the matter, either for court costs or attorney's fees; and I will see that you are absolutely protected in every way from any liability whatever. Thanking you for your permission to bring the suit in your name, I remain." [21]

It was obvious that the private utility was the actual opponent of the Water Commission. Mrs. Wheeler's property interest in Denver was probably too small to make a suit worth her while. In fact it may be reasonable to assume that she had not considered opposing the public water project until the company's attorney approached her and explained that her appear-

20 The case referred to was a proceeding in a Federal Court: *New York Trust Company* v. *The City and County of Denver*, 187 F 890 (CCA 8th 1911).

21 229 US 342, 345.

ance as the nominal plaintiff in the suit would entail no expense and no inconvenience to her. She probably knew nothing of the relative merits of private and public ownership of the Denver waterworks and, especially since she was not a resident of the community, it may be doubted that she cared how the city obtained its water.

Anyone who had not been warned that collusion was a work of art would have experienced little difficulty in applying it to the situation presented by this case. It was readily apparent that the water company and Mrs. Wheeler had worked a scheme designed to permit the former to receive the benefit of federal jurisdiction when its only resort should have been to state tribunals. But the Supreme Court refused to find collusion. Its opinion pointed out that whatever may have been the circumstances which brought Mrs. Wheeler into the suit, she did hold property in Denver and was consequently in a position to maintain the suit in a federal court. In the Court's view of the matter, it made no difference that her action was of primary benefit to someone else: so much so that the litigation was actually being conducted and financed by the private utility which was technically not even a party to the suit.

If we accept the long standing rule of which this case is but one more illustration, namely, that the motives of a party to a litigation have nothing to do with his ability to shift the forum from a state to a national court, it is hard to find anything wrong with the Wheeler Case. Yet one cannot help feeling that it is an instance in which the complexities of our dual judicial system were used to gain a result inconsistent with sound policy and proper administration of judicial affairs. We may indeed wonder whether it is really true that motive is irrelevant in determining the division of power between major organs of national and state government. Mechanical rules have their place in promoting impartial justice, but they cannot solve subtle problems of the relation between states and nation.

The seriousness of these federal encroachments on the state judiciaries is far from easy to determine. The Wheeler Case is somewhat exceptional in its facts and cannot be taken as a fair example of litigation in general. Most of the other cases which supply information relating to the many attempts at creation of diversity jurisdiction are also unsatisfactory because they only give us examples of failure to take disputes out of the sphere of state jurisdiction. Of course, we might conclude that this means that the courts were usually successful in discovering and defeating these frauds. But it is equally probable that cases which should have been tried in state courts found their way into federal tribunals with considerable frequency. Court records and the published opinions of judges are hardly to be taken as reliable guides in this matter. For the reported cases discuss only those instances of fraud and collusion which came to light. The successful schemes were those which escaped judicial eyes and were treated as bona fide instances of diversity of citizenship.

Before 1928 there was reason enough to be concerned about the cynical way in which some litigants jockeyed the rules in order to take full advantage of differences of substantive and procedural law as enforced in the federal and state courts, but at least it could be said that the more flagrant instances of this chessboard maneuvering were frustrated by the federal courts whenever they were discovered. After the Black & White Taxicab Case,[22] one could not even be sure that this was true.

A local taxi company in Bowling Green, Kentucky, had made a contract with the railroad by whose terms the former was to have the exclusive right to park its cabs in and around the depot and to solicit business there. However, it appeared that such an agreement was unenforceable in Kentucky's courts because it violated the State's public policy against monopolies. A rival taxi service, being advised of this defect in its competitor's contract, began to solicit business at the depot notwithstanding the fact that it had no agreement with the railroad. That the family which owned the Black & White

22 276 US 518 (1928).

Taxicab and Transfer Company (the firm which had received the railroad's blessing) was disturbed is understandable. But what was to be done? Under Kentucky law, Black & White was not entitled to the benefit of an exclusive right to solicit business. The lawyers who represented each taxi company and those who were counseling the railroad all knew this, and some of them also knew that there might be a way to evade the Kentucky law, for it so happened that the federal courts looked upon an agreement such as the one between the railroad and Black & White with favor and would enforce it.

The problem, then, was how to get out of the reach of the hostile state authorities into the friendlier hands of federal judges. As the dispute between the rival taxi services was a purely local affair, the only hope was diversity of citizenship. This did not exist because both cab companies were incorporated in Kentucky. With the active assistance of the railroad, the Black & White Taxicab and Transfer Company of Kentucky was dissolved; a corporation of the same name was formed in Tennessee; the railroad made a new agreement with the Tennessee corporation; and all the while, the Bowling Green family which owned Black & White kept on doing business at the same old stand. But in point of law, things were different. Black & White was now a foreign corporation whereas its competitor was still a citizen of Kentucky. This enabled the former to bring suit against its rival in a federal court, which was promptly done. The result was that by some pen-and-paper maneuvering which had nothing to do with the actual operation of a taxi business in Bowling Green, Black & White was able to secure enforcement of its agreement with the railroad thereby denying its rival the right to do business at the local depot. The unfortunate victim might take comfort in the knowledge that this result was in direct contradiction of the laws of Kentucky, but we may doubt that he saw any humor in the situation.

Not one of the elements in the Black & White Case was really new. The cooperation between the railroad company and the taxi service was hardly closer than that between Mrs. Wheeler and the Denver water company. Nor was a change in the state of incorporation for the purpose of creating diversity of citizenship a novelty. This device had almost succeeded in the Lux Case, and its ultimate failure, as we have seen, had nothing to do with the inadequacies of the scheme there attempted. It is a safe assumption that more careful litigants, both before and after that case, had used re-incorporation successfully. Nor was it news to well informed persons that differences in the law as enforced by federal and state courts was at the bottom of maneuvers calculated to bring a particular dispute before one tribunal rather than another. What made the Black & White Case so startling was the combination of all of these features in such a way as to provide the clearest object lesson yet seen of the frictions existing between state and national judiciaries and of the mischief that could result therefrom.

CHAPTER V

RESTRICTIONS ON DIVERSITY JURISDICTION

In 1928 Felix Frankfurter estimated that about one-third of all cases in the federal courts were there because of a difference in the citizenship of the parties.[1] In all fairness, it should be said that not all of these cases represented the same type of danger to the judicial power of the states as that to be found in the Black & White Case. The mere existence of two judicial systems, one state, the other federal—both of them able to serve the needs of litigants—would suggest that some cases would find their way into one set of courts while others were channeled into the competing stream. It is just as reasonable to expect this to happen as it is to expect two stores on opposite sides of the same street carrying similar lines of merchandise to divide the business of a neighborhood between them. In so far as the problem of our rival judiciaries is like that of rival tradesmen, the measure of desirability in the situation is the same—is there enough business to warrant the maintenance of two separate organizations? If this were the crux of the problem its solution would depend on the proper application of routine principles of public administration, and not on basic considerations of public policy. But judicial service to the community presents problems only slightly akin to those found in the realm of private business. Competition in our economy is deemed useful because it is thought to promote long range efficiency. On the other hand, competition in law enforcement is bound to produce a confusion in the administration of justice destructive of a desirable uniformity in the application of the law. However, even when due allowance is made for those cases which wandered into the national courts purely by chance,

---

[1] Frankfurter, *Distribution of Judicial Power Between United States and State Courts*, 13 Corn. L. Q. 499, 523 (1928).

the number of disputes which came to federal rather than state tribunals was still large. The litigants in these controversies chose their forum because they hoped to gain some advantage by their choice. The Taxi Case may have been an unusually graphic example, but it was not an unfair one.

Corporate Preference for the Federal Courts

The unfairness of a system which permits litigants to escape state jurisdiction for reasons which have nothing to do with the merit of their disputes is equally great no matter who the beneficiaries and victims of it happen to be. Nevertheless, the identity of those who took most frequent advantage of the system had much to do with local sentiment against the exercise of diversity jurisdiction by the federal courts. It became an observable fact that large corporations, particularly railroads and insurance companies, regularly removed cases brought against them in state courts to the federal courts. This practice was especially common in the South and West,[2] and its effect was to add to the already considerable reservoir of bitterness against Eastern corporate interests in these sections of the country.

The nature of railroading and insurance makes it inevitable that corporations engaged in these businesses should be defendants in an almost infinite number of suits brought by ordinary citizens. The necessary hazards in travel and the impossibility of transporting millions of tons of assorted freight without damaging some of it make it a certainty that public carriers should face a continuous stream of claims for personal injury and property loss. This passenger has been cut by flying glass, another has been abused by a surly conductor, while a third has sprained an ankle in stepping from a train to the platform. All of these ordinary people have, or believe they have, claims against the railroad. All of them sue the company. Someone else sends his furniture from his present home

2 Frankfurter and Landis, *The Business of the Supreme Court*, p. 65 (1928).

to a distant city in which he intends to take up residence, and on its arrival, all of the glassware is broken and an easy chair is lost. This person also sues the company.

Insurance companies are also habitual defendants in lawsuits. Policies covering all types of risk from death to hurricane damage are widely held by people in all walks of life, and disputes over the insurer's liability on these policies are bound to arise with great frequency. Here, as with the railroads, ordinary citizens who might otherwise have no personal experience with the courts have an opportunity to recognize the effect which judicial processes have on their lives. Especially in the rural communities of the South and West where every man knew his neighbor's troubles, sharp legal practices on the part of the Eastern corporation could more easily become common knowledge than in urban centers of a corporation's home state.

The reasons why these habitual defendants preferred to entrust their fates to national tribunals went beyond the willingness of these courts to make independent interpretations of local law. Of course, corporations were not averse to taking full advantage of differences in the rules of substantive law as expounded by state and federal courts. But if this had been the only reason for the desire to litigate in one place rather than in another, one might expect to find a large number of cases where corporations would prefer the views of state courts. However, there were other motives which led corporations to choose federal courts. Some of them were bound up in the minutia of procedural law and will not be discussed here. Two of the more important reasons, however, deserve notice: they were the desire to compel ordinary people whose resources were limited to undergo the expense of litigation far from home, and the attempt to avoid the effects of local sentiment hostile to Eastern corporations.

Until a generation or so ago, parts of our country were little more than virgin territory. State courts of some kind were usually more or less available in these outlying areas, but federal courts might be several hundred miles apart. As a result, litigation before the latter tribunals was comparatively expensive. The parties to a dispute had to spend the time and money necessary to get them over the distances between their homes and the courthouse. Then too, attorneys and witnesses were compelled to make the journey. Corporations knew that these difficulties would increase their own legal expenses, but they also knew that the ordinary individuals with claims against them would be put to additional expense in prosecuting their suits. The corporate defendants usually had greater financial resources than their adversaries and could better afford the increased burden. Consequently, it was their purpose to make the cost of litigation prohibitive so that most people could not afford the luxury of enforcing their rights in the courts of law. It is probable that many legitimate claims were defeated by these tactics, and it is certain that the communities whose people were victimized harbored considerable ill-will toward the Eastern capitalists who used them.

In thinly settled parts of the United States it is still true that federal courts are much less accessible to many of the people than are the state courts. In Texas, for example, there are twenty-five places throughout the state where a regular session of a United States District Court is held, but there are two hundred and fifty-four places where a regular session of an equivalent state tribunal meets. The situation in California is perhaps even more striking. A United States District Court is to be found at only five places within the state, whereas a California Superior Court is to be found at each of the fifty-nine county seats; and where such county seats are at some distance from outlying areas, a session of the Superior Court is held in towns having as few as seven thousand inhabitants.[3] In the thickly settled Northeastern part of the country this disparity between the geographic availability of federal and state judicial facilities is naturally less, but even so any differ-

3 See table, p. 97, *infra.*

AVAILABILITY OF FEDERAL DISTRICT COURTS

State	No. of U.S. Judicial Districts	No. of Places Where U.S. District Court Regularly Held
Alabama	3	12
Arizona	1	4
Arkansas	2	10
California	2	5
Colorado	1	6
Connecticut	1	2
Delaware	1	1
Florida	2	10
Georgia	3	11
Idaho	1	4
Illinois	3	8
Indiana	2	7
Iowa	2	12
Kansas	1	6
Kentucky	2	12
Louisiana	2	7
Maine	1	2
Maryland	1	1
Massachusetts	1	4
Michigan	2	5
Minnesota	1	6
Mississippi	2	8
Missouri	2	10
Montana	1	7
Nebraska	1	8
Nevada	1	3
New Hampshire	1	2
New Jersey	1	3
New Mexico	1	5
New York	4	13
North Carolina	3	18
North Dakota	1	6
Ohio	2	7
Oklahoma	3	19
Oregon	1	4
Pennsylvania	3	9
Rhode Island	1	1
South Carolina	2	10
South Dakota	1	4
Tennessee	3	9
Texas	4	25
Utah	1	2
Vermont	1	4
Virginia	2	11
Washington	2	6
West Virginia	2	11
Wisconsin	2	8
Wyoming	1	4

The data on which this table is based is to be found in 2 Martindale-Hubbell, " Legal Directory " (1947).

COMPARATIVE AVAILABILITY OF FEDERAL AND STATE COURTS
IN WESTERN UNITED STATES

State	No. of Places Where U. S. District Court Regularly Held	No. of Places Where State Court of General Original Jurisdiction Regularly Held
Arizona	4	14
California	5	59 plus (see below)
Colorado	6	63
Idaho	4	44
Montana	7	55
Nevada	3	17
New Mexico	5	31
North Dakota ...	6	53
Oklahoma	19	87
Oregon	4	36
South Dakota ...	4	71
Texas	25	254
Utah	2	29
Washington	6	39
Wyoming	4	23

In California, sessions of the Superior Courts are held at each of the 59 county seats. In addition, California statutes provide that:

1. In all cities with a population of 125,000 or more, at least three concurrent sessions shall be held.

2. In cities of 50,000 or more a session of the Superior Court shall be held if such city is more than six miles from the nearest regularly held Superior Court.

3. In cities of 35,000 or more a session of the Superior Court shall be held if such city is more than eight miles from the nearest Superior Court.

4. In places of 20,000 or more a session of the Superior Court shall be held if such places is more than thirty-six miles from the nearest Superior Court.

5. In places of 7,000 or more a session of the Superior Court shall be held if such place is not less than fifty-five miles from the nearest Superior Court.

6. In places of 10,000 or more a session of the Superior Court shall be held if such place is eighteen miles from the nearest Superior Court and if certain other conditions are met.

See Ca. CCP (Deering 1941) Sec. 73 and Sec. 73 (b), Supp. 1947.

The data on which this table is based is to be found in 2 Martindale-Hubbell, " Legal Directory " (1947) and the statutes of the various states.

ence is such as to emphasize the convenience of resort to state courts. In Rhode Island, for instance, the only United States District Court is to be found in Providence, whereas state courts of general original jurisdiction sit at seven places within the state.[4]

4 R. I. G. L. Ann. c. 498 (1938) ; 2 Martindale-Hubbell, *Legal Directory* (1947) R. I. Superior Court calendar.

The reluctance of corporate defendants to submit to state authority as exemplified by local courts irritated an already existing bias against big business. The true basis of the sentiment is to be found in the political and economic relation of large corporations, particularly those in the utility field, to the people of the Mid and Far West. The Granger, Populist, and Progressive Movements which loom so large in the history of our nation were directed squarely at state regulation of railroads, grain elevators, and similar enterprises largely owned and controlled by Eastern investors. These targets of agrarian discontent were busily engaged in fighting government control, and it is only natural that they should not wish to have their legal controversies decided by the judicial department of the very state governments which were seeking to regulate their activities. In electing to submit to federal authority, these companies hoped to be judged by tribunals which were insulated against local anti-corporation sentiment. It may be said that such protection was not necessary because the judicial branch of government is concerned, not with the formulation of partisan policy, but only with the administration of an impartial justice. However, the captains of industry and their astute legal advisors were unwilling to rely too heavily on the abstract logic of political theory.

One need only be reminded of one or two salient characteristics of state and federal judiciaries to see the justification for these doubts. In the first place, state judges were bound to be local men who would naturally share the views of their neighbors; this was less likely to be the case with the members of the federal judiciary. Then too, state judges were, as indeed they still are, usually elective officials. They were chosen by the same voters who had put Granger governors and legislatures into office, and they could be turned out by this same electorate. Federal judges, on the other hand, owed their positions to the President and Senate of the United States whose outlook was national rather than provincial. Moreover, federal judges could be removed only by impeachment and were con-

sequently in a better position to champion unpopular causes if
they chose to do so.

In this struggle between Nation and States for judicial
power, the judicial branch of neither government was in complete control of its own battle strategy. Their position as umpires of disputes rather than of participants in them made it
possible for the courts to choose the cases which they were to
decide. Instead, the competing judicial systems were forced to
act on those disputes which private interests wished to bring
before them and to take the occasions which circumstances
might present to formulate the rules and make the interpretations according to which judicial authority would be divided
between the national and local courts. The federal government
had a great advantage in this waiting game. For, so long as the
corporations preferred to litigate in national courts, they could
channel a considerable volume of judicial business in that
direction. As plaintiffs, they could initiate suits in federal
courts, and their adversaries were usually powerless to transfer
them to state tribunals even when they might wish to do so.
As defendants, corporations could remove suits brought
against them from state to federal courts and keep them there
on the plea of diversity of citizenship. What could be done to
improve the position of the states was a vexed question which,
at various times, was puzzled over by interested private litigants, state legislatures, and even the Congress of the United
States.

Litigants' Attempt to Restrict Federal Jurisdiction

We have seen that private individuals and corporations who
wished to bring cases before the national judiciary when they
were properly cognizable only in state courts, could resort to
a number of devices in order to attain their goal. It is also true
that private parties were sometimes able to keep diversity of
citizenship cases out of the federal courts by skillful tactics.
Like the slight-of-hand designed to manufacture federal jurisdiction, the legal magic employed to accomplish the reverse re-

sult was directed at procedural technicalities rather than at the merits of a given controversy. If private persons could bring suits which would normally be tried in state courts before federal judges by changing their residence, it should follow that they could keep suits which did not involve federal questions out of the national courts by a similar device. For it is clear that once national tribunals were closed to litigants they would have to rely on state courts.

In one case, a Minnesota firm had a claim against a Pennsylvania corporation arising out of certain lumbering operations carried on within the State of Minnesota. This claimant preferred to litigate in the local courts, but feared that the corporation would take advantage of its Pennsylvania citizenship and remove the case to a federal tribunal. Accordingly, the prospective plaintiff sold its claim to a resident of Pennsylvania, and the latter successfully resisted the attempt to transfer the case from a Minnesota to a United States Court.[5]

If this device were as effective in keeping cases out of the federal courts as its counterpart has been in getting cases before national tribunals, there would still be reason for complaint. Plaintiffs, regardless of the merits of their claims, would have an undue advantage over their adversaries because they would be able to arrange the facts of citizenship to suit themselves before informing the defendants of their intention to bring suit. This would give them an unhampered choice of forum which no defendant would be able to change. But it cannot even be said that litigants threatened by removal to the federal courts could normally protect themselves by a change of their citizenship. The very lack of parallels for this Minnesota case [6] would tend to indicate that it is markedly more difficult to manipulate citizenship so as to stay in a state court than it

5 *Hayday* v. *Hammer-Mill Paper Co.*, 176 Minn. 315, 223 NW 614 (1929).

6 So far as I have been able to discover, there are only three other reported instances of this practice: *Providence Savings Life Assurance Society* v. *Ford*, 114 US 635 (1885); *Oakley* v. *Goodnow*, 118 US 43 (1886); *Wells* v. *Western Union Telegraph Co.*, 144 Ia. 605, 123 NW 371 (1909).

is to do the same thing with the purpose of appealing to federal authority.

If we take the situation in the Minnesota case as illustrative, we can make several observations which will make this difficulty clear. It should first be noted that had the Minnesotan wished to litigate in the federal courts, he could have done so without disturbing his original circumstances. Even if this would have been of no other advantage to him, he would at least have been spared the search for someone who was able and willing to buy his claim.

But let us assume that the prospective defendant was domiciled in Minnesota, the plaintiff's state. If the latter wished to litigate in the federal courts, he could do so after changing his residence to any one of the forty-seven other states which he might find convenient. Or, should he wish it, he could even move to any foreign country. But if we take the case as it actually arose, we see that the claimant is confronted with a much more difficult situation. If he is to destroy the difference in citizenship, there is only one state that he can consider, Pennsylvania. No other will do because Ohio, Michigan, or any other state he may choose will leave the difference in citizenship unimpaired.

A far more successful, and therefore a far more common way of making sure that cases brought in the state courts would not be removed to a federal docket was to reduce the size of one's claim below the " jurisdictional amount ".[7] This has always been a possible stratagem because our first Federal Judiciary Act provided that cases involving less than five hundred dollars could not be brought in the national courts,[8] and every succeeding Judiciary Act has also contained a provision designed to keep actions involving relatively small amounts of

7 Collier, *A Plea Against Jurisdiction For Diversity of Citizenship*, 76 Cent. L. J. 263, 265 (1913).

8 1 Stat. 78 (1789).

money off the federal docket.[9] But as one may well suspect, the use of this device did not become common until the differences to be expected from litigation in national and state courts became apparent.

If, for example, a man lost a leg in a train wreck during the year 1910, he might have been warranted in suing the railroad for many thousands of dollars; the exact size of his claim would depend upon circumstances—medical expenses, the man's age, loss of earning power, pain and suffering, etc.; it is obvious that the damages for which the railroad company would be liable would be large. But if the man had reason to believe that he could succeed in a state court whereas he would fail before a federal tribunal, he would be forced to consider the wisdom of accepting a small sum as compensation for his serious injury. At that time the " jurisdictional amount " in the federal courts was two thousand dollars. Were the unfortunate victim to claim the compensation to which he was actually entitled for his injury, he faced the almost certain prospect of being forced into a federal court. In order to avoid this danger, he might decide to accept something less than two thousand dollars on the theory that a grossly inadequate recompense was better than none at all. If a present day litigant in a similar situation wishes to keep his case in the state courts, he must also be content with inadequate relief. The only difference is that today the jurisdictional amount is three thousand dollars.

As a result of this set of conditions, litigants were induced to abandon the major portion of just claims which it was the business of the judicial branch of government to protect.[10] Yet

9 An Act of Feb. 13, 1801, commonly called " The Act of the Midnight Judges ", reduced the jurisdictional amount to $400. 2 Stat. 92. But by an Act of March 8, 1802, the Act of 1801 was repealed and that of 1789, including provisions as to jurisdictional amount, was revived. 2 Stat. 132. An Act of March 3, 1887 raised the jurisdictional amount to $2000. 24 Stat. 552. The present $3000 limitation was first introduced in 1911. 36 Stat. 1091, 28 U.S.C. # 41(1) (1927).

10 See Collier, *A Plea Against Jurisdiction for Diversity of Citizenship*, 76 Cent. L. J. 263, 265 (1913). " If a citizen has a claim against a non-

the reduction of claims to a point below the jurisdictional
amount was the only effective protection which suitors wishing to have their rights adjudicated by state judiciaries could
find. The states had a deep interest in the plight of their citizens, for more than the outcome of a few private lawsuits were
involved. To the extent that corporations were able to avoid
submission to the local courts they were able to avoid obedience
to state law. This might ultimately mean an escape from legislation by which the states were seeking to regulate corporate
activities.

States' Attempt to Restrict Federal Jurisdiction

The imbalance of our dual judicial system revealed by these
miscarriages of justice was much more far reaching than the
corporation problem. Any litigant might be forced to reduce
or abandon a just claim because of fear that it would be removed to a federal court where different rules made success
unlikely. This was as true when the prospective defendant was
a non resident individual as when it was a foreign corporation.
Of course, informed opinion in the states knew this, and it is
undoubtedly correct to say that, where enforcement of local
law was concerned, the states would have liked to keep as much
legal business as possible from escaping their jurisdiction. But
any action along these lines had to be tempered by what was
constitutionally possible.

To deny individual citizens the use of the federal courts in
cases within the national jurisdiction was so obviously destructive of the aims which the Federal Constitution was framed to
uphold as to be clearly beyond state power. At the height of
the famous struggle over Nullification in South Carolina, that
State had taken this extreme step in order to prevent federal

---

resident or a foreign corporation, and it is inconvenient to go or be called
into a Federal Court, or he prefers to have applied the state view of his
right, he cannot elect, unless he sues for less than $3,000. This is common
practice in suits against foreign corporations." See also note, *Preventing
Removal of Causes by Foregoing Part of Claim*, 15 Corn. L. Q. 307 (1930).

enforcement of the tariff laws.[11] But the collapse of Nullification before the threat of national force brought an end to this brief episode in South Carolina law, and no other state has ever attempted such a far reaching attack upon the judicial branch of the national government. Indeed, after the Civil War, one could point to a specific provision of the Constitution standing in the way of such state action. The Fourteenth Amendment with its guarantees of due process and equal protection of the laws would certainly be offended by local legislation seeking to close the federal courts to any or all of our people.

In addition to these Constitutional protections, there is the Privileges and Immunities Clause in Article IV which assures the citizens of every state the right to move about and carry on normal activities freely throughout the entire country. Under the protection of this guarantee, an individual citizen of New York is as safe in his person and property and in his right to seek the ordinary assistance of governmental authority in Ohio or California as he is in his native state.

For many years, it was thought that there might be a way to deny these constitutional protections to corporate interests. We have already seen that in the early days, the privilege of incorporation was conferred by special act of a legislative assembly. Occasionally, as in the case of the First and Second United States Banks, the action was that of Congress. But as a general rule, corporations received their charters from state legislatures.

It follows that incorporation was not a right but a matter of grace: something to be granted or withheld by the state at its pleasure. For it would offend our most basic principles of government to suggest that it might be possible to compel a democratic legislative body to make a law that did not have the voluntary approval of a majority of its members.[12] When

---

11 Nullification Ordinance, Nov. 24, 1832, 1 SC Stat. 329, 330 (1836).

12 At first glance, judicial enforcement of the provisions of an interstate compact would seem to be an exception to this statement. In *Virginia* v.

the increasing commercial and industrial development of the country made the corporation an everyday form of business organization rather than the symbol of special legislative favor, it was no longer possible for this original method of incorporation to be continued. No legislature had the time or facilities to consider the deluge of applications for charters that began to descend on all state capitols. Nor was it necessary that a policy-making body such as a legislature pass on the individual merits of these applications. The task was becoming primarily a routine one more fit for administrative functionaries. Accordingly, the "general corporation law" made its appearance and ultimately became universal.

Under this new system for the creation and regulation of corporate enterprises, any business which complied with the requirements established by law and whose incorporators filed the necessary papers with a designated state official could receive a charter. But this did not mean that state governments were surrendering any of their power to control these business enterprises. The "general corporation law" was merely a device tailored to meet the need for mass production of a hitherto seldom used type of business organization. The states could have returned and may still return to the special law as the sole means of conferring corporate charters. In the absence of this unlikely return to outmoded practice, however, they may continue to refuse incorporation to those organizations which fail to meet the conditions set down in the general corporation laws.

West Virginia, 220 US 1 (1911) the State of West Virginia was held liable for an equitable share of the Virginia debt outstanding on January 1, 1861. This liability was in accordance with a compact between the two states. In 1918 the Supreme Court reaffirmed West Virginia's liability and declared that it was able to resort to execution if such a step should prove necessary. 246 US 565. In obedience to this decision the West Virginia Legislature provided for payment of the state's share of the debt. 1919 W. Va. Acts (Ext. Sess.) Ch. 10, p. 19. However, the action of a state legislature in such a case is rendered necessary by the state's previous agreement evidenced in the compact and so may be regarded as the completion of obligations already assumed by the legislature in its prior enactments.

Nor is this all. What a State has granted, the State may normally take away. In the days of special acts, this was abundantly clear. If the legislature of state X had passed a law granting the Y Company a corporate charter, it could take the charter away by the simple expedient of repealing the law. The power to repeal a statute was often exercised, and there was no reason why acts of incorporation could not be undone in the same way that all other laws were changed. When the day of the general corporation law arrived, the legislature no longer found it necessary to expunge specific acts of incorporation. Instead, an administrative official might exercise the power to revoke the charters of corporations which had violated one or another provision of state law.

The state which creates a corporation naturally has the greatest measure of control over its activities, for by revoking its charter, this state may put an end to the organization's existence. But every state into which a corporation wishes to go exercises a similar power of life and death over that portion of the corporate business transacted within its borders. It is, for example, universal practice for a state to require that foreign corporations obtain a certificate of authority to do business and in order to secure and hold such a certificate, the firm must meet certain conditions. Failure to comply results in the denial of the certificate or, where it has already been granted, in its revocation.

Not a few states in the South and West decided to use their power to exclude foreign corporations as a weapon in the struggle between their judiciaries and the federal courts.[13] The plan was to amend their general corporation laws in such a way as to make resort to the federal courts a ground for exclusion from the state. The Secretary of State was directed to revoke the license of any foreign corporation which removed a case brought against it by a local resident to the federal courts pro-

13 See Henderson, *The Position of Foreign Corporations in American Constitutional Law*, Ch. VI (1918).

vided that the removal was without the consent of the local party.

This was indeed a drastic step. So far as the corporation was concerned, the penalty for non compliance was prohibitive, being nothing less than the withdrawal of the right to carry on its activities. One may suspect that many corporations submitted to this coercion by the states rather than run the risk of losing their business. But access to the national courts was too valuable a privilege to be surrendered easily, and it was only natural that these laws should be tested in the courts.

In *Insurance Company* v. *Morse*,[14] the first case involving one of these state laws to reach the Supreme Court of the United States, the law in question was declared unconstitutional. The Court was unable to rest its decision squarely on a specific provision of the Constitution, but apparently believed that to permit the states to decide whether cases could be acted upon by federal authority permitted too great an interference with the power of the national government. According to this view of the matter, it was clearly not intended that local authorities should be able to obstruct the functioning of a major department of the national government. As Article III of the Constitution had given the national government a judiciary and judicial power, it was undoubtedly meant that this power should be freely exercised.

This position had much common sense to recommend it. No less a figure than Chief Justice Marshall had used an analogous argument in deciding that Maryland could not tax the United States Bank because such action was an undue interference with the proper operation of the federal government. But in *McCulloch* v. *Maryland*,[15] the Court could point to the fiscal powers expressly granted Congress as a specific source of national authority, whereas this could not be done in the Morse Case. On the contrary, champions of the states'

14 20 Wall. 445 (1874).
15 4 Wheat. 316 (1819).

position could point to the supposedly well established principle that a state could exclude a foreign corporation from its territory for good reason, bad reason, or no reason at all.

It was, then, not surprising that in the next case to come before the Supreme Court, the result should be different.[16] The Court discovered a slight difference in the wording of the statutes[17] which it was called upon to consider in these two cases and so saved itself the necessity of overruling its former decision. But the effect of this second case was to make it possible for states to restrict the removal of cases to the federal courts where corporations were the defendants.

The Supreme Court might now console itself with the knowledge that superior legal logic was on its side; but what of the common sense embodied in the earlier decision? The Court's task appeared to be an impossible one, for it seemed that whichever way it decided, either legal technicality or practical considerations must be sacrificed. This dilemma explains the somersaults of the next forty years during which the Court alternately held these state laws valid and invalid[18] while it struggled to discover a formula which would conform to the requirements of symmetrical constitutional theory and the practical facts of life in a country organized along federal lines.

Victory of Unfettered Federal Jurisdiction

In 1910 Mr. Justice Harlan supplied the answer for which the Court had been searching. *Western Union Telegraph Co. v. Kansas* [19] did not involve a state statute restricting entry

16 *Doyle* v. *Continental Insurance Co.*, 94 US 535 (1876).

17 The statute in the Morse Case required that a foreign corporation agree not to remove cases into the federal courts as a condition precedent to its entry into the state. The statute in the Doyle Case required no agreement but directed the Secretary of State to revoke a foreign corporation's license if it resorted to the federal courts.

18 *Barron* v. *Burnside*, 121 US 186 (1887), held a statute invalid. *Security Mutual Life Insurance Co.* v. *Prewitt*, 202 US 246 (1906), held a similar statute valid.

19 216 US 1 (1910).

into the federal courts. Instead, it concerned a tax laid on Western Union's business by the State of Kansas. The company claimed that as its business was primarily interstate, the exaction constituted a burden on interstate commerce and could not be levied without violating the Commerce Clause of the Constitution. Kansas argued that as it had the power to prevent the Telegraph Company from doing a local business, it must also have the power to condition its right to do that business upon the payment of the tax. While this argument could have no effect upon the right of Western Union to conduct its interstate operations in Kansas, it was the contention of the State that it was perfectly feasible to require the payment of the tax because of the company's local activities.

In rejecting this argument, Holmes pointed out that it was impossible to separate the interstate and intrastate phases of the telegraph business. Both local and long distance messages were sent over the same lines and the company's facilities would have to be substantially the same whether or not it handled intrastate traffic. If the tax were permitted to stand it must necessarily affect Western Union's interstate activities. As this would necessarily involve a violation of the Commerce Clause, it must follow that the state tax law was invalid. In essence the new doctrine was that whereas a state might have the power to exclude a corporation from its territory, it did not have an unlimited power to circumscribe the activities of corporations already within the state.

Within a few years of its original announcement, this doctrine of "unconstitutional conditions" was applied to cases involving statutes restricting access to the federal courts. It was now decided that just as it was beyond state power to require that corporations engaged in interstate commerce submit to unreasonable burdens on their business, so it was also impossible for the states to make the abstinence from federal protection for their legal rights a condition for corporate entry or continued residence within a state.[20] The vacillation was at an end. With a respectable bit of doctrine to back them up, the courts no longer hesitated to follow common sense to its natural conclusion.

In reality the new doctrine was merely a concise and explicit statement of something implied in *Insurance Co.* v *Morse,* the case which had first brought this particular problem before the high bench. At an early date, the Court had chosen to rest its decision on the fundamental relation between the various sovereignties within our federal system, and that was precisely the basis for this new bit of constitutional theory. But one important thing about its application to statutes of the type under consideration was the express recognition that a state's power over corporations was not so complete as the traditionally doctrinaire slogans seemed to indicate. It was now admitted that there were certain things that the states could not do. This made it unnecessary for the Court to seek spurious distinctions in its efforts to uphold the national judicial power. The day of this kind of coercive legislation was over, and it has not returned. Occasionally, a zealous corporation lawyer trying to save his client from some legitimate form of state regulation has contended that a particular law operated so as to limit a corporation's right of access to the federal courts,[21] but arguments in this vein have been more remarkable for their ingenuity than for their approximation of the true situation.

The indirect attempt to limit the diversity jurisdiction of the federal courts by coercing some of the litigants who habit-

20 *Terral* v. *Burke Construction Co.,* 257 US 529 (1922).

21 *Railway Express Agency* v. *Virginia,* 282 US 440 (1931). A state statute requiring the express company to obtain a local charter before engaging in a purely intrastate business was held valid. The contention that the taking out of a Virginia license would destroy the Company's diversity of citizenship in any suit brought with respect to its local Virginia business, thereby restricting the Company's possible access to the federal courts, was dismissed as frivolous.

ually made use of them and the ultimate failure of the scheme, made it clear that the federal judicial system was beyond state power. As a sovereign, our national government has control over its own judicial branch. Or, to put it more accurately, Congress is the appropriate agency to determine the extent of the jurisdiction to be exercised by the federal courts. Since Congress has chosen to confer both federal question and diversity jurisdiction on the lower federal courts, the area of concurrent federal and state jurisdiction is inevitably a large one. Efforts to restrict a litigant's choice of judicial systems have failed. As a result, the most important question for our judicial federalism is not which court shall hear a case but rather whose law, state or federal, should it apply in reaching its decisions.

PART III

SWIFT V. TYSON: AN EXPERIMENT IN NATION-WIDE UNIFORMITY

CHAPTER VI

THE COMMON LAW

THAT it was obligatory on the states to abide by judgments of the federal judiciary was seriously disputed only during the first generation or so after the adoption of the Constitution. *Martin* v. *Hunter's Lessee* laid the question of open warfare between national and state courts at rest, but that case left a number of equally important matters for later disposition. It should be remembered that neither the Constitution nor *Martin* v. *Hunter's Lessee* stands for the proposition that the state courts are merely inferior members of a national legal organization. Of course, the Supreme Court of the United States has a power of review wherever interests of a federal nature require it. It is equally true, however, that the primary function of our state judiciaries is the enforcement of state law, and in this field their authority is usually final.

If it were possible to keep all questions of local law in the state courts and all matters of federal law in national courts, the relations among our several judicial systems would be fairly simple. Each set of courts would complement the others, but there would be little interrelation of their activities. In all cases coming before them, the judges of Texas or Rhode Island would be obligated to look only to the mandates of their own legislatures and to the guidance of their own precedents. Similarly, judges charged with the administration of law originating in Washington would always center their full attention on the acts of Congress and the decisions of federal tribunals. However, the economic and social frictions that give rise to legal controversy have a way of ignoring pre-arranged classifications. We have seen that where a single piece of litigation presents questions of state and federal law, justice requires that one court hear and determine all of the issues raised by the case. Moreover, the existence of federal diversity jurisdiction makes it inevitable that the national courts decide many questions of local law where there is not even the shadow of a substantive federal right to be protected.

In a country with a unitary system of government, these problems do not exist. If, for example, a vintner from the Garonne Valley and an exporter of Bordeaux maintain business relations, we may confidently expect that it will be done within the legal framework of the French Codes. And if either of the parties requires the intervention of a public authority for the settlement of a dispute, it is clear that the courts of France will apply law made by the Parliament at Paris. But if a Boston shoe manufacturer and a Hartford retailer find themselves in a similar situation, whose law is a federal court to enforce when it comes into the picture only because of its diversity jurisdiction? Shall it be the statutes and common law of Massachusetts, or those of Connecticut? Or shall the federal court ignore both states and administer a rule of its own?

This is more than a question of legal procedure. The power of the State of Massachusetts is only as great as the number and importance of the situations in which its law governs. The Government of Massachusetts has a measure of control over labor, business, health, etc. within its borders because its laws dealing with these subjects will be applied and enforced to disputes in these fields. The State of Massachusetts has no power over these affairs when they are conducted in Connecticut because its laws will not be applied there. And what is true of Massachusetts is equally true of any of our states and of the United States.

EARLY UNIFORMITY IN INTERPRETATION OF SUBSTANTIVE LAW

The situation resulting from the existence of a number of states, each with its own judiciary and its own body of law, is not a unique creation of our federal system. The division of the world into many sovereign nations is, of course, much older than our Republic, and the legal problems that this segmentation of the earth's population and geography presents on the international plane is much the same as that which troubles our federalism. The trading nations of Europe were all aware of the need of reckoning with the laws of foreign territories, and England, as a leading commercial country of the early modern era, had her share of these problems. Starting with Lord Mansfield, English judges began to show a deep interest in the legal aspects of international trade. One of the basic rules that they developed was that the law governing a given transaction was the law of the place where it occurred. From the very beginning, Congress and our courts received this principle willingly. The famous Section 34 of the Judiciary Act of 1789 provided " that the laws of the several states, except where the Constitution, treaties, or statutes of the United States shall otherwise require or provide, shall be regarded as rules of decision in trials at common law in the courts of the United States, in cases where they apply." [1] With this statute as a guide, the federal courts seem to have taken it for granted that in diversity cases " the law of the place " was " the law of the state " where a transaction had occurred. During the first

1 1 Stat. 92 (1789).

half century after the adoption of the Constitution, the cases, except for those in equity,[2] uniformly held to this doctrine. Little purpose would, therefore, be served by rehearsing the details of all of the many opinions relating to this point. It may, however, be of some value to look briefly at a few of the more extreme pronouncements of the Supreme Court in order to understand how unreservedly the federal courts were accustomed to enforce state law.

The most obvious class of cases requiring the enforcement of state law was that involving rights to land. Each state was sovereign within its own territory, and the principle that title to real property derives from the sovereign was as well established in this country as in England. Moreover, to respect local law was the only practicable course. For to countenance a system that permitted two judiciaries, one state, the other federal, to entertain separate notions concerning the true ownership of a single piece of real estate would have been to invite untold and indefensible confusion. The Supreme Court of the United States was so well aware of the soundness of this position that it did not hesitate to respect state law even when faced with somewhat unusual circumstances.

The case of *Mutual Assurance Society* v. *Watts*,[3] decided in 1816, involved an interest in land which, at the beginning of the chain of events leading to the litigation, had been located within the borders of Virginia. Before the action was commenced, however, Virginia had ceded the land to the federal government in connection with the creation of the District of Columbia. One of the parties to the action contended that as

2 At the time of the Revolution and shortly thereafter, a separate equity jurisdiction was barely in its first stage of development in the states. Accordingly, it was later held that the equity jurisdiction of the federal courts came from the English chancery courts. The national judiciary was therefore free to follow its own precedents in preference to those which might be developed in the states. *Boyle* v. *Zacharie*, 6 Pet. 635 (1832); *U. S.* v. *Howland*, 4 Wheat. 108 (1819); *Robinson* v. *Campbell*, 3 Wheat. 212 (1818).

3 1 Wheat. 290 (1816).

the land in question was no longer a part of the State of Virginia, its laws could no longer be consulted to determine the original source of title. Although a tribunal anxious to build an independent federal jurisprudence might conceivably have taken this opportunity to ignore rights which had vested under state law, only two justices of the Supreme Court dissented from an opinion which refused to do so. Since Story, who was later to author the doctrine of an independent federal common law, was one of these two, his reasons for refusing to join in the majority opinion would be interesting. However, neither Story nor Livingston, who also dissented, wrote an opinion. It is therefore impossible to say why there was disagreement on the Court, and it may well be that it had nothing to do with the question of whether to follow Virginia law.

Although the predominance of realty cases in the early work of the Supreme Court may have lent some color to the notion that deference to state law was especially owing in that field,[4] the high bench also accepted state authority in other areas. Chief Justice Marshall's brief opinion in *Mandeville* v. *Riddle* [5] leaves many of the circumstances of that case to conjecture. However, it is abundantly clear that this was a commercial matter in which the plaintiff would have had a remediable grievance if Marshall had thought himself free to apply a general common law to the dispute. But the Chief Justice spent all of his remarkably few words in noting that the laws of Virginia, in which state the case arose, were as yet incomplete. And since the legislature and courts of Virginia had not yet provided for the plaintiff's situation, a federal court could do nothing.

But most striking of all was the Court's holding in *Wheaton* v. *Peters*,[6] decided in 1834. This was a question of copyright—

4 Pepper, *The Borderland of Federal and State Decisions* (1889), p. 74. For an analysis of the change in the character of the business of the Supreme Court between 1825 and 1925 see: Frankfurter and Landis, *The Business of the Supreme Court* (1928), p. 302.

5 1 Cranch 290 (1803).

6 8 Pet. 590 (1834).

a field in which the supremacy of federal law has been recognized from the very beginning. However, because of the unfortunate circumstances of his case, the plaintiff chose to rely largely upon the protection afforded by the common law as developed by the courts of England and inherited in America. The heart of a lengthy opinion by Mr. Justice McLean makes the Court's position clear:

" But if the common-law right of authors were shown to exist in England, does the same exist, and to the same extent in this country? It is clear, there can be no common law of the United States. The federal government is composed of twenty-four sovereign and independent states; each of which may have its local usages, customs and common law. There is no principle which pervades the Union and has the authority of law, that is not embodied in the constitution or laws of the Union. The common law could be made a part of our federal system, only by legislative adoption. When, therefore, a common-law right is asserted, we must look to the state in which the controversy originated. And in the case under consideration, as the copyright was entered in the clerk's office of the district court of Pennsylvania, for the first volume of the book in controversy, and it was published in that state, we may inquire whether the common law, as to copyrights, if any existed, was adopted in Pennsylvania." [7]

The willingness of the Supreme Court to follow local law can be explained in either of two ways. It may be that in obedience to section 34 of the Judiciary Act, the Supreme Court believed itself bound by state decisions on common law subjects. Or, at the very least, it is an illustration of the familiar comity principle which has led the courts of one sovereign to apply the law of other jurisdictions when the circumstances of a particular case make it appear that the ends of justice will be promoted thereby. The passage just cited from Justice McLean's opinion in *Wheaton* v. *Peters* seems to support the former

[7] 8 Pet. 590, 657-658.

view. But an attempt to find a satisfactory answer to this question brings no great reward because so long as the Court was content to follow local law, judges had no reason to choose between plausible explanations of their actions. It was only in 1842 when the Supreme Court began to decide that it was not always necessary to respect the precedents issuing from state courts that an inquiry into the grounds of their action became vital.

EMERGENCE OF FEDERAL INDEPENDENCE OF JUDGMENT

In that year the case of *Swift* v. *Tyson* [8] came to the Supreme Court on a certificate of division from the Federal Circuit Court for the Southern District of New York. The certified question concerned the admissibility of the defendant's evidence, but as this in turn depended upon the validity of a substantive proposition of law, the decision of the Supreme Court dealt with more than a mere matter of procedure.

Two men had sold a tract of land in the State of Maine and had received a negotiable bill of exchange in payment. The defendant, Tyson, had endorsed this bill, and in due time it had been received by the plaintiff, Swift, in New York. Upon maturity, the bill was dishonored and Swift began proceedings against Tyson in the Circuit Court. At the trial, Tyson offered to prove that the original sellers with whom he had dealt were swindlers who did not have title to the land that they had sold. It would, therefore, follow that the bill of exchange had come into existence as the result of fraud, and its payment could not be enforced by the original recipients thereof.

According to well established principles of the common law as they were understood in most jurisdictions, this tale of woe might have caused a judge to shed a sympathetic tear, but its practical value to Tyson would have been nil. A " holder in due course " of negotiable paper may receive satisfaction from an endorser even if the original parties could not have collected

8 16 Pet. 1 (1842).

on the instrument. However, a line of decisions by the courts of the State of New York made it appear possible, although by no means certain, that if the case were to be decided in accordance with the law of New York, Tyson might avoid liability. This was so because in New York it had been held that a holder in due course was one who received a negotiable instrument in " the normal course of trade ".[9] Swift had received the troublesome bill of exchange for a pre-existing debt and, once again according to the then prevailing New York law, this was not considered to be in " the normal course of trade ". Thus, the all important question was whether a federal court sitting in New York was bound to follow the state law.

Mr. Justice Story who wrote the majority opinion in the Supreme Court began with a full review of the facts. He then proceeded to notice that the defendant contended that since the bill of exchange had been accepted in New York, the law of that State should apply. Story next turned to the relevant New York cases, and as a result of his examination of them, he concluded that the state law, although until recently favorable to the defendant's cause, had been thrown into some doubt by two of the latest New York decisions. It appeared, then, that if the federal courts were to follow the state law in this instance, it would not be easy to discover just what the law was. In such a predicament, what was the federal court to do?

The court might have solved its problem in any one of several ways. Story might have likened the situation before him to that in *Mandeville* v. *Riddle* where Marshall had held that in the absence of a remedy under Virginia law, the case was to be dismissed. But such a position would have been hard to justify because *Swift* v. *Tyson* presented a question of sub-

9 For the New York holdings on this point see: *Payne* v. *Cutter*, 13 Wend. 605 (1835) ; *Ontario Bank* v. *Worthington*, 12 Wend. 593 (1834) ; *Rosa* v. *Brotherson*, 10 Wend. 85 (1833). However, the New York courts do not appear to have been entirely satisfied with their own rule. See *Bank of Sandusky* v. *Scoville*, 24 Wend. 115 (1840) ; *Bank of Salina* v. *Babcock*, 21 Wend. 499 (1839).

stance rather than one of remedy. And, even more important, this was not a case of a void in the law but one of uncertainty as to which of two allegedly divergent state holdings to follow.

A less drastic alternative would have been to hold the case in a state of suspended animation until the New York courts had settled the point of substantive law whose indefiniteness was causing the trouble. A year after the Tyson case, Story himself did something like this in litigation which came before him while he was on circuit in Massachusetts.[10] Such a method of procedure had much to recommend it since it permitted the state whose law was in question and whose judiciary was normally charged with its enforcement to have the final word as to the interpretation of its own law. But this approach to the problem would have been possible only where there was some assurance that the litigants in the case would not be kept waiting long for the necessary guidance from a state court. This assurance would only have been forthcoming if it were known that a specific case soon to be decided by the appropriate state judiciary was directly in point. For, unless this were the circumstance, the case which was being kept on the federal docket might hang fire for years while it awaited the accident which would bring an appropriate action before a competent state tribunal.

If the Court had considered these procedures and found them undesirable, there was yet a third road open. The high bench might have recognized the uncertainty of the New York law. It might then have pointed out that because it had the case only by virtue of the constitutionally conferred diversity jurisdiction, it was the duty of a federal court to ascertain as best it might what a state court would do under identical circumstances, and act accordingly.

Any of these dispositions of the case might have been suggested by previous decisions of the Supreme Court, but Story

10 *Springer* v. *Foster*, 2 Story 385 (1843). Chief Justice Marshall had followed this plan in an earlier case. See *Bank* v. *Dudley*, 2 Pet. 492 (1829).

struck out in an entirely different direction. Speaking for all but one member of the Court,[11] he announced that even if the New York decisions had settled the law in that State, that circumstance could not control the actions of the federal judiciary. This stand brought Story into seeming conflict with Section 34 of the Judiciary Act of 1789 which provided that the laws of the several states should be the rules of decision in the federal courts in cases where they apply. But Story used the art of definition to remove this difficulty when he wrote:

" In the ordinary use of language, it will hardly be contended, that the decisions of courts constitute laws. They are, at most, only evidence of what laws are, and are not, of themselves, laws. They are often re-examined, reversed and qualified by the courts themselves, whenever they are found to be either defective, or ill-founded, or otherwise incorrect. The laws of a state are more usually understood to mean the rules and enactments promulgated by the legislative authority thereof, or long-established local customs having the force of laws. In all the various cases, which have hitherto come before us for decision, this court have uniformly supposed, that the true interpretation of the 34th section limited its application to state laws, strictly local, that is to say, to the positive statutes of the state, and the construction thereof adopted by the local tribunals, and to rights and titles to things having a permanent locality, such as the rights and titles of real estate, and other matters immovable and intra-territorial in their nature and character." [12]

After disposing of the Judiciary Act in this fashion, Story proceeded to furnish his own guiding principle. In matters of commercial law, the federal courts were to exercise an independent judgment: to find and expound those general principles of the common law which might govern a particular case

11 See concurring opinion of Mr. Justice Catron in *Swift* v. *Tyson*, 16 Pet. 1, 23.

12 *Swift* v. *Tyson*, 16 Pet. 1, 17-18.

for themselves without any necessary reliance upon judicial opinion in the state from which the case came. And—to apply this rule to the case in hand, the defendant must fail in his attempt to gain the protection of the New York decisions. The Supreme Court of the United States preferred to stay with the weight of judicial authority in most common law jurisdictions which was to the effect that one who becomes the holder of negotiable paper "in due course" is unaffected by the infirmity of the paper as between the original parties.[13]

It has frequently been pointed out that so much of Story's opinion as relates to the freedom of the federal courts to determine questions of common law is dictum. And an analysis of Swift v. Tyson shows this to be true. For, had the Court not strayed from the beaten path, it would have reached a result no different from the one at which it actually arrived. If, as Story took great pains to demonstrate, the New York cases were not clear, it would have been perfectly proper for a federal court to decide the question of substantive law as best it might in the absence of conclusive guidance from the state judiciary. The Supreme Court had done this on a number of occasions prior to 1842. It was, therefore, unnecessary for Story to assume a well settled state law, and equally unnecessary for him to comment upon the independence of the federal Courts. But whether these last pages of the Court's opinion were dictum or holding is, in any but the narrowest academic sense, a matter of little moment, for it is certain that for almost a hundred years, the rule of *Swift* v. *Tyson* was the law of the land. Accordingly, an attempt to discover the source of Story's opinion is more in order than a tirade against its legitimacy would be.

By Story's time the idea that judicial decisions are only evidence of the law and not the law itself was thoroughly familiar to legal philosophy. In medieval England, just as on

13 For a collection of the authorities on this point see *Brush* v. *Scribner,* 11 Conn. 388 (1836).

the continent of Europe, academicians and theologians had decided that law sprang from Nature and Reason. As these are universal phenomena, it seemed to follow that the " True Law " was a body of absolute and universal principles. According to this view of the matter, the common law judge, in every specific case which came before him, embarked upon a voyage of discovery in order to find the law. Sometimes he was like Columbus and announced that he had found the Orient when he had really come upon America; at other times, he was like Vasco Da Gama and actually arrived in India when he intended to go there. His statements were those of an exployer,— to be taken as tentative indications of the actual law but subject to correction by later voyagers whose metaphysics or divine inspiration was of a purer brand.

This theory had already played a part in a celebrated struggle between a judiciary and another organ of government. When King James I sought to ignore a ruling of the courts, Coke told the monarch that he must obey the law because it is the embodiment of Nature and Reason. And when the King opined that he was as fully endowed with reason as his judges and could find the law for himself, Coke found it necessary to answer that the judges were especially qualified to go on voyages of legal discovery:—from which we may gather that even as early as the beginning of the seventeenth century, practical administrators of the law found it expedient to modify the teachings of abstract philosophy.[14]

But the verbal battles between King James and his most eminent jurist were more symbolic than real. Although theoretical discussions sometimes play an important part in winning converts to one position or another, this battle of the sovereign against his courts was a highly practical affair. It is important in the history of government because its outcome helped to establish the independent power of the judiciary.

14 For accounts of the history and importance of this controversy see 5 Holdsworth, *History of English Law* 423-456 (1924) ; Pound, *The Spirit of the Common Law* (1925), Ch. 3.

The same thing may be said of Story's philosophical argument in *Swift* v. *Tyson*. This concept of judicial decision as Evidence of the Law was a hammer which he took from his legal tool chest so that he might drive a practical project toward completion.

Throughout his long service on the bench, Story was anxious to extend the federal jurisdiction as far as the Constitution would permit. In admiralty he was content to let events run their normal course secure in the knowledge that the Constitution had expressly assured the supremacy of the national courts.[15] But other branches of the law required more aggressive attention if the degree of federal control which Story believed essential to our development as a single country were to be attained. Soon after he came to the Supreme Court, that tribunal decided that common law crimes were not offenses against the United States.[16] Consequently, the federal courts were restricted in their criminal jurisdiction. Story believed that the way to remove this obstacle to federally administered justice was to codify and elaborate the federal criminal code. Over a period of years, he drafted and actively sought passage of several bills looking toward the accomplishment of this goal, and the most ambitious of his efforts resulted in the Crimes Act of 1825 which materially expanded the jurisdiction of the national courts.[17]

An even greater part of Story's tremendous energy and scholarship went into his work on private international law. Because his " Commentaries on the Conflict of Laws " was the first systematic and authoritative treatise on this subject in the English language, he had more than the ordinary opportunity to influence the future course of the law and more than the

15 U. S. Constit., Art. III, sec. 2.

16 *U. S.* v. *Coolidge*, 1 Wheat. 415 (1816) ; *U. S.* v. *Hudson*, 7 Cranch 32 (1812).

17 For an account of Story's interest in the criminal code, told largely through his own correspondence, see Story, *Life and Letters of Joseph Story* (1851), I, 242-245, 246-248.

customary need to rely on the writings of Continental Euro-
peans. After noticing the scant attention paid to this branch
of the law in England prior to the time of Lord Mansfield,
Story proceeded to assemble what he considered to be the gist
of the applicable Occidental jurisprudence and to derive a set
of general principles by which to determine the proper law to
be applied to international situations. Under the circumstances,
the " Commentaries " could hardly have been a recital of the
established law of any one jurisdiction, and it certainly could
not have been an attempt to catalog an incomplete common
law. Instead, Story presented a body of conflict-of-laws rules
which he deemed to be capable of universal application. Such
rules are of great value in a branch of practical jurisprudence
whose function is the determination of which national law,
(French, English, Spanish, etc.), shall govern a given international situation.

If we turn from the entire range of the conflict of laws to
that part of the subject which relates to international commerce,
we may find a clear statement of Story's views on the desirability of uniformity in the law. Only a year after the publica-
tion of his " Commentaries ", he wrote as follows:

" As to commercial law. From mutual comity, from the
natural tendency of maritime usages to assimilation, and from
mutual convenience, if not necessity, it may reasonably be expected, that the maritime law will gradually approximate to a
high degree of uniformity throughout the commercial world.
This is indeed in every view exceedingly desirable. Europe is
already, by a silent but steady course, fast approaching to that
state, in which the same commercial principles will constitute
a part of the public law of all its sovereignties. The unwritten
commercial law of England at this moment, differs in no very
important particulars from the positive codes of France and
Holland. Spain, Portugal, and the Italian States, the Hanse-
atic Confederacy, and the powers of the North, have adopted
a considerable part of the same system; and the general disposition in the Maritime States to acknowledge the superiority

of the courts and code of England, leaves little doubt that their own local usages will soon yield to her more enlightened doctrine. What a magnificent spectacle will it be to witness the establishment of such a beautiful system of juridical ethics,—to realize, not the oppressive schemes of holy alliances in a general conspiracy against the rights of mankind, but the universal empire of juridical reason, mingling with the concerns of commerce throughout the world, and imparting its beneficent light to the dark regions of the poles, and the soft and luxurious climates of the tropics." [18]

Somewhat earlier in the same essay, Story addresses himself directly to conditions in the United States. He recognized that the federal character of our government and the existence of separate state judiciaries made some local diversity in our law not only inevitable but desirable. However, he underscored the difficulties which our system placed in the way of judicial administration.[19] It is, therefore, apparent that the uniformity in commercial law which Story thought so advantageous to the world at large should seem even more indispensable to the welfare of a single nation.

Although the majority opinion in *Swift* v. *Tyson* does not rest upon the advisability of uniformity in the commercial law, the case itself contains evidence that this consideration was in the forefront of Story's mind if not in that of his colleagues. Justice Catron concurred in the judgment of the Court, but he wrote a separate opinion,[20] in which he protested the broad doctrine laid down by Story. His objection was partly founded on a conviction that the decision of the case did not require the assumption of a settled New York law, but he also insisted with some vehemence that he did not believe that an attempt

18 MacIntosh (editor), *Law Tracts*, Essay No. 2. Story, *A Discourse on the Past History, Present State, and Future Prospects of the Law* (1835), pp. 23-24.

19 *Ibid.*, p. 21.

20 16 Pet. 1, 23.

to set so wide a precedent as that contained in the opinion of the majority would succeed in producing the desired uniformity.

THE TYSON RULE GROWS

Story had no way of knowing whether his Tyson doctrine would have any effect on the development of our judicial system. The federal courts might subsequently have modified or declined to follow his opinion, and his attempt to expand the federal power would have been to no avail. But it was precisely the contrary that actually happened. In the ninety-six years between *Swift* v. *Tyson* and *Erie Railroad* v. *Tompkins*,[21] Story's original doctrine was so elaborated that even he might have wondered at its eventual scope. Story's opinion contains two principles which can be concisely stated.

1. Where the question is as to the legislative enactment of a state, or as to a well established local custom, or where the title to real estate is at issue, the federal courts will follow the authority of state tribunals.

2. Where the question is one of general commercial law, the federal courts will decide the case in accordance with their independent notions of the common law .

One can see at a glance that most of the cases coming into the federal courts by reason of the diverse citizenship of the parties would afford opportunities for the application of one or the other of these rules. The states might legislate on virtually any subject, and while the body of statute law in mid-nineteenth century America was slim and relatively unimportant when compared with the omnipresent common law, it would not always be so. Disputes over land titles also provided a copious source of litigation in a country which was still in its pioneering days and made its living from agriculture. However, an increase in the number of cases to which this first rule might be applied contained no threat to state authority because these would be cases in which the federal courts would

21 304 US 64 (1938).

follow state laws. On the other hand, prospects for the frequent use of the second principle were also bright. Although overland travel was still difficult, traffic across state lines was an everyday phenomenon and tended to increase in volume as the country became better settled and the production of manufactured goods gave people more things to buy and sell. Increased commercial litigation would necessarily threaten the supremacy of local common law, because according to Story, such cases provided the federal courts with opportunities for the use of their independent judgment.

Despite the breadth of the doctrine announced in Swift v. Tyson, there were classes of disputes requiring judicial attention to which it could not directly apply. There was for example, a vast body of transactions which are personal rather than commercial in nature. Then, too, there was the entire law of torts on which the Tyson Case had nothing to say. The Supreme Court, attracted by the expansiveness of Story's doctrine, early set about the task of filling the voids that he had left.

In 1845 the case of *Lane* v. *Vick*[22] came before the high bench. The relatives of a Vicksburg testator had litigated his will at great length in both state and federal courts, and the highest court of Mississippi had already construed the instrument. But this did not prevent the Supreme Court from giving a totally different construction to the will. Justice McLean delivered a long opinion, but a very few words from it suffice to indicate the point to which the Court, only one member dissenting, had carried Story's doctrine. ". . . it may be proper to say, that this court do not follow the state courts in their construction of a will or any other instrument, as they do in the construction of statutes."[23]

This pronouncement is of particular interest because it is directly counter to the holding in the earlier case of *Jackson* v.

22 3 How. 464 (1845).

23 3 How. 464, 476.

Chew [24] which also involved the interpretation of a will. *Lane* v. *Vick,* together with *Swift* v. *Tyson* and the intervening case of *Carpenter* v. *Providence Washington Insurance Co.,*[25] carried the independence of the federal courts to its greatest possible limit in the class of cases to which they were directly applicable. It was no longer necessary that the writing in a case be commercial in nature. So long as there was any kind of a document, with the possible exception of a deed, to be interpreted, the federal judiciary could ignore state tribunals even though the only reason for the jurisdiction of the national courts was the accidental difference in the citizenship of the parties to a litigation.

Seventeen years after the decision in *Lane* v. *Vick,* the Supreme Court took another step destined to increase the power of a federal court to decide questions of common law for itself.[26] A Chicago property owner had, by the well established common law of Illinois, neglected to observe proper care in protecting passers-by from an excavation which he had made adjacent to a public street. Someone had fallen into this hole, received an injury, and collected a judgment against the City of Chicago. Under familiar principles of law, the City was entitled to reimbursement from the property owner and sued to enforce this right. But the Supreme Court held that it would determine the question of negligence for itself. As it did not agree with the view of the law held by Illinois courts, the federal tribunal proceeded to render judgment against the City of Chicago. This made the independence of the federal courts in matters of common law almost complete. It applied to questions of contract and tort alike.

As the federal power to make independent determinations of state law grew, the final authority of state judiciaries over the remaining portion of their common law became progres-

24 12 Wheat. 153 (1827).

25 16 Pet. 495 (1842).

26 *Chicago City* v. *Robbins,* 2 Black 418 (1862).

sively more uncertain. Story had expressly proclaimed the duty of the national courts to follow local land law, and federal tribunals continued to assure anyone who would listen that the decisions of local courts as to real property law were as binding in diversity cases as they were in the normal run of controversy over land titles. But the general principle was much easier to adhere to in the abstract than it was to enforce in specific instances. The plain truth of the matter was that real estate law could not be put into a box and administered as a thing apart. A dispute would arise because someone thought that he had made an agreement to buy or sell a tract of land. This was as much a matter of contract as of real property, and in contract cases the federal courts followed their own precedents. A deed to land might be given as collateral for a loan, and this transaction would owe as much to the law of security as to that of land. Or, as in *Lane* v. *Vick,* real estate might change hands under the provisions of a will. But here too the national courts used their independent judgment in the interpretation of written instruments.

An analysis of the confusion and inequities attending judicial efforts to administer the Tyson Rule in this most troublesome area of real property would be long and arduous, and the reward for much labor would be slight owing to the fact that *Swift* v. *Tyson* was finally laid to rest in 1938. But two prominent examples of the excesses in which the federal courts indulged are worth examining.

A man named Yates had bought a piece of river-front property in Milwaukee. Taking advantage of his rights as a riparian owner, he built a wharf. Sometime later, the owner of an adjacent property excavated his land causing filler which Yates had placed on the landward side of his wharf to break away, thereby weakening his structure. Accordingly, Yates sued the neighboring owner in the Wisconsin courts only to have the Supreme Court of that State decide that the land at the margin of the river was " a public highway " which he had not purchased when he acquired his property. The result was that Yates lost his suit.[27] A few years later, the City of Milwau-

27 *Yates* v. *Judd,* 18 Wisc. 126 (1864).

kee, acting under power given by the State of Wisconsin, declared the wharf to be beyond its newly established dock line and threatened to remove it as a public nuisance. Yates thereupon sought to enjoin this municipal action declaring that his property could not be taken without just compensation. Although the previous case in the state court was not fully determinative of his rights in his litigation with the City, an examination of that case leaves a strong impression that under state law Yates should not have received his injunction because he did not have title to all of the disputed land. But this second case was brought in a federal court which observed a different rule as to the ownership of water-line property. The matter finally reached the Supreme Court of the United States, and in the course of his opinion Mr. Justice Miller referred to the previous litigation in the Wisconsin courts as follows:

" This question of dedication, on which the whole of that case turned, was one of fact, to be determined by ascertaining the intention of those who laid out the lots, from what they did, and from the application of general common law principles to their acts. This does not depend upon State statute or local State law. The law which governs the case is the common law, on which this court has never acknowledged the right of the State courts to control our decisions, except, perhaps, in a class of cases where the State courts have established, by repeated decisions, a rule of property in regard to land titles peculiar to the State." [28]

The Supreme Court then proceeded to suggest that if the City were to take the wharf, it would have to be by eminent domain. Yates succeeded in obtaining his injunction from a federal court, whereas his chance of getting relief from the local courts would have been, to say the least, dubious.

However, the head-on collision between national and state views of real property law did not come until the decision in Kuhn v. Fairmont Coal Co. in 1910.[29] Kuhn, a citizen of Ohio, had sold the mining rights in a piece of West Virginia land of

28 *Yates* v. *Milwaukee*, 10 Wall. 497, 506 (1870).

29 215 US 349 (1910).

which he owned the fee. His grantee proceeded to conduct mining operations but was careful to take the customary precaution of leaving pillars of coal in the ground in order to support the surface. He then sold the mining rights to the Fairmont Coal Company, a West Virginia corporation. This new owner continued working the property and removed the pillars of coal causing the surface of the land, which Kuhn still owned, to subside. After watching his now unsupported acres settle, crack, and lose their natural water supply, Kuhn decided that he had a cause of action against the coal company.

Some years before the destruction of Kuhn's surface land, but after he had sold his mining rights to the original purchaser, a Mr. Griffin found himself similarly aggrieved by the Fairmont Coal Company and had entrusted his complaint to the not so tender mercies of the West Virginia courts. The highest court of that State had rendered a decision in favor of the defendant coal company in which it was said that the owner of surface land has no protection against the destruction of his property unless he expressly reserves the right to support in the deed conveying the mining rights.[30] As Griffin like Kuhn, had not reserved this right, the Supreme Court of West Virginia ruled against him. Kuhn, however, because he was a citizen of Ohio while the coal company was a corporation of West Virginia, could take advantage of the diversity jurisdiction of the national courts. In reply to a question certified by the lower federal court, a sharply divided Supreme Court of the United States announced that it had long upheld the right of the federal judiciary to make independent determinations in many matters related to real estate titles, and that furthermore, it disagreed with the West Virginia rule and would hold that the owner of surface land was entitled to proper support of his property.[31]

It may well be that in this case the federal rule made better sense than the state law. But it was even more obvious that the

30 *Griffin* v. *Coal Co.*, 59 W. Va. 480 (1905), 53 SE 24.

31 *Kuhn* v. *Fairmont Coal Co.*, 215 US 349 (1910). Mr. Justice Holmes' dissent in this case is one of the landmarks of growing judicial discontent with the doctrine of *Swift* v. *Tyson*.

Supreme Court of the United States had now virtually demolished the supremacy of local real property law in diversity cases. According to the law of West Virginia, Kuhn, by selling the mining rights to his land, had disposed of all his valuable interest in the property. Although he might be the formal owner of the top soil, this could be of no practical significance because his real estate was bound to be swallowed up by the subterranean diggings. But a federal court sitting in the state was able to exempt Kuhn from the fate which had already befallen a local resident, merely because he came from Ohio and did not have to resort to the local courts.

The Supreme Court, and consequently the entire federal judiciary, had traveled a long road since the early days. When, in 1834, Justice McLean had said that there was and could be no national common law, his words could be taken as a reliable indication of the view of the courts. Seventy years later an impressive array of judicial decisions had made McLean's theory misleading if not untrue. For many years the federal courts continued to quote and paraphrase the traditional theory,[32] and even when the weight of changing conditions made McLean's thesis inappropriate, it was modified rather than abandoned. The new view was most concisely stated by Mr. Justice Brewer in *Western Union Telegraph Co.* v. *Call Publishing Co.* where he wrote: " There is no body of Federal common law separate and distinct from the common law existing in the several states in the sense that there is a body of statute law enacted by Congress separate and distinct from the body of statute law enacted by the several States. But it is an entirely different thing to hold that there is no common law in force generally throughout the United States." [33]

This was just as misleading as McLean's outdated theory. Brewer may have meant to say that there was only one body of common law which served as the basis for both federal and

32 See *Murray* v. *Chicago & Northwestern RR. Co.*, 62 F. 24 (1894) and cases cited therein.

33 *Western Union Telegraph Co.* v. *Call Publishing Co.*, 181 US 92, 101 (1901).

state decisions. In a broadly historical sense this may have been an approximation of the truth.[34] But it did nothing to explain the many cases in which local and national tribunals reached opposite conclusions when faced with the same question of law. Or it may be that he meant to say that there are certain rules of the common law which are the same in all jurisdictions and that only these were applied in the federal courts. But even a casual observer could not accept such a statement as this; for it was an indisputable fact that there were many questions which were determined differently in federal and local courts sitting in the same state.

The most obvious inadequacy of the official theory led writers on legal subjects to wonder whether in spite of the denials by the Supreme Court, there was not a federal common law apart from those bodies of precedent administered by the judiciaries of the several states. The argument was long and heated;[35] but the host of metaphysical distinctions invented by Justice Brewer's defenders to sustain his position, and the innumerable specific cases cited by the disbelievers to prove that there was indeed a national common law could not change the simple fact:—*A litigant who would be sure to lose his case in a state court could often succeed in a federal court, and a suitor who stood no chance at all in a federal court might succeed in the local courts.*

---

34 Even the English courts, especially in the times before the American Revolution, recognized local divergences in the common law existing in various sections of England and traceable to ancient local customs.

35 For some of the more informative articles inspired by this controversy see: Eliot, *The Common Law of the Federal Courts*, 36 Am. L. Rev. 498 (1902) ; King, *Is There A Common Law of the United States?*, 24 Am. L. Rev. 322 (1890) ; Parker, *The Common Law Jurisdiction of the United States Courts*, 17 Yale L. J. 1 (1907) ; Prentice, *Federal Common Law and Interstate Carriers*, 9 Col. L. Rev. 375 (1909) ; Street, *Is There a General Commercial Law Administered by the Courts of the United States?*, 12 Am. L. Reg. (N. S.) 473 (1873) ; Von Moschzisker, *The Common Law and Our Federal Jurisprudence*, 74 U. of Pa. L. Rev. 109 (1925) ; Williams, *Common Law in the United States*, 9 Am. L. Rec. 427, 490 (1880) ; Note, 18 Harv. L. Rev. 134 (1905).

For evidence of continued judicial adherence to Brewer's view see *United States v. Central Stockholders Corp.*, 52 F2d 322, 329 (CCA 9th 1931).

CHAPTER VII

STATE STATUTES

VIEWED through the eyes of the states, the great danger in the Tyson Doctrine was to be found in the inter-relation among the various branches of the common law. Commerce blended into contract: contract merged with the whole body of general law; and when this point had been reached, torts and even real property fought an unequal battle against the desire of the national judiciary to free itself from unquestioning obedience to local law. Only the self restraint of federal judges could protect the states from the encroaching national power. In the case of state constitutions and statutes, however, one might have expected local law to fare better. A national court might have to decide whether a given legislative enactment was applicable to the case before it, but once this had been done, the danger should have been passed. In *Swift* v. *Tyson,* Story had expressly remarked on the peculiar deference owing to local statutes and had thereby served notice that he intended no change in this field, for it had been the custom of the federal tribunals to accept a state's interpretation of its own statutes. A number of cases might be detailed in order to support this proposition; but *Green* v. *Neal*[1] is particularly good illustration of the point because it presents the problem with unusual clarity.

Tennessee, during the decades immediately following its separation from the parent state of North Carolina, was largely composed of virgin territory. As a consequence, the number of persons claiming land because of long possession, and not by virtue of any deed, was unusually large. The local statute of limitations that set the conditions under which these squatters became entitled to the land upon which they lived was, therefore, of particular importance. The highest court of the State

[1] 6 Pet. 291 (1832).

had interpreted this statute in 1815,[2] and the Supreme Court of the United States, in a case which was appealed from a federal circuit court in Tennessee a year later, rendered its own judgment in accordance with the holdings of the local courts.[3] Several years later, a second case came before the Supreme Court and it followed its own holding in the prior litigation.[4] In 1825 the highest court of Tennessee was presented with another case involving the State's statute of limitations, and this time it placed a different construction upon the act.[5]

After all of these cases had been decided, the Supreme Court of the United States was again called upon to consider the Tennessee statute in *Green* v. *Neal*. One of the parties contended that the federal courts should follow their own precedent in preference to the later holding of the Tennessee courts. It was conceded that the national judiciary was bound to follow the local interpretation of a statute in the first instance. But it was urged that the federal courts should not be expected to follow every vacillation in the state. In rejecting this contention, Justice McLean, speaking for the Court, wrote:

"If the construction of the highest judicial tribunal of a state form a part of its statute law, as much as an enactment by the legislature, how can this court make a distinction between them? There could be no hesitation in so modifying our decisions as to conform to any legislative alteration in a statute; and why should not the same rule apply, where the judicial branch of the state government, in the exercise of its acknowledged functions, should, by construction, give a different effect to a statute, from what had at first been given to it. The charge of inconsistency might be made with more force and propriety against the federal tribunals for a disregard of this rule, than

2 *Lillard* v. *Elliot*, Tenn. S. Ct. (1815); *Douglass* v. *Bledsoe's Heirs*, Tenn. S. Ct. (1815).

3 *Patton's Lessee* v. *Easton*, 1 Wheat. 476 (1816).

4 *Powell's Lessee* v. *Harman*, 2 Pet. 241 (1829).

5 *Gray and Reeder* v. *Darby's Lessee*, Tenn. S. Ct. (1825).

by conforming to it. They profess to be bound by the local law; and yet they reject the exposition of that law, which forms a part of it. It is no answer to this objection, that a different exposition was formerly given to the act which was adopted by the federal court. The inquiry is, what is the settled law of the state at the time the decision is made. This constitutes the rule of property within the state, by which the rights of litigant parties must be determined.

"As the federal tribunals profess to be governed by this rule, they can never act inconsistently by enforcing it. If they change their decision, it is because the rule on which that decision was founded has been changed." [6]

Had this deference to statutes and their local interpretation continued, it could have been of considerable comfort to the states. Judicial decisions are no less law than statutes, but laymen can most easily appreciate the relation between the work of their legislative assemblies and the processes of self-government. Duly elected representatives gather at the state capitol to make policy. They decide that the state should have a tax system which bears in one way upon certain income groups and in another way upon different economic interests; that the state should have a workman's compensation law which covers one type of disability and not another; an act which requires the presence of seals on certain written instruments and not on others. And it is generally understood that these laws are to be administered by local officials in accordance with local ideas. Nor is this all. So long as federal authority deferred to local statutes as interpreted by state courts, the states had a check on the independence of the national judiciary. If a state did not like a common law rule as it was administered in the federal courts, its legislature could cover the subject by statute, and the national government would follow the local law. Indeed, in a state like California where extensive codification of

6 6 Pet. 291, 299-300.

the common law came into vogue,[7] the protection that the state could give itself in this way might be great.

Early Signs of Federal Independence of Local Interpretations of Statutes

It would be difficult to imagine a more emphatic intention to accept state statutes and their local interpretation than that evinced in *Green* v. *Neal.* Yet it was not long before the policy announced by that case fell into disfavor. *Rowan* v. *Runnels,*[8] decided in 1847, refused to follow an interpretation of the Mississippi Constitution made by the highest tribunal of the State. This was the first time that the Supreme Court had ever taken

---

7 During the middle portion of the nineteenth century, a considerable body of opinion favoring the codification of the common law so as to produce statutory codes like those of Continental European countries was to be found in some of our states. David Dudley Field prepared a number of these codes, and although his native state (New York), rejected one of them after an acrimonious debate over its adoption: see Carter, *The Provinces of the Written and Unwritten Law,* 24 Am. L. Rev. 1 (1890) ; Field, *Codification,* 20 Am. L. Rev. 1 (1886). California adopted a Field Code. The State still uses the Code, but as a result of many years of activity in the California courts, whose judges and lawyers are no less steeped in the traditions of the common law than is the bench and bar of other states, the California practice is little different than it would be without the Code.

The situation in Louisiana, whose legal system bears the marks of the French Civil Code, should also be noted.

8 5 How. 134 (1847). A provision of the Mississippi Constitution dating from 1833 prohibited the importation of slaves for the purpose of sale within the State but allowed their importation for the private use of the importer.

A promisory note was given in payment for slaves brought into the State for sale after 1833, but before 1836 when legislation was enacted implementing this Constitutional provision. Plaintiff attempted to collect the note but was met with the defense that the sale had been illegal and that, as a result, the courts should not enforce payment of the note.

In 1841 the Supreme Court of the United States decided that the State Constitution, unaided by the statute of 1836, was not sufficient to prevent collection of a note similar to that in the Runnels Case: *Groves* v. *Slaughter,* 15 Pet. 422 (1841). At that time, the Mississippi courts had not interpreted this provision of the State Constitution. By 1847, the highest court of Mississippi had made such an interpretation.

such a step and in later years, after federal power to make independent interpretations of state statutes was already an established fact, the case was often cited.[9] But at the time of its decision, it was more easily understood in the light of the slavery controversy of which it was a minor evidence. The major attack to which local statutes succumbed raised important questions of law and politics which must be closely examined if they are to be understood. However, before we embark upon this portion of our inquiry, it will be well to notice several decisions of the Supreme Court which, although relatively unimportant in themselves, furnish interesting examples of a court feeling its way toward new doctrine.

In 1802 a New Yorker died leaving considerable property in trust for the use of certain beneficiaries. Some years later, the last of the trustees also died, and, as the will made no provision for the appointment of successors, the beneficiaries found themselves in a difficult situation. Accordingly, they induced the state legislature to pass a special act empowering the chancery court to provide for the disposition of the property. As a result of this maneuver, the beneficiaries appear to have gotten their hands on the trust property and begun to squander it. As often happens in such cases, a number of prolonged legal battles ensued, and one of them reached the Supreme Court of the United States in 1850. That tribunal was much disturbed by the inept conduct of the beneficiaries and was disposed to save them from their own folly. The Court decided to disregard the New York statute and held that the chancery court had exceeded its power in permitting the disposal of the property.[10]

---

9 *Los Angeles* v. *Los Angeles City Water Co.*, 177 US 558, 575 (1900); *Hartford Fire Insurance Co.* v. *Chicago, Milwaukee & St. Paul Railway Co.*, 175 US 91, 108 (1899); *Burgess* v. *Seligman*, 107 US 20, 34 (1882); *Douglass* v. *County of Pike*, 101 US 677, 686 (1880); *Percy Summer Club* v. *Astle*, 163 F 1, 14 (CCA 1st 1908); *Forest Products Co.* v. *Russell*, 161 F 1005, 1007 (S. D. Miss. 1907).

10 *Williamson* v. *Berry*, 8 How. 495 (1850).

The reasoning employed by the Court in this case was feeble indeed. It was fully aware that local statutes were customarily followed, nor did it appear possible to say that the legislative action was not a statute. However, the Court made much of the fact that this was only a private law dealing with a matter normally left to judicial action. From this it concluded that it would be proper for a federal court to exercise its independent judgment because the word " statute " is usually considered to mean a public act of the legislature. There was no precedent for this distinction between private and public statutes, nor was there any valid reason why the federal government should owe more deference to the one than to the other. A few years later, the high bench recognized its mistake and, in litigation arising out of the same will, accepted the statute.[11] The only difference between the two cases was that in the latter instance, there had been a decision of a New York court upholding the validity of judicial action taken pursuant to the statute. In the days before Swift v. Tyson, this would have been of considerable importance. But the national judiciary no longer considered itself irretrievably bound by local decisions. The later case, therefore, can only be taken as overruling the earlier decision.

A more striking case was *Pease* v. *Peck* [12] which concerned the interpretation of a Michigan statute of limitations. When Michigan was still a territory, its legislature had passed the act in question, and it had been re-adopted when the State was admitted to the Union. Like so many laws of its type, this statute of limitations was borrowed from an old act of the British Parliament. The territorial legislature evidently meant to make a slight alteration in the English model from which it was copying and omitted a short phrase of the original text in order to achieve this design. However, the official printer copied the English statute verbatim with the result that the

11 *Suydam* v. *Williamson*, 24 How. 427 (1860).

12 18 How. 595 (1856).

˜law as published did not accord with the precise enactment of
the legislature. But the error went unnoticed for many years
and legislators, litigants, and courts alike accepted the published
version as correct. It then happened that counsel for a suitor
in a state court came upon the manuscript of the law as actually passed by the territorial legislature. In that case the highest
court of Michigan decided that the correct version of the law
was the one contained in the long forgotten manuscript and
not that appearing in the published statute books. In *Pease* v.
Peck the federal courts were asked to follow this ruling of the
highest tribunal in Michigan, but the Supreme Court of the
United States refused to do so. The Court declared that it
could not agree with the Michigan interpretation. It pointed
out that everyone had accepted the published version of the
statute as authentic for years, and the courts of the State had
enforced the law as printed. Indeed, neither the people of the
State nor non residents having business there had any way of
discovering the law except by reading the official publications,
and to say that these could not be relied upon would be to
work a gross injustice. All of this was undoubtedly true, and
it should also be noted that the Supreme Court could point to
a line of older state decisions applying the local statute of limitations as published. Nevertheless, the case clearly stood for
the proposition that where the provocation is strong enough,
a federal court may disregard a state court's interpretation of
a local statute.

It is far from easy to say what would have happened if the
Supreme Court had been left to work out its new doctrine with
only *Green* v. *Neal* and *Swift* v. *Tyson* as guides. The cases
just reviewed give some indication, although not a very convincing one, that the Court might have developed a theory of
federal independence in any event. It may be that when the
national judiciary became accustomed to a large measure of
freedom in matters of local common law, the urge to exert a
similar independence with regard to the interpretation of state
legislation would have proved irresistible. It is, however, a mat-

ter of indisputable record that the protection originally given to state statutes soon crumbled, and the battering ram which took the fort came from a previously unsuspected arsenal.

A Source of Future Trouble

One of the reasons for the framing of the contract clause of the Constitution was to prevent state legislatures, many of which were under the influence of debtor interests, from repudiating state obligations. As the states had strained their financial resources during the Revolution, this was a very real danger. Half a century and more later, local treasuries were no longer burdened by the cost of military ventures, but this did not mean that state finances were in a prosperous condition. The need for "internal improvements" seemed limitless in nineteenth century America, and public credit was used to aid in the realization of many projects.

The states and their local subdivisions were particularly active in backing the construction of new transportation facilities. New York made its bid for commercial supremacy by building the Erie Canal, and the increasing size and importance of New York City were due primarily to the trading advantages which the canal gave this port in dealing with the landlocked regions beyond the Alleghanies. Boston, Philadelphia, and Baltimore also appreciated the value of access to the commerce of the Midwest and they too encouraged the building of canals. But these cities did not have the advantage which came with location on the Hudson River whose headwaters lay within reasonable distance of the Great Lakes, and for that reason their efforts ended in costly failure.

With rail transportation, however, things were not quite so unfavorable to New York's competitors. While this form of transportation was also cheapest over level ground, the construction of railroads was certainly feasible in the hinterlands of all our Eastern ports. Indeed, the Baltimore and Ohio Railroad received its initial impetus from the attempt of the City of Baltimore to offset the advantage which New York had won through the opening of the Erie Canal. With the civic importance of good transportation becoming ever more apparent, municipalities were anxious to be served by the new railroads. The private promoters of these enterprises were equally anxious to secure subsidies. In this situation, the ingredients of a bargain were not too hard to find. Municipalities began to outdo each other in their efforts to aid in railroading building, and always the object was the same. In return for financial assistance, a city expected to find itself the terminus of an important line. Or if the facts of geography made this impossible, the municipality wished to make sure that at the very least one or more railroads passed through its territory.

The shape taken by this public assistance was much the same wherever it was found. In the case of the federal government, the subsidy took the form of huge grants of land on either side of the prospective right of way. The states, and more particularly their political subdivisions, because they had no public domain to give away, had to find another way to help. The answer proved to be the public credit. Municipalities issued bonds and did one of two things with them. In a limited number of cases, they sold the bonds and lent the proceeds to the railroad companies. In the more usual case, however, the city exchanged these securities for stock in the companies which was to be held until the bonds were retired—it was hoped, by dividends earned from the operation of the completed roads. Upon receipt of these bonds, the private promoters sold them on the open market, sometimes at par value, but not infrequently at much less, in order to realize liquid capital as rapidly as possible.

This kind of wildcat finance was almost sure to cause trouble, and many citizens, some of them doubtful of the benefits to be had from this new-fangled rail transportation, others alarmed at the prodigious waste of public money [13] banded to-

13 For a protest against local aid to railroads, see: *On Municipal Subscriptions to the Stock of Railroad Companies*, 2 Am. L. Reg. 1 (1853).

gether to test the validity of these municipal bond issues. One of these cases reached the highest court of Pennsylvania in 1853. The decision, as was always the case in these early years, upheld the right of the localities to issue securities in aid of railroad construction, but one of the judges was sorely troubled by the economic risks involved. A portion of his opinion ran as follows:

" This is, beyond all comparison, the most important cause that has ever been in this court since the formation of the government. The fate of many most important public improvements hangs on our decision. If all municipal subscriptions are void, railroads, which are necessary to give the state these advantages to which everything else entitles her, must stand unfinished for years to come, and large sums, already expended on them, must be lost. Not less than fourteen millions of these stocks have been taken by boroughs, counties, and cities within this Commonwealth. . . . It may well be supposed that a large amount of them are in the hands of innocent holders, who have paid for them in good faith. We cannot award the injunction asked for, without declaring that all such bonds are as destitute of legal validity as so much blank parchment. Besides the deadly blow it would give to our improvements, and the disastrous effect of it on the private fortunes of many honest men, at home and abroad, it would seriously wound the credit and character of the state, and do much to lessen the influence of our institutions on the public mind of the world.

" The reverse of this picture is not less appalling. It is even more so, as some view it. If the power exists, it will continue to be exerted, and generally it will be used under the influence of those who are personally interested, and who do not see or care for the ultimate injury it may bring upon the people at large. Men feel acutely what affects them as individuals, and are but slightly influenced by public considerations. What each person wins by his enterprise, is all his own: the public losses are shared by thousands. The selfish passion is intensified by the prospect of immediate gain; private speculation becomes ardent, energetic, and daring, while public spirit—cold and timid at the best—grows feebler still when the danger is remote. Under these circumstances it is easy to see where this ultra-enterprising spirit will end. It carried the State to the verge of financial ruin; it has produced revulsions of trade and currency in every commercial country; it is tending now, and here, to the bankruptcy of cities and counties. In England, no investments have been more disastrous than railway stocks, unless those of the South Sea Bubble be an exception. In this country they have not generally been profitable. The dividends of the largest works in the neighboring states, north and south of us, have disappointed the stockholders. Not one of the completed railroads in this state has uniformly paid interest on its cost. If only a few of the roads projected in Pennsylvania should be as unfortunate as all the finished ones, such a burden would be imposed on certain parts of the state, as the industry of no people has ever endured without being crushed. Still, this plan of improving the country, if unchecked by this court, will probably go on until it results in some startling calamity, to rouse the masses of the people." [14]

But for all the country's need of improved transportation, Judge Black of the Pennsylvania Supreme Court, from whose opinion we have just quoted, was right when he observed that railroads were unprofitable enterprises.[15] Some of the trouble may have been due to the fact that builders and operators were dealing with a new product of scientific ingenuity and much had to be learned about the proper ways to construct and run the railways. But even more of the difficulty, especially in the newer regions of the country, came from the sparsely settled character of the land. If railroads were to pay their own way, they needed large and dependable sources of freight, and these could only be had in well inhabited areas. Yet without the rail-

14 *Sharpless* v. *Mayor of Philadelphia*, 21 Pa. 147, 158-159 (1853).

15 For accounts of the difficulties of early railroad finance and construction see: Hafen and Rister, *Western America* (1941), pp. 538-554; Quiett, *They Built the West* (1934).

roads, the Midwest could not attract and support a large population.

In the face of this dilemma, the timidity of private investors is understandable; and in view of the public importance of good transportation, it was appropriate that government should aid in the construction of new railroads. Private promoters made the most of this legitimate claim on the public treasury. They organized monster rallies in a number of inland cities, notably Memphis and Chicago, for the purpose of winning civic support for their enterprises. These meetings were huge successes. To some extent, they undoubtedly induced individual investors to take stock in the railroad companies without asking any security for their risk. But the main achievement of these rallies was in creating enthusiasm for plans under which local governments pledged their credit in aid of the construction and operating companies.

The bonanza spirit in which the entire country embarked upon the task of forging a transportation system adequate to the needs of a large and expanding nation made colossal blunders inevitable. Accordingly, there is good reason to believe that financial disaster would have overtaken many of the companies even if they had been run with scrupulous honesty. But many of the private promoters and their political friends were experts in concocting schemes designed to defraud public and private investors alike.[16] Many railroads were promised

---

[16] "Irresponsible groups as well as legitimate promoters with definite plans for railroads, were allowed to print bonds and stock certificates and sell them wherever they could with little or no restraint. As a matter of fact, most of the capital secured by the sale of stocks and bonds, whether by the state and local governments or by the joint stock companies, was obtained in the East and in Europe. Later when some of these stocks proved fraudulent or when local governments defaulted in the payment of their obligations because no railways were forthcoming, the antagonism between the East and the West was decidedly increased." Clark, *The West in American History* (1937), p. 303.

Another source of vast profit to the promoters and their political supporters was the organization of construction companies. After inducing the federal, state, and local governments to shoulder a large portion of the

but never built; others were started and left unfinished; and those which were actually completed were built at prodigious cost. It was small wonder that the railway companies often failed to pay dividends.

However, this did not excuse the municipalities from liability on the bonds which they had issued in order to encourage railroad construction. Even though the loans were not repaid and many of the promised transportation facilities never furnished, holders of municipal securities insisted on the payment of both interest and principal. When this was not to be had, they resorted to the courts in order to enforce their claims; and the local governments, bitter at the prospect of having to make good losses incurred because of recklessness and fraud, cast about for means of avoiding their heavy financial burdens.

The impulse of local governments to shirk the responsibilites of oppressive debt was natural enough; they had already been duped by unscrupulous promoters. But there is no reason in either sound law or economics why they should have expected to repudiate their obligations. Investors had sought and obtained a pledge of public credit in order to protect themselves against just such eventualities. Communities, however misplaced their trust may have been, had thought to secure great advantages for their residents, and they were now being asked to pay the price of their miscalculations. But local courts in a number of states were disposed to grant relief to hard pressed cities and counties by declaring that securities issued in aid of railway construction were void and that, as a consequence, holders could collect neither interest, nor principal. The judicial histories of these litigations were similar in most of the states where they arose, and no purpose would be served by reviewing each instance individually. However, conditions in

---

expense, these same individuals obtained contracts for the building of the railroads and the supplying of materials. These contracts generally called for the payment of exorbitant prices. The notorious Credit Mobilier Scandal, which occurred during the administration of President Grant, resulted from the unmasking of the most elaborate of these schemes.

Iowa deserve special attention because from that state came the leading municipal bond case in the Supreme Court of the United States.

Starting in 1851, the Iowa legislature passed a series of acts permitting local governments to issue railway aid bonds. It was generally provided that this could be done by the executive organ of a city or county after a special vote of the residents. During the next few years, a number of cities and counties took advantage of this enabling legislation, held the necessary referenda and subscribed to one or more railroad companies.

In spite of the widespread enthusiasm for these undertakings, there were people who did not relish the idea of paying the additional taxes made necessary by these projects. They went to the Iowa courts in attempts to establish the invalidity of the state legislation and of the measures taken by localities in pursuance thereof. But in a series of cases decided between 1853 and 1859, the highest court of the State declared that the railroad aid statutes were in accordance with the Iowa Constitution and sustained local action taken under their authority.[17]

In 1860, however, the Iowa Supreme Court overruled all of these decisions and held that the statutes conferring the power to issue railway aid bonds on political subdivisions of the State were contrary to the Iowa Constitution and that, as a result, bonds then outstanding were void.[18] The opinion of the court was unanimous and well written. It cannot be said for certain that it did not represent a genuine change in the legal opinion of the state judiciary. But observers were natur-

---

17 *Dubuque Co.* v. *Dubuque & Pacific RR Co.*, 4 Green 1 (1853) ; *State* v. *Bissel*, 4 Green 328 (1853) ; *Clapp* v. *Cedar Co.*, 5 Ia. 15 (1857) ; *Ring* v. *County of Johnson*, 6 Ia. 265 (1858) ; *McMillen* v. *Boyles*, 6 IA 305 (1858) ; *McMillen* v. *County Judge and Treasurer*, 6 Ia. 390 (1858) ; *Games* v. *Robb*, 8 Ia. 193 (1859) ; *State* v. *Board of Equalization of the County of Johnson*, 10 Ia. 157 (1859).

18 *Burlington & Missouri RR. Co.* v. *County of Wapello*, 13 Ia. 388 (1862).

ally struck by the fact that this reversal of a supposedly well established position coincided with a growing fear that all was not well with the railroads. This was especially so when it was noticed that the courts of several other states were also reversing previous stands in favor of the validity of these bond issues.[19] On the basis of this circumstantial evidence, it was naturally suspected that the local courts were yielding to local pressures and tempering their justice with politics.

FEDERAL INDEPENDENCE OF JUDGMENT BREAKS THROUGH ITS ORIGINAL BOUNDS

Non resident holders of bonds issued by Iowa municipalities and counties immediately resorted to the federal courts in order to protect their investments. The first of these suits to reach the Supreme Court was *Gelpcke* v. *City of Dubuque*.[20] Justice Swayne, writing for the majority, refused to accept the latest Iowa decision. In view of the highly suspicious circumstances, he may have been justified in doing so, but the wording of his opinion carried far reaching implications: so much so, that it requires extended quotation.

"... However we may regard the late case in Iowa as affecting the future, it can have no effect upon the past. ' The sound and true rule is, that if the contract, when made, was valid by the laws of the State as then expounded by all departments of the government, and administered in its courts of justice, its validity and obligation cannot be impaired by any subsequent action of legislation, or decision of its courts altering the construction of the law.'

19 *People* v. *Salem*, 20 Mich. 452 (1870) ; *Whiting* v. *Sheboygan and Fond du Lac RR Co.* 25 Wisc. 167 (1870). *Cf. Bay City* v. *State Treasurer*, 23 Mich. 499 (1871).

20 1 Wall. 175 (1864). For a favorable analysis of this case see: Thayer, *The Case of Gelpcke* v. *Dubuque*, 4 Harv. L. Rev. 311 (1891). For adverse criticisms see: Reed, *The Rule in Gelpcke* v. *Dubuque*, 9 Am. L. Rev. 381 (1875) ; White, *Some Recent Criticisms of Gelpcke* v. *Dubuque*, 47 Am. L. Reg. 473 (1899).

" The same principle applies when there is a change of judicial decision as to the constitutional power of the legislature to enact the law. To this rule, thus enlarged, we adhere. It is the law of this court. It rests upon the plainest principles of justice. To hold otherwise would be as unjust as to hold that rights acquired under a statute may be lost by its repeal. The rule embraces this case.

" Bonds and coupons, like these, by universal commercial usage and consent, have all the qualities of commercial paper. If the plaintiffs recover in this case, they will be entitled to the amount specified in the coupons, with interest and exchange as claimed.

" We are not unmindful of the importance of uniformity in the decisions of this court, and those of the highest local courts, giving constructions to the laws and constitutions of their own States. It is the settled rule of this court in such cases, to follow the decisions of the State courts. But there have been heretofore, in the judicial history of this court, as doubtless there will be hereafter, many exceptional cases. We shall never immolate truth, justice, and the law, because a State tribunal has erected the altar and decreed the sacrifice." [21]

This passage contains several arguments for the Court's position, and precisely how much weight each of them was meant to carry is an open question.

Swayne's first proposition was that the bonds were contracts between individual investors and the City of Dubuque according to whose terms the latter had agreed to pay interest and principal in return for a loan. It followed that the State of Iowa could make no law depriving the investors of their right to payment; but had the State made such a law? The language of the Federal Constitution deserves exact attention in this regard. " No State shall ... pass any law impairing the obligation of contracts ".[22] The legislature, and only the legis-

---

21 1 Wall. 175, 206-207.

22 U.S. Constit., Art. 1, Sec. 10.

lature passes laws. Therefore, the plain meaning of this provision would appear to be that a state statute could not validly
disturb the bondholders' right to payment. But in this instance,
it was the judiciary of Iowa which by overruling certain of its
previous decisions had raised the obstacle. To declare that
judicial action came within the scope of the constitutional prohibition was, as Swayne himself recognized, an enlargement
of the original scope of the prohibition.

Story's contention that judicial opinions are only evidence
of the law now reappeared—this time in support of a state
court decision. In his dissent, Justice Miller protested that he
had always understood that the law remained the same even
though judicial interpretation of it might change, and that, as
a consequence, the action of the Iowa courts could not be an
impairment of contract in the constitutional sense.[23] But this
remonstrance on a point of theory had little effect at the time
when it was uttered and no greater influence thereafter. Where
the Supreme Court was satisfied that no contract rights had
been violated, it sometimes upheld a local decision declaring
bonds to be void.[24] And even so revered an authority as Oliver
Wendell Holmes, in his dissent from the opinion in *Kuhn* v.
Fairmont Coal Co., distinguished that case from *Gelpcke* v.
Dubuque on the ground that the latter had contained an inti-
mation of constitutional right, thereby granting an oblique
tolerance to the Contract Clause aspect of the bond cases.[25]

At first glance there would seem to be little connection between the Contract Clause and the power of the judiciary to

23 1 Wall. 175, 210-211.

24 *Fairfield* v. *Gallatin County,* 100 US 47 (1879) ; *Town of South Ottawa*
v. *Perkins,* 94 US 260 (1876).

25 See Holmes dissenting in *Kuhn* v. *Fairmont Coal Co.,* 215 US 349, 372
(1910). "I know of no authority in this court to say that in general state
decisions shall make law only for the future. Judicial decisions have had
retrospective operation for near a thousand years. There were enough
difficulties in the way, even in cases like *Gelpcke* v. *Dubuque,* but in them
there was a suggestion or smack of constitutional right."

make independent determinations of local law. Of course, the federal courts have the power to invalidate state laws which contravene the federal Constitution; that was well understood before either *Swift* v. *Tyson* or *Gelpcke* v. *Dubuque* saw the light of day. What brought these two principles together was their common usefulness in attacking the provincialism which occasionally made it difficult for non resident suitors to obtain justice in local courts. When an Eastern investor sought to enforce payment on bonds issued by Midwestern municipalities, he could fall back on the Constitutional protection afforded by the Contract Clause and on his right to bring suit in a federal court because of that tribunal's diversity jurisdiction. These were two separate rights which, in *Gelpcke* v. *Dubuque* and its many successors, were confused and merged into a single theory of federal independence of state courts and legislatures. Because of this merger, Swayne's second and third arguments acquired a strength and a plausibility out of all proportion to their actual merit.

In a very few words, Swayne noted that municipal securities are commercial paper. It may be that this was little more than a chance remark; on the other hand, it is possible that it was meant as a reference to the Tyson Doctrine.[26] But however this may be, later cases elaborated upon this theme [27] and furnished yet another example of the expansive potentialities embodied in Story's original dictum. Bonds are commercial paper; the character of commercial paper is to be discovered by reference to the commercial law; in matters of commercial law, the federal courts exercise their independent judgment. Therefore, whether municipal bonds were validly issued in pur-

26 It is clear that Swayne followed and expanded Story's doctrine of federal independence because he actually cites *Swift* v. *Tyson* as support for the general proposition that a federal court need not consider itself bound by state decisions. 1 Wall. 175, 202.

27 *Supervisors* v. *Schenck*, 5 Wall. 772 (1866). The highest courts of two Eastern states also took this position: *Society for Savings* v. *City of New London*, 29 Conn. 174 (1860). *Cf. Tash* v. *Adams*, 64 Mass. 252 (1852).

suance of provisions of state statutes and constitutions is a question which the national judiciary may decide without reference to the opinions of competent local tribunals in the states where the controversies arise. This argument is so weak as to be almost laughable for the naivete with which it circumvents the whole question of the relation of a state to its political subdivisions. But when the independent action of the federal courts can also be justified by an appeal to the Contract Clause, even the less plausible argument gains a pseudo respectability.

The final portion of Swayne's opinion is notable for its allusions to " immolations ", " altars ", and " sacrifices ". Perhaps these picturesque words makes the Court's opinion more interesting to read. But quite aside from their literary value, these closing lines of the Gelpcke opinion are important for the insight which they give into the crusading spirit which came to characterize the outlook of the national judiciary. The Supreme Court had become so keenly aware of the existence of local prejudice in some sections of the country that it was determined to play the protector's role to the hilt.

The confusion following *Gelpcke* v. *Dubuque* showed our dual judicial system at its very worst. For six years the local courts refused to abandon their interpretation of their own statutes and constitution. In *McClure* v. *Owen,* the highest court of Iowa said:

" We are asked to change the later ruling of this court and abandon the principles of the adjudications so frequently heretofore announced in the cases that have arisen upon these county and city railroad bonds. This we are asked to do, not because the rulings and the principles of construction of our Constitution upon which they are based are unsound, but because the Supreme Court of the United States, which is termed ... the final arbiter upon these questions, has disregarded the decisions of this court, and, in cases before it, has overruled them.

" The questions determined, and upon which there has thus arisen a conflict between this court and the federal courts, are purely those arising upon the construction of the laws and Constitution of our own State . . .

" The Supreme Court of the United States is not in cases of this kind the final arbiter. That august tribunal, the court of last resort in all cases within the federal jurisdiction, as prescribed by the Constitution and laws of the Union, is not charged with the grave duty and great power of construing the Constitution and laws of the State, except where they may be in conflict with the federal laws and Constitution, and of establishing thereby a rule of construction obligatory upon the State courts. In questions of this kind it is, in no sense, the final arbiter, but by a course of adjudications beginning at the foundation of the government and extending to the present time, it is required to look to the courts of the States for the rules of construction of their respective laws and Constitutions. Upon such questions, then, it is, in law and in fact, inferior in authority to the courts of the States. It has the power to disregard the decision of the State courts upon such questions and to enforce its own decisions in a class of cases over which it has jurisdiction; but the superior authority of its decisions upon these questions has not been and never can be admitted. We can not, therefore, be expected to conform our rulings to the opinion of that court upon questions of this character when they are in conflict with the adjudications of this court." [28]

The most obvious result of this deadlock was that non resident bondholders proceeded to satisfy their claims out of the local treasuries by enforcing judgments gained in federal courts while Iowans who held identical securities collected nothing on them. After reading the opinion in the Gelpcke case, one might expect that the way was open for local citizens to extricate themselves from this unequal position. If the federal courts would not accept the interpretation put upon state laws by local courts, at least the local citizens should have been able to join in the parade to the national courts and get their share

---

28 *McClure* v. *Owen*, 26 Ia. 244, 248 (1869).

of whatever municipal assets were available for satisfaction of the outstanding bonds. The Supreme Court of the United States had placed at least a part of its holding upon the Contract Clause of the Federal Constitution. This was a federal question and should have entitled those wishing to litigate it to enter a federal court without having to claim diversity of citizenship.[29] But such was not the view of the Supreme Court. The plaintiff in the McClure Case was one of many residents who tried to come before a national tribunal only to have his suit dismissed for want of jurisdiction.[30]

The reason for this discrimination against local suitors was strange indeed. In *Tidal Oil Company* v. *Flannigan*,[31] the Supreme Court explained that the bond cases in which reference had been made to the Contract Clause had come up on appeal from lower federal courts and had not involved writs of error to state tribunals. This, it was said, showed that *Gelpcke* v. *Dubuque* and the many cases of which it was the prototype were really decided under Article III, Section 2 of the Constitution and the thirty-fourth section of the Judiciary Act. It was still the law that judicial decisions could not impair the obligations of contracts.[32] But, as we have seen, this was only partly true. The curious fact was that the Contract Clause provided a good enough reason for mauling local law when the interests of a non resident were to be protected, but

29 Prior to 1875, when the lower federal courts were given original jurisdiction over suits involving a federal question whether the parties could claim diversity of citizenship or not, local residents would have been compelled to commence their actions in the state courts. However, they would have been entitled to appeal to the Supreme Court of the United States as a matter of right. The litigation of a federal question is discussed, *supra*, ch. III.

30 *Mississippi and M. R. Co.* v. *McClure*, 10 Wall. 511 (1871).

31 263 US 444, 452 (1924).

32 *New Orleans Water Works Co.* v. *Louisiana Sugar Refining Co.*, 125 US 18 (1888); *Lehigh Water Co.* v. *Easton*, 121 US 388 (1887). See *Bacon* v. *Texas*, 163 US 207, 216 (1896). See also Dodd, *The Impairment of the Obligation of Contract by State Decision*, 4 Ill. L. Rev. 155 (1909).

the same Clause could not be invoked for the benefit of persons
who could not claim diversity of citizenship. It is submitted
that this perversion of constitutional theory has no sound justification. All that can be said is that in its anxiety to protect
non residents from local resentment, the federal judiciary had
created two Constitutions: one for the use of non residents,
the other for local citizens.

The people of Iowa were not at the end of their efforts to
extricate themselves from these difficulties. If they could neither
realize anything on their own bonds nor prevent outsiders from
securing federal judgments, perhaps there was another way to
find relief. The constitution and statutes of Iowa, like those of
other states, contained restrictions on the extent of municipal
borrowing and also upon the rate at which property could be
taxed by local governments. The railroad promoters who had
sought local aid for their projects were aware of the problems
raised by these limitations and had attempted to meet them by
insisting on special legislation authorizing city and county officers to lay additional property taxes if this should prove necessary in order to provide the funds to meet payments of interest
and principal on the bonds as they came due. It was now contended that these authorizations for special levies were in violation of the state constitution. Accordingly, taxpayers brought
actions in the state courts for injunctions against the laying
and collection of these assessments. A number of these suits
were successful,[33] and when municipalities were sued in the
federal courts, they defended on the ground that there were no
funds with which to meet payment on the bonds out of normal
revenues, and the local officers could not lay the special taxes
without being in contempt of the local courts.[34]

This was no imaginary danger. At about this time, public
officials in Wisconsin and Louisiana had resigned rather than

[33] See *Lee County v. Rogers*, 7 Wall. 181 (1868); *Moses v. Keokuk*,
6 Wall. 518 (1868); *Riggs v. Johnson County*, 6 Wall. 166 (1868); *Ex Parte
Holman*, 28 Ia. 88 (1869); *McClure v. Owen*, 26 Ia. 244 (1868).

[34] *Butz v. City of Muscatine*, 8 Wall. 575 (1869).

face similar situations, and by so doing, had even succeeded in defeating the bondholders.[35] But events in Iowa were more representative of the situation as it was generally to be found in the states of the Midwest. When confronted with these injunctions, the federal courts paid no more heed to them than they did to other rulings of state tribunals on matters connected with the railroad bonds.[36] Federal judges even went so far as to grant writs of mandamus directed to city and county officers ordering them to levy and collect the special taxes with which judgments secured in the national courts could be paid.[37] The unlucky local tax officers were now caught between Scylla and

35 *Heine* v. *Levee Commissioners*, 19 Wall. 655 (1873); *Rees* v. *City of Watertown*, 19 Wall. 107 (1874).

36 *Butz* v. *City of Muscatine, supra* note 34; *U. S. ex rel. Moses* v. *Keokuk*, 6 Wall. 514 (1868). See *Lee County* v. *Rogers*, 7 Wall. 181 (1868).

37 The first case in which a federal court issued a writ of mandamus to a state officer came from Indiana and was decided before the Gelpcke Case: *Knox County* v. *Aspinwall*, 24 How. 376 (1861). This case was followed in *Von Hoffman* v. *Quincy*, 4 Wall. 535 (1867). This mandamus procedure required two separate stages: 1. The initial action to secure a judgment, and 2. The proceeding to obtain the writ of mandamus. The theory underlying this circuitous method was that a mandamus is not technically an independent action but can only be maintained in support of another action. After *Riggs* v. *Johnson County*, 6 Wall. 166 (1868), however, it was possible to obtain the judgment and the mandamus in a single proceeding. For a discussion of these cases see: Evans, *Jurisdiction in Mandamus in United States Courts*, 19 Am. L. Rev. 505 (1885).

Compare the situation in *Ex Parte* Young, 209 US 123 (1908) where a federal court enjoined the Attorney General of Minnesota from enforcing state legislation regulating railroads on the ground that the state law was unconstitutional. The Attorney General then brought a case in the Minnesota courts wherein it was decided that the legislation was constitutional. The Attorney General disobeyed the federal injunction, and the suit in the principal case was a habeas corpus proceeding to test the legality of his commitment for contempt. Young contended that the suit against him in the federal court was, in effect, a suit against the State and not maintainable without the consent of the State. *Held.* The suit was against the state officer individually. Habeas Corpus denied. This still appears to be the law. *Public Utilities Commission of Ohio* v. *United Fuel Gas Co.*, 317 US 456 (1943); *Herndon* v. *Chicago, Rock Island & Pacific Rw. Co.*, 218 US 135 (1910); *Western Union Telegraph Co.* v. *Andrews*, 216 US 165 (1910). *Cf. Lincoln Electric Co.* v. *Knox*, 56 F. Supp. 308 (D. C. 1944).

Charybdis; if they obeyed the federal writs, they would be subject to punishment for contempt of the local courts, while if they observed the provisions of the injunctions, they would be liable for contempt of the national courts. Nor were they able to navigate safely as the fortunate Ulysses had done. Instead, the local officials over a hundred of them in one series of cases, were committed to jail.[38]

By 1870 Iowa had suffered enough in this unequal contest. Her highest court returned to the early holdings on the bonds and once more declared them valid.[39] So, in this one state, uniformity of federal and local law was finally achieved.[40] The episode demonstrated the superiority of national power, but it did nothing to recommend the drastic modification of the Tyson Doctrine at which the Supreme Court of the United States had now arrived. Municipalities were forced to honor their obligations whether held by local citizens or non residents, and this was all to the good. If it had been accomplished by uniform holdings under the Contract Clause, applicable in diversity and non diversity cases alike, the grounds for complaint would have been much less serious. One might still have questioned the correctness of holding that a state might impair the obligation of contracts within the meaning of the Federal Constitution by the action of its judiciary, but much of the chaos which had resulted from the unequal protection afforded the interests of resident and non resident suitors would have been avoided.

38 See Miller dissenting in *Butz* v. *City of Muscatine*, 8 Wall. 575, 587.

39 *Stewart* v. *Board of Supervisors*, 30 Ia. 9 (1870).

40 Some states refused to change their holdings in order to conform to the decision in the Gelpcke Case. In Michigan, for example, the issuance of railway aid bonds was declared unconstitutional. *People* v. *Salem*, 20 Mich. 452 (1870). *Cf. Bay City* v. *State Treasurer*, 23 Mich. 499 (1871). The Supreme Court of the United States subsequently decided that the Michigan bonds were valid. *Taylor* v. *Ypsilanti*, 105 US 60 (1881) ; *Pine Grove Township* v. *Talcott*, 19 Wall. 666 (1874). However, the highest court of Michigan continued to follow *People* v. *Salem*: *Dodge* v. *Van Buren*, 118 Mich. 189 (1898). *Cf. Township of Grant* v. *Township of Reno*, 114 Mich. 41 (1897) ; *Pierson* v. *Reynolds*, 49 Mich. 224 (1882).

Little purpose would be served by a review of conditions in each of the dozen or more states [41] in which attempts to escape payment on railway aid bonds brought state and national courts into conflict. It has already been pointed out that what has been said of Iowa applies substantially to these other states. Nearly two hundred municipal bond cases came to the Supreme Court of the United States,[42] and many times this number were disposed of in the lower federal courts. Everywhere the story was the same. With the exception of those few cases in which the cities and counties had been so utterly ruined that energetic creditors were unable to find assets appropriate to the satisfaction of their claims,[43] the municipalities lost. However, the course of events in Iowa failed to highlight one aspect of the situation which deserves brief mention.

For a short time, a few southern states thought that they had found a way to outsmart the bondholders. In 1876 the case of *Barkley* v. *Levee Commissioners* [44] came to the Supreme Court from Louisiana. It appeared that a local governmental body in that state had gone into debt in order to finance certain public improvements. When the creditors attempted to enforce payment of their securities, they found that the governmental unit from which they had received their bonds was no longer in existence. It had been replaced by two new levee districts neither of which was particularly anxious to honor the obligations. The defense, which the Court accepted, was

41 The following were the states most seriously affected by litigation over railway aid bonds: Alabama, Florida, Illinois, Indiana, Iowa, Louisiana, Michigan, Missouri, Ohio, Tennessee, Texas, Wisconsin.

42 3 Warren, *The Supreme Court in United States History*, 400 (1922).

43 In a very few cases, the Supreme Court was forced to agree that the defaulting municipalities could not be made to pay. However, this result was reached only because the city in question was in such poor financial condition that no assets suitable for sale on execution could be found out of which to satisfy bondholders' judgments. *Amy* v. *Shelby County Taxing District*, 114 US 387 (1885) ; *Meriwether* v. *Garrett*, 102 US 472 (1880).

44 93 US 258 (1876).

that these new districts were entirely different organizations having no connection with the public body which had incurred the debts. As a matter of legal technicality, this decision was probably sound, and the Court must have been comforted by its belief that the change in the character of the levee districts was not accomplished for the express purpose of cheating the creditors. This would seem to be a necessary inference from the fact that a similar case involving a Florida city, decided at the same time as the Berkley Case, reached an opposite result.[45] In this litigation, the Court made much of the fact that the municipality in question reincorporated for the sole purpose of avoiding liability on its railroad bonds.

However, in spite of this indication that the Court would not respect formal changes in municipal identity if it suspected that the alteration was undertaken in order to perpetrate a fraud, a number of state and local governments took to this new device in the hope that they might be able to fool their creditors and the courts. But these efforts were unavailing. The Berkley Case did not initiate a long line of decisions. When the city of Mobile attempted a reorganization which included a little over half of its former territory, the Supreme Court immediately noted that the new "Port of Mobile" had roughly nine-tenths of the wealth and population of the old city of Mobile and held that the new corporation was the legal successor of the old and liable for all its debts.[46] Indeed, this matter of municipal reorganization proved so transparent a device that not even the state courts were willing to shut their eyes to the realities of the situation and refused to permit the reformed communities to accomplish the repudiation of their securities.[47]

45 *Broughton* v. *Pensacola,* 93 US 266 (1876).

46 *Mobile* v. *Watson,* 116 US 289 (1886).

47 *Amy* v. *Selma,* 77 Ala. 103 (1884) ; *O'Connor* v. *City of Memphis,* 6 Lea (Tenn. 1881), 730.

How Much Respect for Local Interpretation of Statutes?

In time railway aid bonds ceased to be a source of friction between state and federal judiciaries. The country's transportation system was built; the scandals of the early days were almost forgotten; the unfortunate municipalities paid as many of their debts as their resources would permit or as they were forced to pay, and the creditors wrote off the remainder as uncollectible. The importance of this episode in our judicial history, however, lay not so much in the temporary stresses which it produced as in the rules for the conduct of federal-state relations which it developed. Prior to *Gelpcke* v. *Dubuque,* there had been only a few indications of an intention to disregard local interpretations of legislative enactments. By the time the flood tide of bond cases subsided, the exception for state statutes expressly preserved by Story's opinion in *Swift* v. *Tyson* seemed to be gone. No type of statute appeared to be entirely beyond the power of independent federal interpretation. To catalogue all of the proofs of this assertion would be to make a tedious excursion into happily outmoded law. But it may be well to conclude this phase of our study with some mention of the effect which the expanded Tyson Doctrine threatened to have on the movement for uniform state laws.

Watson v. *Tarpley* [48] was an action on a note which had been dishonored before maturity. At common law, the plaintiff was able to commence his suit without waiting until the due date, but under a statute of Mississippi, it was necessary to await the time of maturity before bringing suit. This law was of obvious advantage to debtor interests and may well have been enacted at their behest. Be this as it may, the Supreme Court refused to apply the Mississippi statute to the case. Much of the opinion is couched in terms of a jurisdictional argument. It is said that the state law, by postponing the date for commencing suit, deprived the federal court of jurisdiction of the

48 18 How. 517 (1856).

case during the interval between dishonor and maturity, and that such a limitation on the power of a federal court was beyond the authority of a state. This is certainly a curious proposition and it has not been urged since the time of its original announcement. With this contention as a preface, however, the Court proceeded to say that the Mississippi statute could not be applied in diversity cases because Swift v. Tyson had already determined that in matters of commercial law, the national judiciary would exercise its independent judgment. It followed that a local law dealing with a commercial matter had no greater claim on federal attention than the decision of a local court would have. This was an extreme position; but a modification of it can be seen in the proposition that statutes which are declaratory of the common law may receive an independent federal interpretation.[49] The most widely adopted Uniform State Laws came within this rule. They were intended as codifications of common and statute law and were designed to eliminate the troublesome differences in the commercial law of the several states. That legislative uniformity could be impaired by conflicting state constructions of the same Uniform Act was a real danger.[50] But it would have been even worse if the federal courts had insisted on a separate construction of their own. Luckily the Supreme Court recognized this danger; it disapproved *Watson* v. *Tarpley* and its offshoots and decided that at least in the case of Uniform State Laws it would follow the holdings of local courts.[51]

The many encroachments on the power of the states to control the enforcement of their own laws were too real to be

49 See Fordham, *The Federal Courts and the Construction of Uniform State Laws*, 7 N. C. L. Rev. 423 (1929).

50 *Taylor* v. *American National Bank*, 63 Fla. 631, 57 So. 678 (1912) holds certain notes negotiable. *First National Bank* v. *Bosler*, 297 Pa. 353, 147 A. 74 (1929) holds similar notes non negotiable.

51 The Supreme Court did not decide to follow state interpretations of the *Negotiable Instruments Law until the decisions in Burns Mortgage Co.* v. *Fried*, 292 US 487 (1934) and *Marine National Exchange Bank of Milwaukee* v. *Kalt-Zimmers Mfg. Co.*, 293 US 357 (1934).

doubted. In matters of common law, the federal action was taken in the name of uniformity. In the case of statutes, this could hardly be the reason. The very goal of most legislation is to make desired changes in the common law; to provide for new situations in new ways, or to meet old problems in ways more consonant with changed notions of public policy. The justification for a local statute-making power is the hope that state legislatures will be able to fit their laws to local needs. In the functioning of this process, differences in the treatment given specific problems in the various localities is only to be expected.

In the field of legislative enactment, the purpose of federal disregard of local holdings was quite different, as can readily be shown from an examination of the reasons given for the independent federal determinations. National tribunals would not apply local law because the decision of a state court had been made after the commencement of the instant suit in the lower federal court; [52] or because it had been handed down after the parties made their contract; [53] or because the national courts could not be expected to alter their own previous line of decisions in order to conform to state holdings; [54] or because the local courts had overruled their earlier decisions. [55]

---

[52] *Olcott* v. *Fond du Lac County*, 16 Wall. 678 (1872) ; *Rowan* v. *Runnels,* 5 How. 134 (1847).

[53] An extreme case in which this rule was applied is *Thompson* v. *Perrine,* 106 US 589 (1883). This was a municipal bond case from New York in which the plaintiff had purchased his bonds after the state courts had declared them void and with full knowledge of this fact. For an application of this contract principle in a common law case see Mr. Justice Harlan in *Kuhn* v. *Fairmont Coal Co.,* 215 US 349, 361 (1910). " If, before the rights of the parties in this case were fixed by written contract, it had become a settled rule of law in West Virginia, as manifested by decisions of its highest court, that the grantee or his successors in such a deed as is here involved, was under no legal obligation to guard the surface land of the grantor against injury resulting from the mining and removal of the coal purchased, a wholly different question would have been presented."

[54] *Taylor* v. *Ypsilanti,* 105 US 60, 69 (1881).

[55] *Gelpcke* v. *City of Dubuque,* 1 Wall. 175 (1864).

The suspicions of federal judges were nowhere better stated than by Mr. Justice Grier in *Pease* v. *Peck* when he said that cases might be brought in state courts for the express purpose of affecting the course of litigation in the national courts.[56] The attempt, then, was to prevent non resident suitors from falling prey to local prejudice against outsiders. Just how real this danger is, and to what extent it must enter into present day provisions for the administration of federal justice, we shall consider in Chapter 12 of this study. But whatever the reasons which prompted the evolution of this judicial policy may have been, an overly cynical comment made by George Wharton Pepper in 1889 appeared to reflect the judicial trends of that day: " In spite of such general statements as the Court have seen fit to make from time to time, the cases show that the mere fact of statutory construction is of itself no guarantee that the local holdings will be upheld. That a decision is occupied in construing a statute is an added reason for believing that the state court will be followed in a case in which it would probably have been followed at any rate; but such a fact will not be sufficient to move the Court to follow where in the absence of a statute they would not have done so." [57]

---

56 18 How. 595, 599.

57 Pepper, *The Borderland of Federal and State Decisions* (1889), p. 71.

CHAPTER VIII

THE TYSON RULE IN PRACTICE

THE Supreme Court decisions reviewed in the preceding two chapters of this study brought the doctrine of federal independence to its high water mark. Had *Kuhn* v. *Fairmont Coal Co.* and *Gelpcke* v. *Dubuque* [1] been typical cases instead of outposts of judicial doctrine, state control over local law would certainly have disintegrated. But the national judiciary was not always disposed to exercise its power to the full or to stretch Supreme Court opinions to the outermost limits of their implications.

This was particularly true where state statutes were concerned. Although George Wharton Pepper,[2] writing when the Bond Cases and *Watson v. Tarpley* were current history, correctly interpreted the apparent trends of the time, later decisions of the Supreme Court were less bold in their disregard of opinions rendered by state courts. The Gelpcke Case did not purport to disturb the general rule laid down by Story in *Swift* v. *Tyson* when he said that Section 34 of the Judiciary Act of 1789 directed federal courts to follow local interpretations of state statutes. Instead, the opinion proceeded to except those cases wherein local courts had changed their rulings during the interval between the formation of a contract and the bringing of suit. In this restricted class of situations, state statutes and constitutions were not immune from independent federal scrutiny. But in all other instances, the protection afforded by the Judiciary Act and recognized by Story was to continue. Opinions of the Supreme Court handed down after the turn of the century generally took this view.[3]

1 See Chs. VI, VII, *supra*.

2 See p. 165, *supra*.

3 *Ashe* v. *United States ex rel. Valotta*, 270 US 424 (1926) ; *Douglas* v. *Noble*, 261 US 165 (1923) ; *Thornton* v. *Duffy*, 254 US 361 (1920) ; *Farn-*

Whether one talks of statutory interpretation or of common law decisions, an essential but seldom emphasized characteristic of the rule in *Swift* v. *Tyson* must be borne clearly in mind. It was Story's contention, reinforced by many subsequent opinions, that the federal judiciary was free to make an independent analysis of certain types of local law and make unfettered judgments concerning them. Nowhere is it suggested that federal courts are not to be influenced by the decisions of state courts; no responsible commentator has ever said that the view of state law reached by a national tribunal as the result of its exercise of independent reflection must be different from that announced by local courts when deciding similar questions. If federal courts have differed with state judiciaries concerning specific points of law, we must assume that the federal courts took their stand in the belief that the rule of law which they were espousing was more in accord with sound policy and correct legal reasoning than a proposition favored by state judges. We must also assume, and experience bears us out, that whenever the benches of state and nation came to the same view on a given point of law, their decisions were in complete agreement. As this was clearly the situation, it becomes important to inquire into the day-by-day conduct of the federal courts in order to determine how often their independent power over state law led them to announce results different from those which would have been reached by local judiciaries.

The first observation to be made along this line is that all jurisdictions within the United States, except for Louisiana, have inherited the English common law, and both national and state courts operate in accordance with common law principles.

---

comb v. *Denver*, 252 US 7 (1920); *Erie Railroad Co.* v. *Hilt*, 247 US 97 (1918); *St. Louis & Kansas City Land Co.* v. *Kansas City*, 241 US 419 (1916).

For similar holdings in regard to state constitutions see: *General American Tank Car Corp.* v. *Day*, 270 US 367 (1926); *Palmer* v. *Ohio*, 248 US 32 (1918).

Of course, the long years since our separation from Great Britain have seen the development of a number of rules of substantive law which have found favor in some jurisdictions only to be frowned upon in others. But it has always been true that the acceptance of a common English heritage has produced a high degree of similarity in the law as applied by the judiciaries of the several states and of the nation. This is why treatises like Williston, "Contracts", Meecham, "Agency", Walsh, "Mortgages", Pomeroy, "Equity", and many similar works are as useful in New York as they are in Illinois or Florida and have customarily been relied upon by practitioners in both state and federal courts.

Extent of Uniformity in Attractive Nuisance Cases

We start, then, with the proposition that during the reign of *Swift* v. *Tyson,* there were many situations in which no conflict between the substantive rules of law as applied by local and national courts was likely to exist. In order to see the truth of this generalization, it may help to apply it to a specific class of cases. Throughout the entire judicial history of the United States, it has been a well recognized principle of the common law that a landowner must take certain precautions to protect persons coming onto his property. This duty is not equally exacting in regard to all visitors: a business guest is entitled to one type of protection, a social caller to a different degree of safety, and a trespasser to a third and lower order of consideration. Concurrent with this set of principles is another policy of the law which recognizes that trespassing children, because of their immaturity, should receive more protection from the landowner than adults. Such a point of view received its first authoritative exposition in a case decided by the Supreme Court of the United States in 1873.[4] This "Attractive Nuisance" doctrine was bottomed on a

---

[4] *Sioux City & Pacific R. Co.* v. *Stout,* 17 Wall 657. For a comprehensive discussion of this and subsequent cases see Hudson, *The Turntable Cases in the Federal Courts,* 36 Harv. L. Rev. 826 (1923).

social policy of wide appeal: the securing of added protection for the health and safety of our children. When similar cases came before state courts, as they did with considerable frequency, many of them chose to adopt the opinion of the Supreme Court and evolved rules similar to those made obligatory on lower federal courts by the decision in the original "attractive nuisance" case.

Eventually, about two-thirds of our state judiciaries agreed that children were not to be held as strictly accountable for their actions as adult trespassers.[5] The result was that "attractive nuisance" cases arising in these jurisdictions would receive a sympathetic hearing in either state or federal courts. Unless the attorney for an injured child or his parents found some other reason to prefer one judicial system over the other, there was no special inducement to try such cases in a federal rather than in a local court. A doctrine originating in the Supreme Court had brought substantial uniformity of substantive law in two-thirds of the country's jurisdictions. Of course, one-third of the states never subscribed to the "attractive nuisance" doctrine, and whenever litigation arose in such localities, the difference in substantive law was a likely source of confusion and injustice.

EXTENT OF UNIFORMITY—A CROSS SECTION OF LITIGATION IN FEDERAL COURTS

It is possible to gather many examples like the foregoing from all corners of the common law. To the extent that repetition improves understanding, such illustrations would probably be helpful, but an accurate picture of the use made of the rule in *Swift* v. *Tyson* by the federal courts must be gained from an inquiry of a different kind. First, it is necessary to take a substantial sample of the cases coming through the federal courts before 1938.[6] The complete records of all these cases

---

5 See Prosser, *On Torts* (1941), p. 618.

6 In 1938 *Swift* v. *Tyson* was overruled by *Erie Railroad Co.* v. *Tompkins*, 304 US 64.

should be studied in order to make an accurate count of the suits in which a question of state law was raised. This examination should be followed by a careful reading of the court opinions in order to discover how the local questions which did arise were handled. It would also be necessary to reconstruct the factual and legal situation presented by each case wherein jurisdiction was based on diversity of citizenship so that the investigator could decide what result would have been reached had the litigation taken place in a state court. On the basis of such a study, it would then be possible to say precisely how national tribunals were accustomed to deal with local law.

So far as I am aware, this type of research project has never been undertaken. It could not be accomplished by a single investigator with limited time and resources at his disposal. Until someone with the requisite zeal and facilities for such an inquiry presents the results of his labors, we must be satisfied with less complete, and for that reason, less conclusive investigations.

In the hope of assembling sufficient data upon which to found some observations of at least a tentative nature, I have examined the contents of one volume of the Federal Reporter covering a portion of the cases decided by the lower federal courts during 1930. The material thus presented has the advantage of being a random sample of the work then in progress in the nation's courtrooms. Petitions in bankruptcy appear side by side with prosecutions under the then operative National Prohibition Act. And these litigations are interspersed with disputes over land titles, suits on insurance policies, cases arising under the patent laws, and every other type of litigation processed by the national judicial machinery of that time. The order in which these cases follow one another has been dictated only by chronology. Consequently, we may be sure that in so far as the size of the sample studied permits, the lawsuits considered represent a fair cross section of the cases subject to federal jurisdiction. I selected a volume from the year 1930 because *Swift* v. *Tyson* was then at the height of its vigor. All the Supreme Court decisions expanding its principles had already been recorded, and none of the opinions limiting the scope of federal independence of local law had yet been written.

Volume No. 40 of the Federal Reporter, Second Series, reports on seven hundred and seventy-six cases in United States District and Circuit Courts of Appeals. As is customary with legal reports, it contains little or no information in addition to the actual opinions of the judges. In some instances these are more illuminating than in others. They make only haphazard references to the arguments of counsel; they contain only so much of the factual background of a case as the judge believes it necessary to give in order to make the disputed points of law and his decision on them clear.

Of the seven hundred and seventy-six cases covered, nineteen were decided in the District of Columbia and two in our Territorial Possessions. As these are areas exclusively within the national jurisdiction, no question of conflict between federal and state law of the kind here discussed could be presented by any of these twenty-one litigations. One case concerned an unsuccessful attempt to confer jurisdiction on a federal court through a plea of diversity of citizenship. As the court refused to entertain this dispute, no friction with a state judiciary could be present here. Most of the remaining cases arose under acts of Congress and it was obvious that federal law was to be applied. In some few instances, the court's opinion was so brief that it contained no indication of the facts on which federal jurisdiction rested. In the remaining cases, fifty-eight in number, it was clear that the only disputed points were questions of state law, and that a difference in the citizenship of the parties to the suit presented the only ground for an exercise of federal authority. All of these cases were possible subjects for the application of the Tyson Rule.

In only four out of these fifty-eight cases do the opinions disclose a conflict between substantive rules of law prevailing in state and federal courts. In each instance, the court emphasized its independence of local opinions and proceeded to follow federal precedents in arriving at its decision. Assuming that a more thorough study along the line suggested above would show four out of fifty-eight to be a fair ratio, it appears that in seven percent of the cases brought to national tribunals because of diverse citizenship the outcome was different from what it would have been had the litigants been compelled to make use of state courts. This is not so large a body of litigation as to deprive the states of effective control over their own legal processes, but it is a sufficient factor to produce a measure of uncertainty in the enforcement of local policy. Moreover, we shall soon see that seven percent may be too low a figure, although it is not possible to calculate the extent of error.

In a much larger group of cases, twenty out of the fifty-eight or roughly thirty-five percent of the total, the court relied on precedents of the appropriate state judiciary in deciding the suit before it. Whether results would have been any different in these cases had the courts chosen to exercise their independent judgment and follow federal precedents is not to be learned from a scrutiny of any of the opinions, but the fact that state authorities were cited in preference to federal decisions seems to indicate a willingness to defer to local views when deciding questions of local law. This is not to say that the federal court reached the same result that would have been obtained from a local tribunal in every instance. It may be that in a small fraction of the cases the federal judges interpreted state precedents to mean something quite different from what local judges would have thought them to mean. But this is the same phenomenon which is occasionally to be observed in different parts of the same judicial system. Trial and intermediate courts of the same state sometimes disagree over the interpretation to be placed on a decision of their highest court, and when this happens, various parts of the state experience a difference in the enforcement of a supposedly uniform law. To the extent that the presence of federal courts increases the number of tribunals administering the same laws, these irregularities are multiplied. However, such of these twenty cases as may be examples of this condition do not present serious problems in the relation between state and federal authority because any harm which was done resulted from the vagueness of the local law. All that could reasonably be asked of the federal courts was that they abide by state rules and state policy in so far as these could be discovered. In the cases of which we have been speaking, this was done.

The instances of obvious conflict between federal and state law together with the cases in which state law was followed account for less than half of the fifty-eight diversity suits. The remaining thirty-four disputes represent the rule of *Swift* v. *Tyson* in what appears to have been unchallenged operation. In all of these cases, the federal courts acted as any common law judiciary would when called upon to interpret its own jurisprudence. As the United States Supreme Court stands at the apex of the national judicial system, its opinions received first allegiance. When no applicable pronouncements of that Court could be found, the decisions of lower federal courts were consulted and followed. Of course, the opinions of state courts, not necessarily those of the state whose judiciary would have settled the controversy had there been no diversity of citizenship, were sometimes cited. But this was done in precisely the same spirit that state courts sometimes refer to decisions in other jurisdictions: merely to show a preponderance of learned opinion in support of some point of law or to throw some light on a matter which had not been thoroughly canvassed by domestic decisions. Such outside sources of legal learning did not command the obligatory attention of the federal courts, and whether they were to be given any weight was a matter of complete discretion.

These thirty-four cases in which the decisions were based on considerations of general law contain no reliable evidence of their probable outcome had state law been applied. However, the failure to consider local decisions is significant as an indication of the normal relation of national courts to the enforcement of state law. It may be that experience had taught the lawyers representing both sides of these litigations that federal tribunals were not likely to hold local law in high regard. Believing it utterly futile to urge the opinions of local judiciaries on the federal courts, these attorneys may have resigned themselves to the necessity of fighting their cases with whatever ammunition was provided by federal precedents. If this is not the explanation, we must assume that any points of state law relied on by the parties were not deemed sufficiently important to merit notice in the court's opinion.

LIMITING THE TYSON RULE

For over ninety years after its original formulation, the rule of *Swift* v. *Tyson* was changed only to permit of its extension to new fields. Each of the Supreme Court decisions expanding the principle of federal independence of state law, with but a single exception,[7] was reached over the objection of one or more members of the Court. But opposition from within was never strong enough to prevent the steady growth of Story's famous doctrine. Shortly before the decision in the Black & White Taxi Case [8] pointed up the mischief which an over zealous disregard of local law and policy might cause, Professor Charles Warren conclusively proved that Story's construction of the Judiciary Act of 1789 was not correct.[9] An

7 *Yates* v. *Milwaukee*, 10 Wall. 497 (1870). All of the other Supreme Court decisions extending the Tyson Rule were rendered by a divided Court. In *Lane* v. *Vic*, 3 How. 464 (1845), Justices M'Kinley and Taney dissented; in *Williamson* v. *Berry*, 8 How. 495 (1850), Justices Nelson, Taney, and Catron; in *Gelpcke* v. *City of Dubuque*, 1 Wall. 175 (1864), Justice Miller; in *Baltimore & Ohio R. Co.* v. *Baugh*, 149 US 368 (1893), Justices Field and Fuller; in *Kuhn* v. *Fairmont Coal Co.*, 215 US. 349 (1910), Justices Holmes, White, and McKenna; and in *Black & White Taxicab and Transfer Co.* v. *Brown & Yellow Taxicab and Transfer Co.*, 276 US 518 (1928), Justices Holmes, Brandeis, and Stone dissented.

8 *Black & White Taxicab and Transfer Co.* v. *Brown & Yellow Taxicab and Transfer Co.*, 276 US 518 (1928). For the facts of this case see pp. 79-81, *supra*.

9 Warren, *New Light on the History of the Federal Judiciary Act of 1789*, 37 Harv. Law Rev. 49 (1923).

examination of the recently discovered original drafts of this statute showed that Congress had intended federal courts to apply local court decisions as well as local statutes. But nearly a century of judicial usage had implanted the misconception too firmly to be ousted by so unofficial an authority as an article in a legal periodical. Moreover, by the time Professor Warren wrote his piece for the *Harvard Law Review,* the incorrectness of the Tyson Doctrine was no longer a simple matter of fact needing nothing more than historical research to accomplish its overturn. On the one hand, it was possible to argue with Professor Warren that Story's interpretation of the Act of Congress was contrary to the evidence of legislative intent. On the other hand, one might invoke the oft-used canon of statutory construction which is to the effect that a judicial interpretation of a statute long acquiesced in by Congress must have the sanction of that body. Indeed, the late Senator Norris of Nebraska led several attempts to legislate Swift v. Tyson out of existence, but all of them were unsuccessful.[10]

But in response to growing dissatisfaction with the Tyson Rule, a slow change in judicial sentiment began to take place. *Brinkerhoff-Faris Trust Co.* v. *Hill,*[11] decided in 1930, gave the Supreme Court an opportunity to explain with particular clarity that *Swift* v. *Tyson* could be applied only where a case had been litigated in a lower federal court. Although this case was ultimately decided on a question of federal law, Mr. Justice Brandeis wrote the following during the course of his opinion: " Our present concern is solely with the question whether the plaintiff has been accorded due process in the

10 S. 3151 (Senator Norris) 70 Cong. 1st Sess. See Sen. Rep. 626 of Committee on the Judiciary, March 27, 1928, S. 4357 (Senator Norris), 71 Cong. 2d. Sess. See Sen. Rep. 691 of Committee on the Judiciary, May 20, 1930.

A bill designed to abolish the rule of *Swift* v. *Tyson* was also introduced (Senator Walsh), S. 4333, 70th Cong., 1st Sess.; S. 96, 71st Cong., 1st Sess.

For a general discussion see Yntema and Jaffin, *Preliminary Analysis of Concurrent Jurisdiction,* 79 U. of Pa. L. Rev. 869 (1931).

11 281 US 673 (1930).

primary sense . . . . Undoubtedly the state court had the power to construe the statute dealing with the State Tax Commission; and to re-examine and overrule the *Laclede* case." (a decision of the Missouri Supreme Court) " Neither of these matters raises a federal question; neither is subject to our review." [12] And in a footnote to this passage, Mr. Justice Brandeis continues: ". . . The doctrine of *Gelpcke* v. *Dubuque,* and *Butz* v. *Muscatine,* like that of *Swift* v. *Tyson,* is, if applied at all, confined strictly to cases arising in the federal courts.[13]

It would be too much to say that the Brinkerhoff decision signaled a departure from the Gelpcke and Tyson Rules, because the cases originating in state courts had naturally been decided in accordance with the views of local judiciaries, and it was not customary for the Supreme Court to reopen state determinations of local law on appeal. In the Brinkerhoff Case, the Court did not decide the questions of state law on their substantive merits as the earlier cases had done, but this difference was due to the nature of the case rather than to a change in attitude. The only question presented by *Swift* v. *Tyson* had been the one relating to the law of negotiable instruments, and the Supreme Court could hardly avoid addressing itself to the matter actually before it. In *Gelpcke* v. *Dubuque* the sole question was as to the validity of certain municipal bonds: if the Court decided anything at all, it had to decide the question of substantive law. But the Brinkerhoff Case presented a constitutional question whose decision was preliminary to a consideration of the disputed issues of state law. As a practical matter, it was perfectly feasible for the Supreme Court to decide the federal question while leaving possible questions of Missouri law for clarification in subsequent legal proceedings. However, Brandeis' remarks in reference to *Gelpcke* v. *Dubuque* and *Swift* v. *Tyson* are interesting as an indication,

12 281 US 673, 681 (1930).
13 *Ibid.*

albeit a feeble one, that the Court was no longer likely to continue to expand the Tyson Rule.

The first real limitation of the Tyson Doctrine came when the Supreme Court handed down its opinion in *Mutual Life Insurance Co.* v. *Johnson* [14] during 1934. This was a dispute over the interpretation of an insurance contract delivered and to be performed in Virginia. By the ordinary principles of conflict of laws, such a contract was normally to be construed in accordance with Virginia Law; but as the Johnson Case was tried in the Federal Courts, it was possible for those tribunals to, exercise an independent judgment and decide the case on principles of general law. Indeed, this was the customary procedure and had the Supreme Court followed it when the case came up for review, no one would have been surprised.

But the high bench took another tack. Mr. Justice Cardozo, who wrote for a unanimous Court, began by noting that the particular insurance policy clause then before him was giving the courts a deal of difficulty. He was able to cite decisions from ten jurisdictions agreeing on one interpretation of the clause, and decisions from eight other jurisdictions holding to quite another construction. This indicated, so Cardozo said, that the point to be decided was " balanced with doubt ". As a matter of layman's common sense, this conclusion seemed natural enough. But Cardozo's reason for making the observation was hardly a commonplace one.

Fifty years earlier, when writing the opinion for a case in which the United States Supreme Court refused to accept a local interpretation of a state statute,[15] Mr. Justice Bradley had remarked that federal courts lean to an agreement with the views of state judiciaries and follow local decisions whenever a case is " balanced with doubt." By 1934, Bradley's words had received many quotations. But it seemed as though federal judges were especially fond of using them when deciding to

14 293 US 335 (1934).

15 See *Burgess* v. *Seligman*, 107 US 20 (1882).

ignore the opinions of state courts; perhaps they thought to soothe local feelings by reminding observers that state law would have been followed if only the circumstances had been different.

Cardozo also had fine words for the state courts. With his customary eloquence, he wrote: " The *sumum jus* of power, whatever it may be, will be subordinated at times to a benign and prudent comity" [16] But the difference between this case and other occasions on which federal courts had expressed respect for local judiciaries was that in this instance, the Court had actually demonstrated such respect in full operation. It so happened that one of the jurisdictions which had made an interpretation of the troublesome insurance policy provision was Virginia,[17] and Cardozo had just announced the Supreme Court's intention to accept the Virginia precedent in the following words:

" In this situation we are not under a duty to make a choice for ourselves between alternative constructions as if the courts of the place of the contract were silent or uncertain. Without suggesting an independent preference either one way or the other, we yield to the judges of Virginia expounding a Virginia policy and adjudging its effect. The case will not be complicated by a consideration of our power to pursue some other course." [18]

Of itself, the Court's willingness to be influenced by precedents from another jurisdiction was not unusual. When faced with a difficult or novel question, it is in the best common law tradition for a court to draw upon all the fountainheads of legal learning that it can find and adopt what seems to be the most convincing view as its own. Had the Supreme Court done this, it would have subscribed to the Virginia Rule and, in the future, all federal tribunals would have been bound to

16 293 US 335, 339.

17 *Swann* v. *Atlantic Life Ins. Co.*, 156 Va. 852, 159 SE 192 (1931).

18 293 US 335, 339.

follow the sanctioned construction of the insurance policy. In short, the federal law would have become coincident with the Virginia Rule, by a process of adoption; but this is not what was done in the Johnson Case. Cardozo declined to announce a federal rule of substantive law. The condition of substantive insurance law, as applied by national courts, was precisely what it had been before the decision.

The new feature in *Mutual Life Insurance Co. v. Johnson* was Cardozo's use of the " balance with doubt " formula. As a note in the Harvard Law Review [19]saw the situation, one might have expected the Supreme Court to make an independent investigation of the question in the case with a view to deciding which of the conflicting constructions of the insurance policy met with its approval. If the Court could not make up its mind, it might then have said that the question was " balanced with doubt " and permitted the Virginia law to prevail. But to Cardozo, the mere fact that ten jurisdictions held one view while eight took a contrary position, was enough to raise the doubt. In the opinion of the writer in the Harvard Law Review, such reasoning opened the door to constant evasion of the rule in *Swift* v. *Tyson* without the need for overruling Story's long standing doctrine. There were many questions in the common law whereon courts divided sharply, some adhering to one view of the law—others supporting a divergent or even a contradictory rule. All of these sectors of the law could easily be returned to complete state control if only the federal courts found questions in these areas to be " balanced with doubt ".

It is interesting to speculate on how completely this approach would have succeeded in undermining *Swift* v. *Tyson*. Much would have depended on the lengths to which the courts were willing to carry the " balanced with doubt " formula. Cardozo applied it when he found an almost equal division among the

19 Note, *Some Recent Implications of Swift v. Tyson*, 48 Harv. L. Rev. 979 (1935).

authorities. Would it have been applied if seventy-five or eighty percent of the authorities opposed the Virginia view? Would it have been applied if all other jurisdictions disagreed with the Virginia interpretation of the insurance policy? Indeed, it is logically possible, although not at all likely, that the courts would ultimately have said any question was "balanced with doubt" if opposing sides in a litigation appeared to be genuinely convinced that they were in the right. Had *Swift* v. *Tyson* not been squarely overruled within a few years after the Johnson Case, the Supreme Court might have found an opportunity to explore some of these possibilities. However, as matters now stand, it would serve little purpose to do more than point them out. It is now unnecessary for opponents of the Tyson Doctrine to vindicate state authority by courting the art of technical legal argument.

PART IV
ERIE v. TOMPKINS: A MORE MODEST UNIFORMITY

CHAPTER IX
THE CASE

THROUGHOUT our history as a nation most commercial law has emanated from local courts and legislatures. As a result, each of our states has come to have a body of commercial law somewhat different from that to be found in each of the other states. It has been said that these local variations correspond to differences in local conditions and that a system which permits each state to fashion its commercial law to meet its peculiar needs is more workable than a single national commercial code would be. However, a system of uniform statutory and common law throughout all of the forty-eight states would have certain advantages over present conditions. Businessmen who deal with out-of-state suppliers or customers as well as those who carry on simultaneous operations in many states would be among the first to notice the comparative simplicity of such an arrangement. In deciding whether a contract provision offered them proper protection for their interests, they would no longer have to wonder whether one rule would be applied to it in Illinois, a second in Indiana, and a third in Michigan. It would be sufficient for them to know what *the legal significance* of the provision was because it would be the same everywhere. It is likely that interstate transactions would be consummated with greater speed; bills for legal counsel would be reduced; and some of the negotiations which falter because of uncertainties in the law would be carried to successful conclusions. To the extent that more efficient business operations would be attained under a standardized body of law, increased prosperity for the country as a whole might result.

Dubious Success of the Tyson Rule

As we have seen, the blessings of uniformity in the law were probably of first importance to Story when he decided Swift v. Tyson. And it is even more certain that believers in the doctrine of that case have thought its chief value to lie in the promotion of a more uniform view of the law throughout our many separate jurisdictions.[1] Accordingly, it may be well to give a moment's attention to this matter of harmony in the common law and to see how the power of federal courts to make independent interpretations of state law was supposed to induce a greater consistency in legal administration.

Decisions of the Supreme Court of the United States are always binding on the lower federal courts; this is a natural consequence of the former's position at the apex of the national judicial hierarchy. Supreme Court precedents are also binding on state tribunals whenever they are called upon to interpret the Constitution of the United States or federal statutes; such is the case because the high bench at Washington is the ultimate authority in questions of federal law. But in most other matters state judiciaries make final determinations which are

---

1 See Green, *The Law as Precedent, Prophecy, and Principle: State Decisions in Federal Courts*, 19 Ill. L. Rev. 217 (1924) ; Moore, *The Passion For Uniformity* in *International Law And Some Current Illusions* (1924), pp. 333-334; Schofield, *Swift v. Tyson: Uniformity of Judge-Made State Law in State and Federal Courts*, 4 Ill. L. Rev. 533 (1910).

not subject to federal review. In extreme circumstances, like those surrounding the Railway-Aid Bond Cases, local courts may be coerced into following federal authority. It will be remembered that in those cases local power was insufficient to prevent non residents from collecting on their bonds by securing judgments from federal courts, and the Iowa judiciary finally yielded so that local citizens might recover what they could before outsiders completely stripped municipal treasuries. But such situations are rare and play no part in the normal relations between federal and state judicial systems.

There has never been any serious doubt concerning the Supreme Court's ability to bring uniformity to the administration of law by the lower federal courts. To be sure, there have often been conflicting decisions by two or more Circuit Courts of Appeals and by various District Courts; but these have persisted only until such time as the Supreme Court has found an opportunity to make an authoritative pronouncement of its own on the troublesome point. Thereafter, federal tribunals in all parts of the country have recognized their duty to apply the law as expounded by the highest court in the national system. So long as the national judiciary made independent determinations in matters of general law, the influence of the Supreme Court on inferior national tribunals was naturally as great here as in other fields, and the securing of a uniform administration of the common law by all sectors of the federal judiciary was a comparatively simple project. But the attainment of this goal was only a small part of the benefit expected to flow from the opinion in *Swift* v. *Tyson*. The vast body of litigation on common law subjects has always taken place in state courts. Consequently, if any real uniformity in the bodies of common law was to follow from the Tyson Rule, it would depend on the willingness of local tribunals to accept principles embodied in the decisions of the Supreme Court.

Story had good reason to hope that such voluntary obedience would be forthcoming. He knew that the opinions of English judges like Mansfield, Holt, and Coke were almost as important to the bench and bar in America as they were in England. Surely, this was not due to any obligation on the part of American courts to follow British precedents; any compulsion of this kind had terminated when we won our Independence. Instead, the continued influence of English law was traceable to the high reputation of the King's Bench and to the acknowledged learning of the more talented British judges. Story may well have believed that the United States Supreme Court was coming to enjoy an equal respect and that, in the future, state judiciaries would look to it for guidance in much the same way that they looked to the courts of England. Although it had once been a serious question whether the highest court in the national system was greater in prestige than appellate tribunals in the states,[2] the excellent work of the former, done under the masterful direction of Chief Justice Marshall, had established the primacy of the high bench at Washington. In the light of these conditions, it may have been reasonable to expect that pronouncements of the Supreme Court on common law topics would have an eager audience and following in the states.

Supporters of the Tyson Rule have indeed always claimed that this was actually the result. In support of their view, they can point to many opinions delivered in state courts which declare pronouncements made by the Supreme Court at Washington to be highly persuasive.[3] But it is impossible to say

---

2 See Ch. II, *supra*.

3 There were innumerable cases to this effect. The following are a few examples. *Santee River Cypress Lumber Co.* v. *Query*, 168 SC 112, 167 SE 22 (1932) (Federal decision interpreting state statute persuasive and followed). See *Dicken* v. *Missouri Pacific R. Co.*, 188 Ark. 1035, 69 SW 2d 277 (1934); *People* v. *Herbert's of Los Angeles*, 3 Ca. App. 2d 482, 39 P2d 829 (1935); *Board of Com'rs of Boulder County* v. *Union Pacific R. Co.*, 89 Col. 110, 299 P 1055 (1931); *Parsons* v. *Federal Realty Corp.* 105 Fla. 105, 143 So. 912 (1932); *Detroit Trust Co.* v. *Detroit City Service Co.*, 262 Mich. 14, 247 NW 76 (1935); *McNary* v. *State*, 128 O. St. 497, 191 NE 733 (1934).

But there are also many cases to the contrary. *First National Bank of Lyndhurst* v. *Bianchi & Smith*, 106 NJE 333, 150 A. 774 (1930); *American*

whether *Swift* v. *Tyson* fostered uniformity where discord would otherwise have prevailed. In order to make a conclusive test of this assertion, it would be necessary to turn back the calendar to 1842, permit Story to erase his opinion from the books, and wait fifty or a hundred years to see what the course of history would bring. We could then compare what really happened with what might have been. However, as such an experiment is obviously impossible, it may be best to suspend judgment in the matter.

In any event, it was easy to see that even if the Tyson Doctrine had brought some degree of uniformity into the common law, the operation of a principle of federal independence had not always brought desirable consequences. By way of a start, we may note that the New York courts, whose rule concerning negotiable instruments Story had refused to follow, did not change their holdings because of the decision in *Swift* v. *Tyson*. On the contrary, they adhered to their own views as though nothing had happened.[4] The result was not uniformity in the administration of the common law, but serious disagreement. Federal courts sitting in New York followed the Tyson Case while local tribunals presiding over the same territory continued to insist on their right to disregard Story's opinion.

Some forty years after *Swift* v. *Tyson* was decided, legal research disclosed twenty-eight kinds of cases wherein federal and state judiciaries customarily held different views of specific questions of common law.[5] These classifications covered many fields, and it may be ironic that a number of them were

---

Fidelity & Casualty Co. v. *Newman* (Tex. Civ. App.), 60 SW 2d 482 (1933); *Seaboard Air Line Ry. Co.* v. *Sarman,* 38 Ga. App. 637, 144 SE 810 (1928). See *State* v. *Risty,* 51 SD 336, 213 NW 952 (1927).

4 *Lawrence* v. *Clark,* 36 NY 128 (1867); *Moore* v. *Ryder,* 65 NY 438 (1875); *Potts* v. *Mayer,* 74 NY 594 (1878); *Phoenix Ins. Co.* v. *Church,* 81 NY 218 (1880); *Leach* v. *Flack,* 31 Hun (NY 1884) 605. See *Mayer* v. *Heidelbach,* 123 NY 332, 339, 25 NE 416, 417 (1890).

5 Holt, *The Concurrent Jurisdiction of the Federal and State Courts* (1888), pp. 159-188.

squarely within the commercial law whose uniformity was especially necessary in Story's eyes. Had a systematic study of this field been made forty or fifty years later, it is likely that something like these same results would have been duplicated. Nothing seems to have happened in the interim to change the earlier situation. Indeed, we have considerable evidence of continued dissimilarity in the judge-made law of our several states.

During the late 1920s, The American Law Institute began work on the series of " Restatements " of the law now familiar to all lawyers. One of the avowed purposes of this work was to provide attorneys and judges with unofficial codifications of various segments of the law in the hope that courts would be inclined to accept the views of the Restatements in areas of conflicting opinion. If *Swift* v. *Tyson* had succeeded in promoting as high a degree of uniformity as its supporters hoped, this work would have been at least partly unnecessary.

THE TYSON RULE OVERTURNED

Despite a rising stream of criticism in legal periodicals, complete abandonment of Story's long-standing doctrine did not appear to be an immediate prospect. As late as 1937, the Supreme Court cited *Swift* v. *Tyson* in the usual way and took advantage of an opportunity to decide a question of general law.[6] Then, in 1938, came *Erie Railroad Co.* v. *Tompkins.*[7]

The facts of that case were unfortunate and all too familiar. On a dark night, a man named Tompkins was walking along a well used path beside the tracks of the Erie Railroad in Pennsylvania. The open door of a passing freight car, which stuck out from the side of a moving train, hit and injured Mr. Tompkins. In the suit commenced by him, his right to a recovery depended on the measure of care owed to him by the Erie Railroad.

6 *Boseman* v. *Connecticut General Life Ins. Co.*, 301 US 196, 204 (1937).
7 304 US 64 (1938).

Tompkin's quest for the most propitious tribunal before which to bring his suit was a project in itself; his more obvious range of choice lay among a state court in Pennsylvania, a federal court in Pennsylvania, a state court in New York, and a federal court in New York. The first of these alternatives was appropriate because the plaintiff was a resident of Pennsylvania, the Railroad did business in Pennsylvania, and the accident had occurred in Pennsylvania. But chances of success were heavily against Tompkins if he chose the courts of that State: a decision of the highest court in Pennsylvania had held that persons using longitudinal footpaths on railroad rights-of-way were to be considered as trespassers, and only persons crossing the tracks were properly on the right-of-way.[8] Tompkins could have resorted to a state court in New York because the Erie Railroad was incorporated there. However, this would probably have been to no avail because the New York court would have applied its conflict of laws rule, discovered that the accident had occurred in Pennsylvania, and followed the substantive law of that state in judging Mr. Tompkins' rights. A federal court in Pennsylvania was also open to the plaintiff, and litigation in that forum offered a more hopeful prospect because the court would not be bound to follow local decisions, but could decide the case on principles of general law. But Mr. Tompkins evidently thought that a federal court in New York would be even less likely to apply Pennsylvania decisions,[9] and so he chose to commence his action in the Federal District Court for the Southern District of New York. This proved to be a wise choice, for by the time the case had been fought through the Circuit Court of Appeals, Tompkins had a $30,000 judgment in his favor. This result was brought to the Supreme Court for review.

8 *Falchetti* v. *Pennsylvania R. Co.*, 307 Pa. 203, 160 A. 859 (1932).

9 The local law supposedly most familiar to a federal court sitting in New York was the law of New York. In order to apply Pennsylvania law such a court would first have to apply the New York conflict of laws rule.

The Erie Railroad was naturally anxious to persuade the Supreme Court that it should follow state law and that it should not exercise its power to use an independent judgment on the question of general law. However, the Erie's attorneys evidently believed it futile to request a repudiation of Story's doctrine. In arguing to the Court counsel said:

" We do not question the finality of the holding of this Court in *Swift* v. *Tyson,* that the ' laws of the several States' referred to in the Rules of Decision Act do not include state court decisions as such.

" It would be idle to deny that this Court, in matters of a general nature, has exhibited a marked reluctance to recognize nonconformist state rules as settling the question of state law." [10]

Having decided to make this apparently inevitable concession to solidly entrenched legal doctrine, the best that Erie could do was to argue: " The Pennsylvania Decisions should have been recognized as controlling because they had established the rules of law with sufficient definiteness and finality to constitute it a local rule of property, action or conduct, even though the question might otherwise have been regarded as mainly one of general law." [11] This was an appeal to the Court to employ some of the " benign comity " to which Justice Cardozo had referred in *Mutual Life Insurance Co.* v. *Johnson.*[12]

Tompkins, on the other hand, felt all the comfort that the support of a well used and familiar rule of law can bring. The Circuit Court of Appeals had acted in a perfectly normal fashion when it treated the case as a dispute on a question of general law, and all that Tompkins wanted was an affirmance of a well worn legal principle. As a matter of precaution, counsel deemed it wise to say a few words in the hope of convincing the Court that, should it perchance decide to follow the state

10 304 US 64, 66.

11 *Ibid.*

12 See Ch. VIII, *supra.*

law, the Pennsylvania opinions did not really mean what the
Railroad said they did;[13] but Tompkins' fort was *Swift* v.
Tyson, and he had good reason to be satisfied with its strength.
In this situation, imagine the surprise of the litigants and of
all informed readers of the advance sheets from the United
States Reports when they saw the opening sentence of Justice
Brandeis' opinion as he wrote for a majority of the Court.
" The question for decision is whether the oft-challenged doc-
trine of *Swift* v. *Tyson* shall now be disapproved." [14]

By way of prelude to its solution of the problem, the Court's
opinion made a brief survey of the ninety-six years under the
Tyson Rule. It referred to all of the major law review articles
criticizing Story's doctrine adversely, and agreed that conditions were unsatisfactory. The inability of the federal courts
to coerce or persuade state tribunals to accept a national version of the common law was certainly the moving force behind
judicial disapproval of existing practice, and the embarrassing
situations resulting from attempts to take advantage of disparate national and state rules was undoubtedly the primary
reason for the Court's desire for a change. Justice should not
be made to depend on whether litigants chanced to appeal to a
federal rather than to a state forum. Nationwide uniformity in
the common law might still be highly desirable, but it was
fully as desirable that courts sitting within the same state apply
the same rules of law whether they were part of federal or state
judicial systems. The Court was now anxious to shift the
emphasis from interstate uniformity to a federal-state uniformity to be obtained within the boundaries of each state by permitting local rules of law to prevail. But the conduct of the
Supreme Court is circumscribed by the Constitution and the
laws of Congress. In this particular instance, the legal doctrine
was based on Story's construction of the Rules of Decision
Act. Consequently, the repudiation of federal independence in

13 304 US 64, 68-69.
14 304 US 64, 69.

matters of local law required more than judicial displeasure with established rules. In his concurring opinion,[15] Mr. Justice Reed submitted that it was perfectly proper for Swift v. Tyson to be thrown into the discard, and that the Rules of Decision Act offered ample support for such a course. He cited Warren's work [16] in uncovering the true legislative history of Section 34 of the Judiciary Act of 1789, and said that with the correct information at hand, there was no longer any excuse for perpetuating Story's error. The majority of the Court also recognized the importance of Professor Warren's researches, but rested its decision on a more fundamental ground. As they saw the matter, the many acts of the federal judiciary in obedience to the Tyson Rule were nothing less than unconstitutional.

Unusual Character of the Constitutional Argument

This idea had first made its appearance in a dissenting opinion written by Mr. Justice Field for *Baltimore & Ohio R. Co. v. Baugh* [17] in 1882. That case was important because it helped to extend the Tyson Doctrine into the field of torts. In declaring the Court's action to be an unconstitutional exercise of power, Field said that he himself had many times cited learned authority to justify his concurrence in Story's doctrine, but that he was now convinced that he had been in error.[18] At a later period, Mr. Justice Holmes also seems to have believed that federal independence of state law was contrary to the Constitution,[19] but he was more inclined to stress the practical mischiefs of the Tyson Rule than to make a searching inquiry

15 304 US 64, 90.

16 Warren, *New Light on the History of the Federal Judiciary Act of 1789,* 37 Harv. L. Rev. 49 (1923).

17 149 US 368, 399 (1893).

18 *Ibid.,* p. 401.

19 Holmes expressed this view in his dissents to *Kuhn* v. *Fairmont Coal Co.,* 215 US 349, 370 (1910) and *Black and White Taxicab and Transfer Co.* v. *Brown and Yellow Taxicab and Transfer Co.,* 276 US 518, 532 (1928).

into its specific constitutional basis. However, in *Erie Rail-road Co.* v. *Tompkins,* the constitutional question became the foundation of the Court's opinion.

The part of the Constitution offended by *Swift* v. *Tyson* is the Tenth Amendment which provides that all powers not given to the federal government are reserved to the states or to the people. As the power to bypass state law when deciding diversity cases is not specifically conferred upon the national judiciary, it is argued that local law must necessarily be applied by national courts in appropriate cases. Moreover, the Constitution recognizes the sovereignty of the states, and an element of that sovereignty is the ability to proclaim and control the content of state law. To permit the federal government to undermine the power of the states in this regard, would be to contradict the basic division of authority between States and Nation made by the Constitution.

This is plausible doctrine, and since it has been accepted by the Supreme Court, it is currently valid constitutional theory. But its correctness is not of precisely the same order as that exhibited by the axioms in geometry. It is possible to doubt, as indeed Mr. Justice Reed did when he wrote his concurring opinion, that the constitutional argument was altogether called for in the Erie Case.

In the first place, the reversal of *Swift* v. *Tyson* was accomplished in a highly unusual manner. As we have seen, the parties to the litigation had not uttered so much as a syllable in criticism of the established rule, and while it is possible for a court to reverse a prior position without prodding from the suitors, such a practice is hardly encountered in the normal course of events. Even more unusual was the Court's decision of a question in constitutional law. It is a familiar principle that a court will avoid the decision of a constitutional issue wherever possible,[20] and in the Erie Case, it was certainly pos-

20 Mr. Justice Brandeis concurring in *Ashwander* v. *Tennessee Valley Authority,* 297 US 288, 341 (1936) ; Weaver, *Constitutional Law* (1946), pp. 82, 83.

sible. Mr. Justice Reed reached the same conclusion as the majority of his colleagues by making a simple reinterpretation of the Rules of Decision Act. This alternative was not lost to the majority of the Court because its opinion mentions the researches of Professor Warren, and the Court would have been following a traditional path if it had joined Reed in accepting the legislative intent of 1789 as determinative of the issue.

In the realm of constitutional doctrine, critics of the Erie Decision may use an argument which, if it is not more plausible than that advanced by Mr. Justice Brandeis on behalf of the Court, also has its merit. Article III, Section 2 of the Constitution gives the Supreme Court appellate jurisdiction over cases and controversies between citizens of different states, and by Act of Congress, the lower federal courts are empowered to take original jurisdiction over such cases.[21] The power to entertain such disputes necessarily involves the power to decide questions of common law presented in them. This is certainly recognized by the Constitution; yet that document is silent concerning whose law is to be applied in the federal courts. Why, then, is it not proper to assume that federal courts should apply the common law as they themselves interpret it? But whether one prefers this line of reasoning or that advanced by the Supreme Court, we must all agree that the views announced by the majority in the Erie Case are the law.

The grounds for the Erie Decision are of the utmost importance to federal-state judicial relationships. If it is true that the Constitution, of its own force prevents national courts from doing otherwise than to accept local interpretations of state law, the Rules of Decision Act is merely declaratory of pre-existing Constitutional law. Moreover, a Congressional attempt to change present policy would be to no avail. In the 1920s, there was some talk of modifying or repealing *Swift* v. *Tyson* by legislation;[22] under the holding in the Erie Case,

21 1 Stat. 73 (1789).

22 Yntema and Jaffin, *Preliminary Analysis of Concurrent Jurisdiction,* 79 U. of Pa. L. Rev. 869 (1931).

there is no longer a need for such statutory changes. Should serious dissatisfaction with present federal obedience to local precedents develop, there might be talk of returning to the old rule by way of the legislative route. But this would be impossible. If the development and interpretation of principles of common law is a power reserved to the states, Congressional action cannot reach it. Nothing less than a constitutional amendment would bring Story's doctrine back to life.

The knowledge that our courts occasionally brand some governmental act with the stamp of unconstitutionality is universal among students of government and widespread among laymen. Indeed, this function of our judiciaries is so well known to us that we seldom take the trouble to remark on some of its characteristics. One of the things that we accept as a matter of course is the notion that acts of legislation or of the executive branch of government are the only objects of challenge in the courts. For example, cases wherein the Supreme Court has declared minimum wage [23] or child labor [24] laws unconstitutional are celebrated episodes in our judicial history; so are instances wherein the President has been said to have exceeded his power when removing officers of the federal government.[25] But we are not accustomed to think of a decision of the United States Supreme Court as unconstitutional. That tribunal is the highest authority we have on the interpretation of our fundamental law. From time to time, the Supreme Court may overrule its own precedents and replace them with new doctrines. We do not consider this to mean that the former decisions were illegal when announced. Instead, we explain such changes in our constitutional law by observing that concepts like free speech, due process of law, and interstate

23 *Morehead* v. *New York ex rel. Tipaldo,* 298 US 587 (1936).

24 *Hammer* v. *Dagenhart,* 247 US 251 (1918).

25 *Humphrey's Executor* v. *U. S.,* 295 US 602 (1935).

commerce have altered in substantive content as the social, political, and economic condition of the country has grown more complex. So, a minimum wage law which once interfered with an employer's liberty of contract is no longer held to do so.[26] Manufacturing was, at an earlier period of our history, a local activity; today it may be a part of interstate commerce.[27]

The declaration that *Swift* v. *Tyson* was unconstitutional made the Erie Case unique. It is the only instance to date wherein the Supreme Court has so characterized one of its own precedents.[28] Logically, there is no reason why a rule of law created by judicial opinion cannot be as invalid as a rule of law created by an Act of Congress. Each prescribes the relationships between individuals, between individuals and their

26 *West Coast Hotel Co.* v. *Parrish*, 300 US 397 (1937), overrules *Morehead* v. *New York ex rel. Tipaldo, supra*, note 23.

27 The earlier view is represented by *Hammer* v. *Dagenhart, supra*, note 24. In 1941 the Supreme Court overruled the Dagenhart Case in *U. S.* v. *Darby*, 312 US 100 (1941).

28 In *U. S.* v. *Darby*, Mr. Justice Stone said: "*Hammer* v. *Dagenhart* has not been followed. The distinction on which the decision was rested that Congressional power to prohibit interstate commerce is limited to articles which in themselves have some harmful or deleterious property—a distinction which was novel when made and unsupported by any provision of the Constitution has long since been abandoned. The thesis of the opinion that the motive of the prohibition or its effect to control in some measure the use or production within the states of the article thus excluded from the commerce can operate to deprive the regulation of its constitutional authority has long since ceased to have force. And finally we have declared, ' The authority of the federal government over interstate commerce does not differ in extent or character from that retained by the states over intrastate commerce.'

"The conclusion is inescapable that *Hammer* v. *Dagenhart*, was a departure from the principles which have prevailed in the interpretation of the Commerce Clause both before and since the decision and that such vitality, as a precedent, as it then had has long since been exhausted. It should be and now is overruled." 312 US 100, 116-117.

The language here used by the Court comes close to declaring that the decision in *Hammer* v. *Dagenhart* was unconstitutional. However, that case, although disapproved in no uncertain terms, is merely characterized as a mistaken and untrustworthy precedent.

government, or between various governments within our federal union; each must conform to the fundamental pattern outlined in the Constitution. But the usages of judicial protocol generally militate against such drastic handling of precedent. Occasionally, a court may criticize a former decision as a departure from sound doctrine, but this is not done lightly. The etiquette of legal parlance, like the language of diplomacy, induces courts to refer to their predecessors and, indeed, to judges in other jurisdictions as our " learned brethren" without distinguishing between individual wearers of the judicial robe. The courts of any period represent the best available authority on the Constitution. Because they are composed of human beings, they are fallible. But it is not customary to think of their errors as being so grave as to violate the basic tenets of our fundamental law. Yet, this is the assertion made by six out of the nine judges of the Supreme Court in regard to Story's doctrine. Only Justice Reed chose to put his disapproval of *Swift* v. *Tyson* on the narrower statutory ground. Justices Butler and McReynolds were in favor of the old rule, and their argument was simply that such a well established precedent should not be cavalierly overthrown.[29]

Many doctrines vanish by degrees: this is the evolutionary process traditional with the common law system of jurisprudence. The first sign of a change is an increasing tendency on the part of the courts to avoid the application of a venerable principle. They explain that the case in hand, for all its apparent similarity to preceding cases, is not really like them at all. Instead of emphasizing points of similarity between the new cases and the old ones, the courts light on differences between the factual situation presented by the precedent which is to be explained away and that existing in a current litigation. The more a precedent is distinguished in this way, the smaller it becomes. Formal obedience to the old doctrine may continue

29 304 US 64, 80.

for years or even decades, but ere long, informed observers realize that the once powerful principle is weak or altogether dead.

When this happens, it is comparatively easy to trace the decline of an old rule of law and to detail the rise of its successor. All that one needs to do is to spot the growing list of exceptions to a supposedly invulnerable doctrine and draw whatever conclusions seem appropriate. By placing these developments in their historical setting, it is often possible to evolve elaborate explanations of the forces behind a particular change. It is possible to make this kind of analysis of the Tyson Rule and its decline, but the result is not as satisfactory as it would be if *Erie Railroad Co.* v. *Tompkins* had come at the end of a longer judicial trend away from the doctrine of federal independence of state law. However, the forces behind the Erie Case and the reason why it came upon the judicial scene when it did can be shown. In order to gather all the threads of the explanation together, it will first be necessary to see how the courts have implemented their decision to accept and administer local law as interpreted by state authorities.

CHAPTER X
IMPLEMENTING A POLICY

Erie Railroad v. *Tompkins* is of much broader significance than most precedent-forming decisions. If, for example, the highest court in a particular jurisdiction has decided that under given circumstances a motorist exercises a reasonable degree of prudence when he decreases his speed to twenty miles an hour while approaching and crossing a railroad track, this is the law. All courts of the jurisdiction are bound to follow this precedent. They may have difficulty in discovering whether subsequent cases actually occurred under substantially similar circumstances or whether later drivers really took the required care, but once these questions of fact have been established, there is no difficulty in administering the principle of law. A precedent in the field of contract law is normally of equal simplicity. A court of last resort has determined that certain acts on the part of an offeror followed by another set of actions performed by an offeree produces a binding contract. It may not be easy to evaluate the conflicting stories of opposing sides in a dispute; but once this has been done, it is seldom difficult to apply the precedents so as to discover the appropriate legal solution of the case.

Of course, when an appellate court decides to change the law, it is faced with a question of policy: Are motorists who drive across railroad tracks at twenty miles an hour taking sufficient precautions to safeguard themselves and other people? Should a man be allowed to wait three weeks before accepting an offer without losing the right to accept? These are important problems for the protection of personal and property rights, and their solution may be difficult. However, once the highest court of a jurisdiction has written the change into precedent, inferior tribunals have little discretion whether or not to apply a rule of substantive law. The policy has been made for them and the tasks which remain are largely routine.

The Erie Case made no changes in specific rules of substantive law. It dealt specifically with a narrow question in the law of torts, but even in this field, it did not decide upon the rights of the parties to the suit.[1] Instead, the Supreme Court centered its attention on a matter of procedure or method. It was not, however, the type of procedure that one meets in a Civil Practice Act. The significance of the Erie Case is of an entirely different order from that of decisions shedding light on proper methods for the service of legal process, or the prescribed way to draw pleadings. The Supreme Court was setting an objective for the national judiciary and directing all member courts in the federal hierarchy to conduct themselves so as to attain the goal. Brandeis and his colleagues were redistributing judicial power between the tribunals of State and Nation. This was a task larger than the law of torts or the law of negotiable instruments. It was as large as the whole common law. It was obvious that the Court could not deal with all the segments of this vast subject in one opinion. All that it could do was to indicate a desired pattern of future events.

If Brandeis had given these new instructions to federal judges at a meeting called for the purpose, he might have addressed them in something like the following words. " Until now we have exercised considerable freedom when interpreting state law. When we have agreed with the common law precedents of a jurisdiction, we have decided cases much as an appropriate state forum would have done. But where we have been persuaded that local rules of substantive law were not as good as those which we could devise ourselves, we have felt free to make our own precedents. This is not to be our practice in the future. Our function is to act precisely as an appropriate state would if it were deciding the case. Of course, we must protect litigants from the ill effects of hostile local sentiment, but even where this is the reason for the exercise of our

1 The case was remanded so that state substantive law could be applied. 304 US 64, 80 (1938).

jurisdiction, it is the precedents of the states that we must enforce. Our duty, then, is to discover what a state court would do in a particular situation, and do it."

FINDING STATE LAW: EASY OR DIFFICULT?

Since 1938, the federal courts have experienced little difficulty in applying state law to ordinary run-of-the-mill questions of substantive law. Even in our newer states, local judiciaries have been in operation for many years. Their work has proceeded in all phases of the common law and, somewhere in the course of their day-by-day operations, the appellate tribunals in all our states have made at least one authoritative decision on most points of law. When such a point of state law is contested before a federal bench, the judge need only consult the reported opinions of the judiciary of the state in which he sits and act accordingly. This is no more than the inferior local courts are constantly doing, and a satisfactory performance of the task requires only an ordinary degree of legal skill. To employ Justice Cardozo's simile, following precedent is like matching colors.[2] When a judge has found a hue in his catalogue which is similar to the shade of the case before him, his work is successfully accomplished.

Although they are small in numbers, litigations presenting novel or difficult questions of state law are of the greatest importance. It is when deciding such cases that judges participate in the law making process, and it is then that courts have the opportunity to modify or change the common law so as to keep it abreast of conditions in a rapidly changing modern society. Advances in the field of science and technology provide the most striking examples of this process at work. Only a few decades ago, the automobile was a newcomer on American roads. Like the horse, it is a means of transportation. But this is probably the only similarity between the two conveyances. Increased speed and peculiarities in the construction of the

2 Cardozo, *Nature of the Judicial Process* (1922), p. 20.

motor car have made it necessary for judges to revise many of the rules of substantive law which were appropriate to the regulation of horse-drawn traffic. For example, behavior which is perfectly safe when indulged in by a rider perched high on the back of a slow moving animal may be gross negligence if copied by the driver of a fifty-mile-an-hour, low slung automobile. This has made it necessary for courts to modify or abandon many of their horse-and-buggy precedents in order to build new ones specifically relating to motor borne traffic. Similar processes of legal change have been set in motion by the development of the airplane and by the introduction of every mechanical device which has materially affected some phase of human life.

Since *Erie* v. *Tompkins,* the state courts have been charged with primary responsibility for the creation and clarification of whatever rules of substantive common law appear to be needed. This is no simple task, and it is almost inevitable that judges should make many mistakes before they settle upon the appropriate rule for a new or complex situation. This method of trial and error is the very essence of systems of common law jurisprudence, and where it is used by the most appropriate judiciary, it works reasonably well. However, the federal courts, which no longer have power to mold principles of general common law are often called upon to decide cases involving questions supposedly covered by state law. What happens when a federal court is faced with a situation wherein state decisions furnish no guidance has been a troublesome question.[3] It is still a long way from complete solution, but in the ten years since the Tompkins Decision, much progress has been made.

According to the teachings of ancient theory, this problem should never arise. As we saw when discussing Story's opinion in *Swift* v. *Tyson,* judicial precedent is sometimes thought of

3 For discussions of this point see: LaSalle, *The Problem Facing Federal Courts Where State Precedents are Lacking,* 24 Texas L. Rev. 361 (1946); Note, 24 Wash. U. L. Q. 132 (1938).

as merely " evidence " of the law and not the law itself. When regarded in this light, the common law is an omnipresent body of just principles sufficient unto every occasion. All that a judge must do to solve new problems is to apply correct legal reasoning and the proper answer must surely appear. But this philosophy smacks too much of abstract metaphysics to be a practical answer to the specific question of policy presented by the Erie Rule. If federal judges were to create principles of substantive law by the use of their independent powers of reason whenever state precedents were lacking, the result would be to revive a national general common law on a small scale.[4] This would be a direct violation of the Erie Doctrine which declares that there is no federal general common law.

The federal courts might have decided to apply a principle of conflict of laws to this type of situation. In legal parlance, it is known as the doctrine of " forum non conveniens ", and its operation can best be understood in terms of a simple example.

The Inconvenient Forum Test

Let us assume that Mr. X, a resident of Pennsylvania, comes into a New York State trial court and says that three months ago he was in San Francisco. While crossing at an intersection with the light in his favor, he was struck by a car driven by Mr. Y, and was injured so badly that he was forced to spend six weeks in the hospital. This, so he claims, entitles him to a judgment against Mr. Y in the sum of fifty thousand dollars. In support of his contentions, he is ready to prove, among other things, that Mr. Y had drunk a pint of whiskey shortly before the accident, was obviously driving while under the influence of liquor, had passed through two red lights before hitting him, and fell into a drunken stupor immediately after the accident.

All of this may be true, and it is possible that the attorney for Mr. X has been fortunate enough to find the " culprit " in

---

4 The creation of rules of substantive law in diversity cases was the precise evil thought to be corrected by the overruling of *Swift* v. *Tyson*.

Grand Central Station ready to board a train back to the Pacific Coast and has taken advantage of this opportunity to serve him with a summons. But it is also possible that Mr. X is a congenital liar. He actually was injured in San Francisco three months ago and did spend six weeks in the hospital. However, the accident was all his fault. According to Mr. Y's story, it was X, and not he, who had been drinking and who had crossed against the light. Moreover, it is Mr. Y's contention that although he is a resident of San Francisco and was there at the time of the accident, it was not he who hit the unfortunate plaintiff.

The New York State court would have jurisdiction over this case because of the temporary presence of both disputants, but it would very likely refuse to entertain the suit. The reasons for this failure to act would be entirely practical in nature. In the first place, the law to be applied to the case would be that of California because the accident occurred there.[5] While this is not of itself sufficient to make the New York court reluctant to proceed with the case, a number of additional factors would influence the judge before whom the action would come. To name only a few of these, witnesses to the accident would be in San Francisco, three thousand miles from the courtroom. Of course, it would be possible to take their testimony by written deposition, but this is hardly as satisfactory as personal testimony. This is especially true where opposing litigants are in complete disagreement as to the facts. Cross examination is the only effective means of evaluating conflicting stories, and this technique cannot be managed through the mail. Another device which is sometimes helpful in personal injury cases is the juror's view. When the circumstances of a particular accident make it advisable, the jury is permitted to inspect the scene of the mishap so that it may gain a clearer idea of what actually happened. As a practical matter, this can only be done

5 Restatement, *Conflict of Laws*, Sec. 383 (1934).

if the locale is reasonably close to the courtroom: a condition which would not prevail in our hypothetical case.

In order to relieve itself of these difficulties, the New York court might tell the plaintiff that it did not have the facilities necessary to accomplish justice in this particular instance and that the courts of California would undoubtedly be in a better position to handle the matter. The Supreme Court has decided that district courts may use the doctrine of " forum non conveniens " in dismissing suits. However, such dismissals rest on the likelihood that some other federal court would be in a better position to administer justice.[6]

In recent years, the Federal Supreme Court has exhibited some tendency to employ an analogous practice in cases where federal jurisdiction is based on grounds other than diversity of citizenship. The most instructive of these instances is *Herb* v. *Pitcairn:*[7] a suit under the Federal Employers' Liability Act. That statute permits injured workmen who come within its protection to bring their actions in state courts whenever they choose to do so, and further provides that such suits may not be removed to federal courts despite the fact that the disputes arise under an act of Congress.[8] An Illinois railway employee elected to sue in the Illinois courts and, because of procedural

6 *Gulf Oil Co.* v. *Gilbert,* 330 US 501 (1947) (Action brought in S. D. New York dismissed with direction that case might be brought in a court *in* Virginia—presumably either a federal or a state court).

Koster v. *Lumbermen's Mutual Casualty Co.,* 330 US 518 (1947) (In a stockholder's derivative action, the fact that the suit was brought in the plaintiff's home jurisdiction, may of itself be insufficient to prevent dismissal on the ground of forum non conveniens.)

An amendment to the Judicial Code, effective Sept. 1, 1948, embodies the forum non conveniens principle.

" For the convenience of parties and witnesses, in the interest of justice, a district court may transfer any civil action to any other district or division where it might have been brought." Pub. Law 773, 80 Cong., 2nd Sess. (1948). Sec. 1404A, 28 US C 1404A (1948).

7 324 US 117 (1945).

8 36 Stat. 291 (1910).

difficulties, the litigation was long and confused. Finally, the case was passed upon by the highest court in Illinois and brought to the Federal Supreme Court for review.

The decision in the case had been against the employee, but the reason for the Illinois decision was not clear. The opinion of the State Supreme Court [9] contained an inclusive discussion of two possible grounds for its holding. One possibility was that under the Court's interpretation of the Federal Employers' Liability Act, the employee was not entitled to relief; the other conceivable reason for the result was that, under Illinois law, the action may have been improperly begun with the result that jurisdiction over the case had never been conferred on any court.

The Federal Supreme Court decided that the Illinois interpretation of the federal statute was incorrect,[10] and if the case had been decided on that ground, the state decision must be reversed. There is no doubt that the interpretation of the Federal Employers' Liability Act presents a federal question on which the high bench at Washington is the ultimate authority. For the Supreme Court to correct a faulty state construction of a Congressional enactment would not disturb state power in any way. However, if the state court had rested its ruling on an interpretation of the Illinois Civil Practice Act, the matter concerned state law. In this field, the opinion of the Supreme Court of Illinois would be controlling, and the only proper course was to affirm the decision of that tribunal.

At times, judges in all courts, whether state or federal, encounter ambiguous precedents. This increases the difficulties of the judicial function, but it cannot excuse judges from their duty to decide cases as they arise. Courts do the best they can; take as much guidance from extant opinions as they can find; and try to decide each case in a sensible way. Physical and legal circumstances usually make it impossible for a court to ask

9 *Herb v. Pitcairn,* 384 Ill. 237, 51 NE 2d 277 (1943).

10 *Herb* v. *Pitcairn, supra,* note 7.

judges of another time and place to rewrite their opinions so as to make them more intelligible. However, the peculiar conditions presented by a case in its appellate stages make such procedure possible. In this particular instance, the Federal Supreme Court continued the case on its docket and asked the Supreme Court of Illinois to clarify its opinion so as to remove any doubt concerning the ground of its decision. The state court answered that it had decided against the employee because he had not complied with Illinois procedural law. With this information at hand, the Supreme Court of the United States remanded the case to the Supreme Court of Illinois.[11]

However, the device used by the Supreme Court in *Herb* v. *Pitcairn* would not be appropriate in cases involving difficult questions of state law when these are presented to the lower federal courts solely because the parties to a litigation are citizens of different states. In such instances, the judiciary of a state whose law is to be applied has no connection with the dispute. Local judges could not be asked to explain their previous handling of the case because they have not handled it. The state law exists in a body of local statutes and judicial precedents entirely independent of a suit now in progress. If the existing body of law did not furnish sufficient guidance to the federal court, all it could do would be to apprise the appropriate state court of the facts in a current litigation and ask that tribunal what it would do if the case had been brought to it instead of to the national tribunal.

There would be at least two serious objections to such a procedure. In the first place, the state court would not gain jurisdiction over the suit in question. Consequently, any opinion which it might give would be purely advisory. It so happens that most state judiciaries are not empowered to render advisory opinions [12] and could, therefore, not provide the desired

---

11 *Herb* v. *Pitcairn*, 325 US 77 (1945).

12 Only seven states empower their courts to render advisory opinions. Anderson, *American Government* (3rd Ed. 1946), pp. 158-159.

information. In the second place, the most meritorious reason of policy supporting the continued existence of federal diversity jurisdiction is the hope of mitigating the undesirable features of provincialism. Suitors who fear to trust their rights to local courts may resort to the national judiciary, but this protection would be ephemeral indeed if the latter were to ask the very state court which the litigant sought to avoid how to decide the case.

In *Meredith* v. *City of Winter Haven*,[13] the Supreme Court of the United States said that it could not shirk the decision of questions of state law merely because they were difficult. That was a case involving the right of holders of bonds issued by the City of Winter Haven in 1933 to the payment of deferred interest on their investment. The questions related solely to matters of Florida statute and the Florida Constitution, and the case was in a federal court solely because of a diversity in the citizenship of the parties to the suit. In form, the action was one in equity and it might have been argued that the Erie Rule was of doubtful application. However, as we shall see, since 1938 the Supreme Court has virtually obliterated the distinction between law and equity so far as these classifications might affect federal independence to examine questions of state law.

The difficulty in the Meredith Case arose from conflicting decisions of the Florida Supreme Court. Petitioners urged that the last pronouncement of that tribunal was not controlling authority because counsel in that case had not called the judicial attention to relevant principles of Florida law and that, as a consequence, the case had been wrongly decided. It was further averred that the case had not been fought with proper diligence because although it had been an adversary proceeding in form, it was really not of that character. For these reasons, petitioners urged that if given an opportunity to pass upon the questions involved once more, it would repudiate its latest precedent and return to earlier holdings on the points at issue.

13 320 US 228 (1943).

The Circuit Court of Appeals had been sufficiently impressed by this line of argument to dismiss the case on the ground that the state law was so much in doubt that a federal court was not an appropriate forum for the decision of the suit.[14] But the Supreme Court of the United States refused to take this view. Its opinion, written by Mr. Justice (later Chief Justice) Stone, ran in part as follows:

" . . . While the rulings of the Supreme Court of Florida in the *Andrews* case must be taken as controlling here unless it can be said with some assurance that the Florida Supreme Court will not follow them in the future, . . . we assume, as the Court of Appeals has indicated, that the Supreme Court of the State may modify or even set them aside in future decisions. But we are of opinion that the difficulties of ascertaining what the state courts may hereafter determine the state law to be do not in themselves afford a sufficient ground for a federal court to decline to exercise its jurisdiction to decide a case which is properly brought to it for decision.

" The diversity jurisdiction was not conferred for the benefit of the federal courts or to serve their convenience. . . . In the absence of some recognized public policy or defined principle guiding the exercise of the jurisdiction conferred . . . it has from the first been deemed the duty of the federal courts, if their jurisdiction is properly invoked, to decide questions of state law whenever necessary to the rendition of a judgment . . . denial of that opportunity by the federal courts merely because the answers to the questions of state law are difficult or uncertain or have not yet been given by the highest court of the state, would thwart the purpose of the jurisdictional act." [15]

There is little room for argument with the Court's position. The Constitution and laws of Congress certainly empower the federal judiciary to adjudicate diversity of citizenship cases; nor is there any indication that the courts themselves were

14 *Meredith* v. *City of Winter Haven*, 134 F 2d 202 (CCA 5th 1943).

15 320 US 228, 234-235.

intended to have any discretion in deciding whether or not to take jurisdiction of suits wherein the parties are actually citizens of different states. The choice between a federal and a state tribunal in these cases has been left entirely in the hands of the private litigants.

However, the correctness of the view presented by Justice Stone in the *Winter Haven* case does not solve the problem. In fact, it does just the reverse: for the more certain it becomes that federal courts cannot reduce the number of diversity suits coming before them by the use of discretionary power, the more inevitable it is that those courts must decide questions of state law. It naturally follows that some of this vast flood of litigation will concern matters not yet considered by the highest courts of the states. Yet it is also clear that under the Rule of *Erie* v. *Tompkins,* the federal judiciary is bound to seek out state interpretations of local law and apply them. Where these are to be found when courts of last resort are silent has been a question of some difficulty.

LOWER STATE COURT DECISIONS AS GUIDES
TO STATE LAW

The problem facing a federal court may be put into simple language; where may it look for authoritative expositions of state law? The opinions of the highest court of a particular state are most valuable when they can be shown to throw light upon the legal question in hand because, insofar as our governmental machinery provides definitive sources of law, our highest courts are certainly the organs of government appropriate to the formulation of reliable doctrine. But it must be remembered that the tribunals of last resort are only a few among many judicial bodies constantly engaged in the interpretation of state law. Back of each court of last resort is an extensive network of lower courts. Each of them plays an important part in the administration of the law; each of them adjudges cases arising under state law. Why, then, should not the federal courts follow the decisions of tribunals on the lower rungs of the state judicial hierarchy when there are no pertinent rulings of an appropriate higher court?

This thought occurred to judicial minds at an early date after the decision of *Erie* v. *Tompkins,* and in *Vandenbark* v. *Owens-Illinois Glass Co.*[16] the Supreme Court of the United States found no difficulty in holding that declarations as to state law made by inferior local courts should be heeded when no better evidence of the true interpretation of state law was available.

This apparently reasonable doctrine has been subjected to a hail of criticism. The difficulty does not come from anything which was said in the Vandenbark Case, but springs from the highly unfortunate situation revealed in *Fidelity Union Trust Co.* v. *Field.*[17]

Before proceeding to relate the circumstances surrounding that litigation, it is advisable to point out some of the principles prevailing in the law of trusts. It is common practice that notice of the existence of a trust be given to all parties who may be affected by its creation or continuance. Accordingly, it is usual to notify a bank in writing when opening an account in trust for another person. Not only does this precaution serve to provide additional evidence of the existence of the trust, but it also eliminates certain objections which may arise under the law of gifts.[18]

However, it is a fact of everyday experience that many people open bank accounts which they signify are to be in trust for some named person other than the depositor. They intend to relinquish none of their rights to use the money so deposited for themselves during their lifetimes. In such instances, the only evidence of the existence of a trust is to be found in the form of the bank account.

16 311 US 538 (1941).

17 311 US 169 (1940).

18 The problem of proving that a gift was actually intended is often a difficult one and where it cannot be surmounted, the gift fails. Restatement, *Trusts* (1935). Sec. 41c, 42d; 2 Williston, *Contracts* (rev. ed. 1938) Sec. 438-440.

Wishing to make such bank accounts valid trusts, the New Jersey legislature passed a series of statutes [19] in 1932 designed to accomplish this end. But on two separate occasions, the lower courts of the State held the statutes ineffective to accomplish their purpose.[20] Neither case was appealed to the Court of Errors and Appeals and, as a result, that tribunal had not construed the legislation.

A New Jersey woman, who was almost certainly unaware of these technicalities, opened a bank account and placed it in trust for Ethel Field. She did not give notice of the trust to the person named as beneficiary and in the course of time she died. Mrs. Field naturally claimed the money which had been left to her and, in order to overcome the difficulties posed by her benefactress' neglect, pointed to the New Jersey statute. Since Mrs. Field was not a New Jersey resident, she chose to entrust her claim to a federal court.

The Circuit Court of Appeals for the Third Circuit proceeded to interpret the New Jersey statutes for itself and decided that as those Acts of the State Legislature had clearly been intended to cover a situation like the instant one, Mrs. Field was entitled to her money.[21] But in reversing this decision the Supreme Court of the United States, speaking through Chief Justice Hughes, said:

" . . . . It appears that ordinarily the decisions of the Court of Chancery, if they have not been disapproved, are treated as binding in later cases in chancery, but there is always, as respondent urges, the possibility that a particular decision of the Court of Chancery will not be followed by the Supreme Court or even by the Court of Chancery itself. It is a function of the court of last resort to resolve such conflicts as may be created by decisions of the lower courts. . . . Here, however, there is

19 17 N. J. Stat. Ann. (Soney & Sage, 1939) Sec. 9-4.

20 *Thatcher* v. *Trenton Trust Co.*, 119 NJ E 408, 182 A. 912 (1936); *Travers* v. *Reid*, 119 NJ E 416, 182 A. 908 (1936).

21 *Field* v. *Fidelity Union Trust Co.*, 108 F 2d 521 (CCA 3rd 1939).

no conflict of decision. Whether there ever will be, or the Court of Errors and Appeals will disapprove the rulings in the *Thatcher* and *Travers* cases, is merely a matter of conjecture. At the present time the *Thatcher* and *Travers* cases stand as the only exposition of the law of the State with respect to the construction and effect of the statutes of 1932, and the Circuit Court of Appeals was not at liberty to reject these decisions merely because it did not agree with their reasoning.

" The question has practical aspects of great importance in the proper administration of justice in the federal courts. It is inadmissible that there should be one rule of state law for litigants in the state courts and another rule for litigants who bring the same question before the federal courts owing to the circumstance of diversity of citizenship. In the absence of any contrary showing, the rule of the *Thatcher* and *Travers* cases appears to be the one which would be applied in litigation in the state court, and whether believed to be sound or unsound, it should have been followed by the Circuit Court of Appeals." [22]

This decision of the Supreme Court raised a storm of criticism. Those who believe that the task of a judiciary is to do justice in each case as it arises were appalled by Chief Justice Hughes' opinion. In his own guarded fashion, the Chief Justice had recognized that the two New Jersey decisions might very well be incorrect, but that it was not the place of a federal tribunal to undo this bad law and that federal courts were bound to misread the New Jersey statutes until a state court saw the light.

It is not particularly useful to speculate on the reasons why the Thatcher and Travers Cases had not been taken up to the highest court of the state for review. Because of their patent failure to give effect to the express intent of the New Jersey Legislature, these decisions might well have been reversed in the Court of Errors and Appeals. But the plain fact is that

[22] 311 US 169, 179.

neither case went further than the Chancery Court. It may be that the litigants in them did not have the financial resources necessary for further legal proceedings; or, it may be that the cases were settled by private agreement among the parties before an appeal could be taken. But whatever the reason, the cases stood unchallenged by any state tribunal.

Left in the pages of the local law reports, these questionable examples of state administered justice would probably have remained buried in obscurity. Their capacity for mischief would have been limited to the locality in which they were decided and, as adverse critics of the Fidelity Union Case apparently assume, would likely have been eventually disavowed by the New Jersey courts. However, once the two state holdings became the basis for an opinion by the Supreme Court of the United States, they were subjects of attention in legal circles throughout the country.

What disturbed some observers was not that a court had rendered a mistaken decision; the most learned of judges is sometimes the architect of error. The seemingly ridiculous part of the situation was that the Supreme Court had knowingly allowed bad law to stand. The most eloquent of the critics of the Fidelity Union Case, put his objections into this language:

" Thus, it appears that in determining the law of a state the federal judiciary, including the Justices of the Supreme Court themselves, are forbidden to use their own ' reasoning '. They are restricted to no more than a good clear reading glass. . . . It appears, further, that Ethel Field has been deprived of all opportunity to question the validity of the Vice-Chancellor's opinion, rendered in a case to which she was not a party. Had she been before the Vice-Chancellor himself she could have questioned it. In any other court of New Jersey, she could have questioned it; and she could have appealed to the Court of Errors and Appeals. But in the federal courts, it is inviolate. Be it remembered that under our Constitution she can be dragged into the federal court wholly against her will. She must submit her fortunes to the decision of a court that can read but must not reason. Even its reading is limited. It must not read the act of the legislature, if a Vice-Chancellor has decided in a collateral case that it is meaningless or invalid. Is this ' due process of law '? Is this a day in court? " [23]

Professor Corbin's fundamental disagreement with the Fidelity Union Case stems from his conviction that the Supreme Court was knowingly permitting incorrect law to stand and to spread its influence into the federal courts. There is clearly something disturbing about a judicial process which produces such a result. The primary duty of our courts is certainly to bring justice to the parties in a dispute and to do so in accordance with their best capabilities for determining sound principles of substantive law. Wherever this is not done, there is room for a suspicion that a judiciary has dispensed something less than justice and has not fulfilled its responsibility to the private citizens who submit to public settlement of their disputes according to law rather than private argument and violence.

This objection to the Fidelity Union Decision would be just as strong if it had been the New Jersey Court of Errors and Appeals which had decided the Thatcher and Travers Cases. Judicial nullification of the legislative policy with regard to trust accounts could hardly have been more defensible if practiced by the highest court of the state than it was when indulged in by an inferior tribunal. The injustice is the same in both instances: subversion of the legal rights of private citizens who rely on the protection of the state statute. This becomes clear if we ask whether Professor Corbin would have complained if the Supreme Court, and the lower federal courts before it, had followed the opinions of Vice Chancellors enforcing the New Jersey statutes in accordance with their plain meaning. The answer must surely be in the negative because

23 Corbin, *The Laws of the Several States*, 50 Yale L. J. 762, 768 (1941).

judicial opinion in the state would then have been in accord with the common sense in behalf of which Corbin makes so eloquent a plea. In his view of the matter, it would have been better if the Court of Errors and Appeals had furnished a precedent for the guidance of the federal judiciary because that tribunal might have been less obtuse than the two unfortunate Vice Chancellors. But this is no more than Professor Corbin's hope and can have no decisive part in fixing a general rule to govern the attitude of the federal courts toward local judicial precedents. As a matter of fact some lower court opinions have criticized the Thatcher and Travers Decisions but have done so only by way of dictum.[24] The highest court of New Jersey has not yet found an opportunity to pass on the point disputed in *Fidelity Union Trust Co.* v. *Field;* it has come closest in *Passaic National Bank & Trust Co.* v. *Taub.*[25] But in that case the alleged trustee was still alive and the suit was by a creditor seeking to satisfy a debt out of the bank account. Consequently, the effect of the New Jersey statutes was not in issue and the Court of Errors and Appeals did not even mention the legislation.

Another argument, made in the passage from Corbin above quoted but more fully developed elsewhere,[26] questions the value of lower court decisions as indicia of state law. This objection to the doctrine of *Fidelity Union Trust Co.* v. *Field* is best understood in terms of a hypothetical example and will be discussed by the use of such an illustration.

Let us inspect State X with a particular eye for the organization and functioning of the judicial branch of its government. The first thing that strikes our notice is that the state contains thousands of square miles of territory and a large number of

24 See *Abruzzese* v. *Oestrich*, 138 NJE 33, 47 A 2d 883 (1946); *Hickey* v. *Kahl*, 129 NJE 233, 19 A 2d 33 (1941).

25 137 NJE 544, 45 A 2d 679 (1946).

26 See Broh-Kahn, *Uniformity Run Riot*, 31 Ky. L. J. 99 (1943).

inhabitants. Some of these people live in cities; others reside in rural areas. The size and economic activity within State X is so great that its government is broken up into a number of subdivisions each serving a particular locality. This decentralization is a universal phenomenon and it is accepted as necessary to the systematic administration of governmental affairs. What is true of administration in general is equally true of the enforcement of our laws. A single courthouse is insufficient to serve the needs of the entire state, and this is so obviously true that no one has ever voiced a contrary view. From the very beginning, State X has had a number of courthouses, each of them presided over by a different judge or set of judges, scattered throughout the territorial expanse of the state. Such a decentralization in the administration of justice has naturally raised problems concerning the coordination of the work done in these dispersed courthouses, for it is generally recognized that uniformity in the administration of the law throughout the state requires some supervision and direction by a central authority.

In order to meet the dual needs of decentralized administration and coordination, State X is divided into fifty judicial areas, each of them having one trial court of general jurisdiction in which cases of all kinds are initiated. These judicial areas are arranged into five judicial departments or circuits composed of ten judicial areas each, and each presided over by an intermediate court of appeal. From the point of view of the private litigant, these intermediate courts provide facilities for the correction of errors made by the lower courts. From the standpoint of judicial organization, these tribunals provide the necessary supervision over courts of first impression in their part of the state and also dispose of much of the business which would otherwise overburden the court of last resort. Finally, there is the Supreme Court of State X which sits at the capital and hears appeals from the five courts of intermediate appeal. This pattern for the organization of the judicial branch of

State X's government varies in detail from the situations prevailing in neighboring states. Some of them may find it to their advantage to have somewhat less than fifty judicial areas and fewer than five circuits, while others may have more courts of first impression and a larger number of departments than State X. But all state judiciaries are organized substantially on this hierarchical principle and operate in much the same way.

Now let us imagine that the legislature of State X has passed the New Jersey statute relating to trust accounts, and that the Thatcher Case is before one of the trial courts in the First Department. What is the law of State X? Clearly it is the statute; the court, the members of the local bar, and the citizenry can all see that plainly enough. But now the court of first impression does what a New Jersey Vice Chancellor did and interprets the statute out of existence. What is the law of State X now?

This question is not so easy to answer. So far as the single trial court rendering the decision is concerned, its opinion is the law and, at least for the time being, will continue to be so throughout the judicial area served by this tribunal of first impression. *But remember:* this court serves only one-fiftieth of the state, and what the law is in the remaining forty-nine fiftieths of the state must still be determined. The first proposition that calls for our recognition is that none of the forty-nine judicial areas need follow the lead of the judge in the fiftieth. They are of equal rank with him in the judicial hierarchy and cannot be bound by his rulings. This is even the case in regard to the other judges of trial courts within the same department. Moreover, if the common sense for which Professor Corbin pleads is to have any place in State X, we may hope that other judges will be inclined to read and understand the act of the legislature and come to a result at complete variance with that reached by the first judge. At any rate, there is the statute and, until we discover the contrary, we are justified in believing that in forty-nine fiftieths of the state it is the law.

But the difficulty does not end here. What is the law of State X if, as happened in New Jersey, a second judge reads the statute out of existence? Clearly, if all the courts of the state eventually follow suit, the uniform result of these judicial interpretations is the law. But if Professor Corbin is right in saying that the interpretation is utterly ridiculous, it is likely that many judges will refuse to agree with the original decision. The result will be a conflict of judicial opinion in various parts of the state. In effect, the law will be different in one section of State X from what it is in an adjoining section. In so far as an observer can determine, there will be no single law of the state, but only divergent views concerning what the law is.

In time—a year, five years, twenty years—it is difficult to say how long—this confusion will probably disappear. Eventually a number of these cases will be appealed from the trial courts to the courts of intermediate appeal. There are only five of these in State X, and there is a much greater likelihood that five courts will agree than there is that fifty will espouse the same legal opinion. Moreover, each of these five intermediate courts has the power to bind the ten trial courts of its department and so to enforce uniformity throughout the portion of the state under its jurisdiction. There may, of course, be disagreement among the intermediate courts and, as none of these have power to bind the others, the confusion can be prolonged. But given sufficient time, the question will probably come to the Supreme Court of State X, and an authoritative precedent will then be established.

Comforting as this thought may be to observers who are satisfied to know that everything will turn out properly in the long run, it is of absolutely no help to a federal court which must decide specific cases as they arise. It must decide what the law of the state is at a given moment; at a time when there may be conflicting precedents in the lower state courts or before all of these courts have had the opportunity to rule upon a point of law. At such times, so the argument runs, there is no way of telling whether a lower court decision is actually state law or not.

So long as the discussion remains pitched on a plane of generalized legal argument, there is little to choose between the merits of each side in this controversy. It is certainly true that even the lowest of state courts is engaged in interpreting and enforcing state law. Their decisions are binding on the individuals over whom they obtain jurisdiction. On the other hand, it is equally true that such decisions may not be followed in other parts of the state and may, in some instances, be unacceptable to the highest court in the state. In applying the Fidelity Union Rule much depends on whether the federal courts are to consider themselves bound in equal measure by the decisions of all local courts. The Supreme Court has recently shed some light on this question in *King* v. *Order of United Commercial Travelers of America* [27] where the question was as to the interpretation of a clause in an insurance policy. The case arose in South Carolina and was tried by a federal court sitting in that state. The only applicable South Carolina decision was one of dubious correctness made by a local Court of Common Pleas. When the King Case reached the United States Supreme Court, it was decided that the Fidelity Union Rule did not necessarily require federal courts to follow all decisions of local trial courts even where no other local precedents were available. The Court pointed out that other state courts in South Carolina were not bound by Common Pleas decisions and reasoned that a federal court sitting in the state was under no greater obligation to accept local precedents than were courts within the state judicial system. In deciding questions of local law federal courts must determine what a state tribunal of competent jurisdiction would do and act accordingly. Only where trial court precedents seem likely to be followed by other courts of the state need federal courts be guided by them.

[27] 333 U. S. 153 (1948).

The Fidelity Union Rule presents peculiar difficulties in South Carolina because that state has no courts of intermediate appeal. As it applies to South Carolina then, the King Decision means that only precedents from the highest state court are necessarily to be followed by federal tribunals. Were the judicial systems of other states like that in South Carolina the Fidelity Union Rule would have no area in which to operate and would now have to be taken as discarded. The confusion foreseen in a jurisdiction like our hypothetical State X would be at an end. Even in most states the King Decision simplifies the problem because it reduces the number of courts from which a federal tribunal must accept guidance in its attempt to determine state law. But at least part of the difficulty remains because so long as a number of intermediate Appellate Courts continue to function within a state it is possible and even likely that disparities between precedents will be found in various parts of the same state.

Since the goal has become identity in the administration of justice as between federal and state courts, it is necessary to ask how far the tribunals within the national judiciary can or should go in their efforts to discover what their counterparts in the judicial systems of the various states would do in specific cases. At the very threshold of this inquiry, we are met with the proposition that no matter how diligent federal judges are, they probably cannot make their decisions conform to those that local courts would give in every case. This becomes increasingly true as the complexity of a case increases, and as the judge is called upon to break new ground or to decide close questions of law. Legal rules, although many of them are precise and clear, are seldom exactly like the mass-produced parts of an automobile—certain to yield the same finished product no matter who puts them together. One of the chief tools of the law is argument, and where a case is doubtful, convincing briefs can be built on both sides of a disputed question. A judge may sometimes choose either of the proposed answers to the question before him, and in deciding which it is to be, subtle differences in personality and background may come to the fore.

In order to appreciate this fact, one need only recognize that dissenting opinions, although they are not the general rule, are none the less frequent in our appellate courts. Five to four decisions in the Supreme Court of the United States are not unknown and have caused some wonderment in both lay and professional circles. A brief examination of a well known case of this sort may be most illuminating.

Adkins v. *Children's Hospital* [28] concerned the validity of a minimum wage law for women workers in the District of Columbia. Justice Sutherland who wrote the majority opinion holding the statute to be in violation of the Fifth Amendment to the Constitution, began his opinion by admitting that there had been instances of legislative regulation of terms and conditions of employment, and that the Supreme Court had declared the statutory goals legitimate and the means employed to be constitutional. Such cases, he said, were of four types: [29] 1. Those relating to industries affected with the public interest. 2. Those relating to conditions to be insisted upon in the performance of public contracts (contracts between a government agency and private business firms). 3. Laws providing that wages were not to be paid in kind or in script. 4. Laws regulating hours of labor.

Justice Sutherland proceeded to argue that a statute providing minimum compensation for workers, whether they were women or men, in private employ did not come within any of these established categories. Consequently, the law under review must be unconstitutional. In summarizing the general principle underlying his decision, Sutherland said: " There is, of course, no such thing as absolute freedom of contract. It is subject to a great variety of restrictions. But freedom of con-

28 261 US 525 (1923).
29 261 US 525, 546.

tract is, nevertheless, the rule and restraint the exception; and the exercise of legislative authority to abridge it can be justified only by the existence of exceptional circumstances." [30] The majority of the Court did not believe that the Adkins Case presented any exceptional circumstances.

There were, however, two dissenting opinions written in the case; one by Chief Justice Taft,[31] the other by Mr. Justice Holmes.[32] The reasoning in each of these dissents led to a conclusion opposite to that reached by the majority; yet each was written by a hand fully as competent as Sutherland's. The Chief Justice examined the same precedents relied on by the Court [33] and found that some of the cases falling within Sutherland's four categories of sanctioned legislative action were governing precedent for the situation presently under scrutiny. Accordingly, as a matter of unembroidered stare decisis, a minimum wage for women was valid. Justice Holmes agreed that precedent supported the legislation, but he went even further. Instead of minimizing the restrictive nature of law as Sutherland had done, Holmes reiterated an argument which he had used in dissenting from the Court's decision in the Lochner Case.[34] In his view, the whole purpose of the law was to keep people from doing things that they might otherwise do and so was primarily restrictive in nature. Addressing himself directly to the question before him, Holmes remarked: " To me, notwithstanding the deference due to the prevailing judgment of the Court, the

30 261 US 525, 546.

31 261 US 525, 562.

32 261 US 525, 567.

33 Both Sutherland and Taft rested their opinions on principles drawn from the following cases. *Bunting* v. *Oregon,* 243 US 426 (1917); *McLean* v. *Arkansas,* 211 US 539 (1909); *Lochner* v. *New York,* 198 US 45 (1905); *Knoxville Iron Co.* v. *Harbison,* 183 US 13 (1901); *Holden* v. *Hardy,* 169 US 366 (1898).

34 *Lochner* v. *New York,* 198 US 45, 74 (1905).

power of Congress seems absolutely free from doubt. The end, to remove conditions leading to ill health, immorality and the deterioration of the race, no one would deny to be within the scope of constitutional legislation." [35] *Notice:* not only does Holmes say that the majority opinion is wrong, but he *is absolutely sure that it is wrong.* This sharp disagreement persisted despite the opportunity of the members of the Court to discuss their differences of opinion before the decision was announced.

Let us suppose that the Adkins Case had concerned a troublesome question of state law rather than an act of Congress and the Federal Constitution. Further, imagine that Mr. Justice Holmes occupied a state bench and that Mr. Justice Sutherland were sitting in a federal court. This difficulty of producing uniformity of view would have been even greater because Sutherland would only have had reported precedents to guide him and would probably have been completely unaware that Holmes was not likely to agree with him. Because of diversity in the citizenship of the parties to a particular lawsuit, the case comes before Holmes rather than before Sutherland. Would the latter make the same disposition of the case as the former?

If federal judges were required to answer questions such as this one, their attempts to find out what state courts would do in any given situation could end only in uncertainty. We know that different judges may not agree when asked to decide a difficult question. All that can be expected of them is that they use the same legal tools in arriving at their decisions. In deciding to accept the opinions of some lower courts as well as those emanating from the highest court of a state, the Supreme Court has made a rule designed to aid in the determination of state law and so to make it easier for federal judges to carry out the policy announced in *Erie* v. *Tompkins.* It is, of course, true that the decisions of inferior tribunals are sometimes disapproved by the higher state courts. Indeed, it is also true that precedents made by courts of last resort are themselves over-

35 261 US 525, 567.

ruled. In failing to recognize situations which, had they arisen in state courts, would produce such changes in state law, federal courts undoubtedly fall short of their aim to achieve complete identity of result in the enforcement of state law. But surely it is safer to assume that state courts will continue to decide cases in conformity with already recorded precedents even if these be only opinions of inferior courts. Experience and legal theory teach us that such practice is far more common than disapproval of prior decisions.

If the complaint is that the doctrine expounded in *Fidelity Union Trust Co.* v. *Field* does not guarantee complete uniformity of action as between state and federal courts, there is certainly merit in such a contention. But we may wonder whether any set of rules, however ingenious, can achieve the goal so long as two independent judicial systems are concurrently engaged in the enforcement of state law. The only sure way to find out what a state court will do with a particular case is to let the state court decide it.

CHAPTER XI

THE SCOPE OF THE ERIE RULE

IT is now a full decade since the Supreme Court overturned Story's doctrine of federal judicial independence and supplanted it with the Erie Rule. As we have seen, the present doctrine is not free from difficulty. Some problems, like those springing from an absence of applicable local precedents, will probably decrease as the passing years multiply the number of reported decisions available from state courts. Other difficulties are inherent in our federal system of government and may never be completely conquered. However, there appears to be general agreement with the aim of *Erie* v. *Tompkins*.

The exercise of legislative power by the states is an essential feature of our federal system. In order to make this state power meaningful, it would seem only natural that the states should exert control over the content of their own laws. So far there is no controversy; but what constitutes control? Everyone will agree with Calvin Coolidge's minister who declared that he was against sin. But what is or is not sinful is a much vexed question on which even competent moralists differ. Similarly, there can be many notions concerning what constitutes state control over the content of its laws. It follows that while informed opinion, both on and off the bench, holds it to be desirable that local conceptions of state law prevail, general acquiescence in this underlying principle does not necessarily insure the realization of the goal. We must, therefore, ask whether the Erie Case has increased state authority.

FEDERAL ACCEPTANCE OF LOCAL PRECEDENTS IN EQUITY

A significant indication of the importance which the Erie Rule has assumed may be seen in its extension into the field of equity. It will be remembered that *Swift* v. *Tyson* governed only in matters of common law. It is, of course, true that the federal courts asserted their independence of state precedents in equity as well,[1] but they did so for a different reason. The Rules of Decision Act specifically mentions only "trials at common law" and so does not apply to cases in equity.[2] Indeed, during the early decades after 1789 local equity jurisprudence was either scanty or non-existent in the states. By specific statutory direction, however, the federal courts were given jurisdiction in equity[3] and national tribunals considered themselves to have inherited the powers of English Courts of Chancery.[4] Accordingly, it was possible that *Erie* v. *Tompkins* did not apply to proceedings in equity and that the federal courts could continue to go their own way in questions relating to this large and important segment of our jurisprudence. But *Erie* v. *Tompkins* was not to be confined within so narrow a scope. In *Ruhlin* v. *New York Life Insurance Co.*,[5] decided very shortly after the Erie Case, a question relating to the interpretation of a clause in an insurance policy was at issue. In writing for a unanimous Court, Mr. Justice Reed said:

" It was stated in *Carpenter* v. *Providence Washington Ins. Co.* that questions concerning the proper construction of contracts of insurance are ' questions of general commercial law,' and that state decisions on the subject, though entitled to great respect, ' cannot conclude the judgment of this court '. A limitation was put on this doctrine in *Mutual Life Ins. Co.* v. *Johnson*. Putting aside all questions of power, the Court interpreted a specific provision of an insurance contract in accordance with the decision of the highest court of the State of Virginia, where delivery was made. ' All that is here for our decision is the

1 *Robinson* v. *Campbell*, 3 Wheat. 212 (1818).

2 *Ibid.*, pp. 221-222.

3 1 Stat. 73, 78-79 (1789).

4 *Robinson* v. *Campbell, supra,* note 1.

5 304 US 202 (1938).

meaning, the tacit implications, of a particular set of words, which, as experience has shown, may yield a different answer to this reader and to that one. With choice so balanced with doubt, we accept as our guide the law declared by the state where the contract had its being.' The decision in *Erie Railroad Co.* v. *Tompkins* goes further, and settles the question of power. The subject is now to be governed, even in the absence of state statute, by the decisions of the appropriate state court. The doctrine applies though the question of construction arises not in an action at law, but in a suit in equity." [6]

How far did the Ruhlin Case go? Justice Reed clearly says that the Erie Rule applies to cases in equity as well as to cases at law, but he also refers to *Mutual Life Ins. Co.* v. *Johnson* and the " balanced with doubt " formula.[7] There are certainly points of similarity between the Ruhlin and Johnson Cases, and it appears that the Court could have reached its result simply by following the precedent set in the latter case. This would have required no mention of *Erie* v. *Tompkins.* Consequently, it may be argued that any disapproval of *Carpenter* v. *Providence Washington Ins. Co.* was merely by way of dictum. However, it is obvious from an examination of the passage just quoted from Mr. Justice Reed's opinion that the Court did not wish to stand on so narrow a ground. Nevertheless, the different reasons traditionally assigned for federal independence in the interpretation of equity principles has given rise to the lingering thought that a greater degree of federal freedom might yet remain in the field of equity despite the Erie Case.[8] Subsequent decisions of the Supreme Court have shown such a view to be untenable [9] and it now appears to be correct to say that in diversity of citizenship cases, the national judiciary

6 304 US 202, 205 (1938).

7 See Chap. VIII, pp. 177-180, *supra.*

8 Note, 44 Col. L. Rev. 915 (1944).

9 *Guaranty Trust of N. Y.* v. *York,* 326 US 99 (1945), rehearing denied 326 US 806 (1945).

looks to local judicial opinion whenever a question of either equity or law is involved.

DIFFERENCES IN PROCEDURE SUPPLANT DIFFERENCES IN SUBSTANCE

As we have seen, the attempt of federal courts to follow local precedents removes the most serious danger to the integrity of state law. But it is not always possible to achieve a complete identity of result between federal and state administration of local law. If *Erie* v. *Tompkins* had removed all possibility of litigating questions of state law in federal courts, it would be obvious that the policy which that case inaugurated assures the desired restoration of state authority. But one does not have to look far to discover that the Erie Case does not prevent suits involving state law from coming before national tribunals. Diversity of citizenship jurisdiction still stands as before, sanctioned by the Constitution [10] and authorized by an act of Congress.[11]

The next possibility is that present doctrine discourages resort to the federal courts. It can be argued that since the federal courts now apply state law as interpreted by local courts, litigants no longer have any incentive to evade local judicial determination of their cases. The law is the same in both state and federal judiciaries and the outcome of any case should be the same no matter where it is brought. There is probably a measure of truth in this contention, but it is far from being completely true. So far as we know, there has been no actual decrease in the volume of business which comes to the national judiciary through the diversity of citizenship route.[12]

10 US Constit. Art. III Sec. 2.

11 1 Stat. 73, 78-79 (1789).

12 A recent volume of the Federal Reporter (158 F2d 1946-1947), which was selected at random, contains 778 cases. These were analyzed in the same way as 40 F2d (1930). (See pp. 170-174, *supra*). Thirty-one cases arose in the District of Columbia and so presented no problems of the type

It may be that this source of federal jurisdiction would furnish even more cases if the Tyson Rule were still in operation, but any reduction in the total number of diversity suits has probably been discouraged by an amazing coincidence in the development of judicial policy for the federal courts.

From 1872 until 1938, that is to say during the major part of the Tyson Era, a federal statute known as the Conformity Act [13] was in force. By the terms of this Congressional enactment, it was provided that, wherever practicable, federal courts should conform to the rules of procedural law in use in the state courts. This meant that while national tribunals were free to exercise their independent judgment on substantive questions of local law, they were generally expected to employ the same modes of pleading, the same pre-trial procedures, etc., existing in appropriate state courts. However, in 1938 the Conformity Act was repealed. In response to a widespread clamor for procedural reform,[14] the Supreme Court, in pursuance of authority given to it by an act of Congress,[15] promulgated the present Federal Rules of Civil Procedure. It is now the duty of the federal courts to act in accordance with these rules rather than with those which may be in use in the states.

Under Story's rule, the all important question was whether a matter could be fitted into the classification of " general law "; for if it could, federal courts might exercise their independence of local precedents. There is no doubt that this might affect the outcome of a case. In the notorious Black & White Taxicab

---

under consideration. Three cases arose in the territories and are therefore not to be considered. Many of the remaining cases contain no indications as to the citizenship of the parties. But in forty-nine cases it is clear that diversity of citizenship was the only basis for invoking federal jurisdiction.

13 17 Stat. 197 (1872).

14 See Clark and Moore, *A New Federal Procedure—I. The Background*, 44 Yale L. J. 387 (1935); Hughes, *Address*, 21 ABAJ 340 (1935); Mc-Caskill, *One Form of Civil Action, But what Procedure, for the Federal Courts*, 30 Ill. L. Rev. 415 (1935); Note, 36 Yale L. J. 853 (1927).

15 48 Stat. 1064 (1934).

Case [16] for example, a contract which was contrary to the public policy of Kentucky and so illegal, was enforced there because the decision was rendered by a federal rather than a state court. Since *Erie* v. *Tompkins* and the new Federal Rules of Civil Procedure, the all important question has become whether something is substance or procedure.[17] If it belongs to the former category, national courts will follow state decisions; if the dispute is over a matter in the latter category, the federal judiciary will not apply state law but will follow its own rules.

Theoretically, differences in the procedural law pertaining in state and federal courts should be of little consequence. People who find themselves in Mr. Tompkins' position want to know whether they can obtain judgments entitling them to compensation for their injuries. Litigants like the Erie Railroad wish to establish their freedom from liability. These are matters of substantive law and, according to current doctrine, are to be determined by reference to state law as interpreted by local courts. Procedural rules are only the mechanics of legal administration designed to promote the efficient dispensing of justice. Provided that a rule is suited to its purpose, it should not matter that there may be another rule equally well adapted to the performance of the task. A state judiciary may use one procedural approach, the federal judiciary another; but both should arrive at the same result.

In practice, however, these differences in procedural rules can be of the utmost importance. Pedestrians who are injured by passing trains, businessmen who have made contracts, public utilities whose rates are regulated by government boards may have legal rights, but they cannot enforce them unless they can convince a court of the merits of their cases. By giving litigants greater or less freedom in the preparation and prosecu-

16 *Black and White Taxicab and Transfer Company* v. *Brown and Yellow Taxicab and Transfer Company,* 276 US 518 (1928).

17 Cook, *The Logical and Legal Bases of the Conflict of Laws* (1942), Ch. VI.

tion of their cases, procedural rules determine the degree of forcefulness with which a suitor may explain his legal rights to a court and so have a bearing on a person's ability to convince the courts that his cause is just and that there is a remedy for his grievance.

Differences in federal and state procedural law encourage litigants to shop for the forum before which they are likely to make their best showing in much the same way that they were accustomed to do when *Swift* v. *Tyson* held out the promise of different interpretations of substantive law. As lawsuits are in the nature of battles between adversaries, it is often a safe principle that what helps one party to the dispute will harm his opponent, and so the tug of war is on, each litigant will try to bring the case before the court whose procedures offer him the greatest advantage. It may be that this consideration explains the apparent failure of the diversity business in the federal courts to decrease.

It would, of course, be unfair to attribute these continuing frictions between federal and state judicial systems to *Erie* v. *Tompkins*. By removing differences in the administration of substantive law, the Supreme Court has attempted to reduce the attractiveness of the federal courts for those litigants who should really rely upon the states for the vindication of their legal rights. How much greater is the flow of business to local courts because of the Erie Decision is, however, difficult to say. Critics of *Swift* v. *Tyson* appear to have assumed that litigants were to be found in federal courts only when they believed that their cases would receive more favorable treatment there. This is undoubtedly true in some cases. But many observers appear to overlook what must be a large number of situations in which it does not make, and has never made, any real difference which court is called upon to act. Important as a proper distribution of litigation between national and local judiciaries is to the smooth functioning of our governmental machine, explanations of the existing division of judicial power between the nation and the states are of practically no interest to private suitors.

The ordinary citizen who happens to have business with the courts is interested in winning his case. Frequently it makes no difference to him whether the agency to which he applies is state or federal provided only that the judicial system to which he entrusts his rights has the facilities to help him. So long as there are two courts to which he can come, one state, the other federal, it is only reasonable to assume that sometimes he will chance to use the one, and sometimes, the other.

But this is not to say that *Erie* v. *Tompkins* has been of little consequence. On the contrary, it has worked a basic alteration in federal-state relations. From the point of view of individuals and government alike, the all important question is: whose law will govern a dispute? If it is state law as made and interpreted by organs of state government, any question concerning which court is to go through the formal motions of handing down the judgment is of only secondary importance. The state is in substantial control of its own policy and law. An owner of mineral-bearing lands will not be able to find a different law of real property merely by walking into a federal courthouse.[18] When he sells his mining rights, both he and the buyer will know that their rights are determined by state law. When Kentucky decides that certain types of contracts create monopolies which are not in the public interest, Kentucky may know that its policy will be respected even if a federal court is called upon to enforce the law.[19]

AREAS WHEREIN THE ERIE RULE DOES NOT APPLY

Erie v. *Tompkins* did more than overrule *Swift* v. *Tyson*. It virtually swept away an almost endless mass of precedents which the federal courts had raised in the decision of cases at common law. Now that the rules of substantive law to be ap-

18 This was the result in *Kuhn* v. *Fairmont Coal Co.*, 215 US 349 (1910). See Ch. VI, *supra*.

19 The result in the Black and White Case, *supra*, note 16, would have been different.

plied are those of the states, it matters little what the federal rule in regard to negligence, offer and acceptance, rescission, etc., may have been in the days prior to 1938. This truth has been well recognized; in fact, it may be that it is too well recognized and that students and practitioners of the law have fallen into error and exaggerated the magnitude of the change wrought by *Erie* v. *Tompkins*. Some writers seem to believe that Brandeis meant to say that there is no national common law. While this is almost an accurate statement of the Erie Opinion and serves well enough for most purposes, it is not really correct. In speaking for the Court, Brandeis wrote, " There is no federal general common law ".[20] The word " general " must not be overlooked because it marks out a significant limitation on the operation of the Erie Rule.

Now that the Erie Doctrine has received some elaboration by the courts, it is plain that a body of federal common law does exist. How extensive it is depends, to a degree, on one's breadth of definition because even when interpreting legislation, the federal courts all proceed in the common law tradition. They refer to and consider themselves bound by previous decisions construing statutes. Consequently, they may be said to follow judicial precedents in many instances where they are primarily engaged in giving effect to legislatively created policies. An extreme case in point is supplied by federal anti-trust laws. The Sherman Act provides that " *Every* contract, combination, or conspiracy in restraint of trade " is illegal.[21] Yet it was early determined that despite its obvious dictionary meaning the word " *every* " did not include a number of restraints of trade permissible at common law.[22] In 1911 judicial decision also produced the famous " Rule of Reason " and thereby intro-

20 304 US 64, 78 (1938).

21 26 Stat. 209 (1890).

22 *United States* v. *Addyston Pipe & Steel Co.*, 85 F 271 (CCA 6th 1898).

duced a further qualification into the law.[23] Neither of these two judicial interpretations of the Anti-Trust Law are narrowly restricted to the words of the statute and they even appear to do violence to the literal meaning of the Sherman Act.

In an address delivered when he was an Associate Justice of the Supreme Court, Harlan Fiske Stone once said that statutes could be used as springboards of judicial interpretation in somewhat the same manner as judicial precedents.[24] Where this is true, the judicial additions to the law grow by the same procedures as the common law and are of a similar nature. In this view the Constitution has been the source of a large and extremely important body of common law.[25] Almost all of the key provisions of the Constitution have been elaborated, or changed, depending on one's point of view, by hosts of Supreme Court opinions. To document this assertion fully would require a book in itself, but two or three of the more obvious illustrations may be in order. In *McCulloch* v. *Maryland*[26] Chief Justice Marshall announced that the states could not tax an instrumentality of the federal government. Marshall's decision was undoubtedly in harmony with the objectives cherished by the founding fathers, but the broadness of the doctrine cannot be fully supported by a mere reference to the literal words of the Constitution.

The extent of state power over interstate commerce has given the Supreme Court an even wider opportunity for judicial creation in the common law manner. The Constitution does not in terms provide for any state control over interstate commerce; indeed it is possible to argue that it does just the reverse. Article I says that Congress shall regulate commerce

---

23 *Standard Oil Co. of New Jersey* v. *United States*, 221 US 1 (1911).

24 Stone, *The Common Law in the United States*, 50 Harv. L. Rev. (1936).

25 Such a suggestion has been made by Dowling, *Interstate Commerce and State Power—Revised version*, 47 Col. L. Rev. 547, 559 (1947).

26 4 Wheat. 316 (1819).

among the states, and by virtue of the Tenth Amendment the states retain power not expressly delegated to the central government or to the people. It is well settled that as a result of these two provisions the Congressional power is plenary.[27] One might also think it possible to contend that the federal power is exclusive because the regulation of interstate commerce is expressly delegated to the central government. However, it has been well established ever since *Cooley* v. *Board of Port Wardens of Philadelphia* [28] that some state power does exist in this field. Mr. Justice Curtis declared that some kinds of interstate commerce require uniformity of regulation and must necessarily be within the sole province of national regulation. Other types of interstate commerce, on the other hand, permit of diverse treatment and so may be regulated by the states when there is no contrary Congressional policy. The distinction made in the Cooley Case has certainly been a useful one because it has permitted localities to deal with many problems of vital concern to them despite the presence of interstate factors. But the Constitution itself knows nothing of *two types* of interstate commerce. The only commerce mentioned in that document is commerce " among the several states, with foreign nations, and with the Indian tribes." [29] This commerce is to be regulated by Congress. The Cooley Doctrine is a judicial addition to the Constitution which has been followed by the federal courts in much the same way that they used to follow the rule of negotiable instruments law laid down in *Swift* v. *Tyson*.

If the elaboration of constitutional doctrines is to be considered a part of the common law process, there can be no doubt that courts enforce a federal common law in this area. Adherence to the decisions of the Supreme Court in matters of constitutional interpretation is incumbent on federal and state courts alike. The reason for accepting federal precedents is to

27 2 Willoughby, *On the Constitution* (1929), p. 761.

28 12 How. 299 (1851).

29 U. S. Constit. Art. I, Sec. 8, Cl. 3.

be found in the federal nature of the subject matter. Whether it is by the literal translation of the words of the constitution or by judicial precedent building, disputes over the effect to be given principles derived from the United States Constitution raise federal questions. Even though state courts also interpret the Constitution and enforce its provisions as the supreme law of the land, there has never been a distinct body of national constitutional law evolved by state judiciaries.

There is another type of situation wherein it would be difficult or impossible to claim that state law should be enforced as a matter of right but where, unlike the cases of constitutional interpretation, it is necessary to consider the advisability of applying state law in preference to an independently developed federal rule. This is the kind of situation which finds the United States as a party to a civil suit. The national government owns property, purchases supplies, engages in financial transactions, and does a host of other things done by individuals and business enterprises. In the course of these operations, the United States is just as likely to find itself involved in legal proceedings as are the private persons who carry on similar activities. As a matter of political theory it is, of course, impossible to conceive of a lawsuit brought by or against the United States which does not raise a question of federal concern. Nevertheless, when the United States appears in the capacity of an ordinary litigant, there is a body of state law which, if *Erie* v. *Tompkins* is controlling, should be applied. Two cases in the Supreme Court are particularly worthy of notice in this connection because they illustrate the position of the United States in the class of suits under discussion, and because they decide that federal common law is to govern.

In *Clearfield Trust Co.* v. *United States* [30] suit was brought to recover a sum equal to the face amount of a government check. This check had been made out to a WPA worker, but had been intercepted and forged. The Clearfield Trust Co., of

[30] 318 US 363 (1943).

Clearfield, Pennsylvania, had honored the check because it had no reason to suspect that anything was wrong. Moreover, the Government delayed for a considerable length of time in notifying the Company of the forgery, a circumstance which under Pennsylvania law was sufficient to relieve Clearfield Trust of any liability.[31] Nevertheless, when the Supreme Court was faced with the problem of applying local law, it decided that *Erie* v. *Tompkins* did not govern where the United States was a party and proceeded to hold the Trust Company liable as a matter of federal common law. The practical reason advanced in justification of this decision appears to be that the United States is the author of much commercial paper and that it is of federal interest that financial transactions engaged in by the National Government be adjudged by a single uniform rule of law rather than by diverse state rules.[32]

A declaration in favor of applying federal common law in tort cases to which the United States is a party has also been made.[33] A soldier was injured in Los Angeles by a truck belonging to the Standard Oil Company of California. The injured man was hospitalized for some time, and the Government brought suit against Standard Oil to recover for the loss of the soldier's services during the period of his incapacitation. Suits for loss of services were known to the California Law,[34] and, although they are customary where the plaintiff is a relative of the injured person rather than a participant in the unique relationship occasioned by army service, it may be that an interpretation of California law would have allowed the Government

31 *Market Street Title & Trust Co.* v. *Chelten Trust Co.*, 296 Pa. 230, 145 A. 848 (1929).

32 Note, *Exceptions to Erie v. Tompkins: The Survival of Federal Common Law*, 59 Harv. L. Rev. 966, 970 (1946).

33 *United States* v. *Standard Oil Company of California*, 332 US 301 (1947).

34 *Karr* v. *Parks*, 44 Ca. 46 (1872); *McManus* v. *Arnold Taxi Cab Corp.*, 82 Ca. App. 215, 255 P 755 (1927). See *Finnerty* v. *Cummings*, 132 Ca. App. 48, 50, 22P 2d 37, 38 (1933).

to succeed. However, the Supreme Court characterized the question in the case as one of federal fiscal policy and said that it was not prepared to create a new cause of action unknown to the federal common law.[35]

Both the Clearfield and Standard Oil Cases are alike in that they exempt the United States from the application of local law where private suitors would not receive an exemption. But the reasons given for the results are different. When a government check is involved, it would seem that the federal interest requires uniformity of law. It is undoubtedly more burdensome for the United States to observe the requirements of forty-eight possibly divergent state rules than it is for the government to adjust its practices to a single federal rule. Perhaps its special status makes it wise to grant the United States this privilege not enjoyed by other litigants, but the advantages of uniformity should be urged with caution. For it is also true that private citizens who engage in transactions in two or more states would find it easier to keep abreast of a uniform rule of law, but under the Erie Rule they must adapt themselves to local conditions. The reason for refusing to consider the possibility of compensation for the United States when one of its soldiers is injured by the negligence of a private person is simpler. The long and short of the matter seems to be that where the Government is the plaintiff, federal law does not look with favor upon the creation of new common law rights. Of course, it is possible that the state courts would not so interpret their law as to afford the United States relief. But this speculation is not particularly in order because *Erie* v. *Tompkins* does not apply, and the question is one of federal common law.

Important as constitutional cases and suits by or against the United States undoubtedly are, they do not threaten the effectiveness of state law. In the one instance there is no body of state law to be applied, and the obvious supremacy of national interest makes it clear that constitutional questions are beyond

35 332 US 301, 310.

the scope of the Erie Rule. Where the United States is a litigant it can receive special treatment without leaving the way open for ordinary citizens to claim similar privileges. Consequently, the most serious practical problems concerning the scope of *Erie* v. *Tompkins* and the continuance of national common law are to be found in areas outside the two just considered. As we have already seen, cases presenting real or colorable elements of both federal and state law raise unusual difficulties. In such situations both national and state governments have a recognizable interest and a choice of law must be made.

Strange as it may seem at first glance, the administration of many federal statutes produces a mingling of national and local law. The reason is to be found in the relation of Congressional enactments to the entire body of American jurisprudence. Few statutes can be relied upon to give a complete answer to any given legal problem. Even the more comprehensive ones are merely parts of a larger context and are expected to operate in association with other laws. The Bankruptcy Act, for example, is an elaborate statute, but it deals with only one phase of commercial law. The bankrupt of today has engaged in a long series of transactions, most of them before he had any thought of approaching financial ruin. Almost all commercial law emanates from state courts and legislatures, and so it is local law that would be applicable to them if it were not for the chance fact of bankruptcy. In order to determine the respective rights of the bankrupt and his creditors, it is frequently necessary to establish the legal significance of these prior transactions. Since they took place within a framework of local rather than of national law, the need for federal courts to take some account of this local law is evident. Indeed, it is not at all unusual for national tribunals to draw upon state law to some extent when adjudicating petitions in bankruptcy. However, the Supreme Court has said that *Erie* v. *Tompkins* does not control in these cases and that federal courts accept guidance from local law only where such a course will better effectuate the policy underlying the Bankruptcy Act.[36] When the application of local law does not advance the purposes of the federal statute, national courts are at liberty to decide collateral questions for themselves. Where this is done, the principles evolved belong to the federal common law.

A similar situation arises in the application of federal employers' liability legislation, but here the national common law is in the field of torts. These statutes provide for the liability of employers under given circumstances, but do not make it clear how an injured workman is to prove his case. According to general principles of Anglo-American common law, the mere occurrence of the injury may establish the inference of negligence.[37] This doctrine of " res ipsa loquitur " has been accepted by the Supreme Court as applicable to employers' liability laws,[38] but this is not due to the prevalence of the doctrine in states where accidents have occurred. Instead, the Court has reached this result by creating and following federal precedents. Here is a considerable field wherein a national common law survives *Erie* v. *Tompkins*. Where the decision of questions of common law is necessary in order to elaborate provisions of federal statute, it is national common law that is to be applied.

This national common law which grows in the interstices of federal statutes may relate to a variety of subjects,[39] but so long

36 3 Collier, *Bankruptcy*, Sec. 63.03 (1941). *Cf. Deitrick* v. *Greaney*, 309 US 190 (1940).

37 Prosser, *Torts* (1941), pp. 292-293.

38 *Johnson* v. *United States*, 333 US 46 (1948).

39 In *Federal Crop Ins. Corp.* v. *Merrill*, 68 S. Ct. 1 (1947), the Court decided that representations made to farmers concerning the insurability of their crops are not binding in the face of regulations appearing in the Federal Register. See Mr. Justice Jackson dissenting: " The Government asks us to lift its policies out of the control of the States and to find or fashion a federal rule to govern them. I should respond to that request by laying down a federal rule that would hold these agencies to the same fundamental principles of fair dealing that have been found essential in progressive states to prevent insurance from being an investment in disappointment." 68 S. Ct. 1, 5. The decision to which Jackson objected reversed a holding to the effect

as it comes into play only when a case is primarily concerned with adjudicating rights dependent on federal statute, the sphere of its operation is severely limited. There is, however, one field wherein a body of common law developed in the federal courts primarily because of the passage of a federal statute bids fair to survive independently of the Congressional enactment. The statute in question is the law permitting the registration of trademarks and giving such registered marks a protected status.[40]

Business enterprises have naturally made wide use of this registration because the protected trademarks are valuable advertising devices. Suits for the misappropriation of registered marks have always been brought in federal courts because they arise under federal statute and because state courts do not exercise concurrent jurisdiction in this field. However, the same facts which make out a case for trademark infringement can usually be made to support a separate count of unfair competition. The latter is a common law cause of action which encompasses a number of unethical business practices. In order to obtain the full benefit of both statute and common law, litigants long ago adopted a practice of combining counts for trademark infringement and unfair competition in the same suit and trying the two claims in the federal courts as part of the same proceeding. In the days of *Swift* v. *Tyson* this practice raised no serious questions concerning the application of local law because the federal courts were free to develop their own common law of unfair competition. Due to the trademark statute, the national judiciary had many more opportunities to consider

---

that Idaho insurance law applied to federal crop insurance in the state. *Merrill* v. *Federal Crop Ins. Corp.* (Id.) 174 P2d 834 (1946).

For an independent federal definition of the familiar term used in insurance law "in loco parentis" when relevant to a determination of rights under the *National Service Life Insurance Act* see *Niewiadamski* v. *United States*, 159, F2d 683 (CCA 6th 1947).

40 First Trademark Act, 21 Stat. 502 (1881), and 22 Stat. 298 (1882). Superseded by Trademark Act of 1905, 33 Stat. 724.

unfair competition cases than did local tribunals. The result was a more complete development of federal law on the subject than was possible in each of the separate states. This more extensive and therefore more predictable body of law in turn attracted cases wherein the only complaint was one of unfair competition. Where no right was asserted under the trademark laws, it was impossible to bring such cases into federal courts by pleading a federal question.[41] However, diversity of citizenship would also support federal jurisdiction, and unfair competition cases which could not come before federal tribunals in one way usually got there by the other route. This further channeling of litigation away from the state courts produced a still more complete national law of unfair competition and an even more scant local law on the subject.

The advent of *Erie* v. *Tompkins* threw the law of unfair competition into utter confusion.[42] We have already seen something of the problems besetting federal courts in their efforts to find state law when precedents are unclear or totally lacking. But generally speaking, these difficult situations have been the exceptions rather than the rule. In unfair competition, however, the absence of state law was almost universal. Some states had no judicial precedents at all, and in many of the others a handful of antiquated decisions was all that could be found.[43] Yet it need hardly be said that unfair competition cases continued to come into the federal courts. It would seem that the Erie Rule was squarely applicable to these cases, but neither federal judges nor private citizens could see any advantage in abandoning a reasonably satisfactory federal common law in order to play guessing games in the vacuum of non-existent state decisions. The result was that in one way or another federal law

41 Zlinkoff, *Erie* v. *Tompkins: in Relation to the Law of Trade-Marks and Unfair Competition*, 42 Col. L. Rev. 955 (1942).

42 Chafee, *Unfair Competition*, 53 Harv. L. Rev. 1289 (1940); Zlinkoff, *op. cit., supra*, note 41.

43 See notes 41, 42, *supra*.

continued to be applied. In the absence of local precedents, litigants continued to build their cases around federal decisions and judges, adhering to a well known principle in the conflict of laws, assumed that since the contrary had not been shown, the law of the foreign jurisdictions (states) was the same as the law of the forum (federal courts).[44] At other times, national tribunals have merely applied federal precedents without mentioning *Erie* v. *Tompkins*.[45] Although the Tyson Rule has been dead long enough to permit the emergence of some new local law in the field of unfair competition, any such development has been retarded by the continued use of federal courts for this type of litigation so that national common law has suffered no appreciable diminution of vitality.

The case of *Bulova Watch Co.* v. *Stolzberg* [46] demonstrates that there may be additional difficulties in the way of enforcement of state law even if local precedents eventually become sufficiently numerous to furnish satisfactory guides to the federal courts. The facts on which that suit was based revealed a misappropriation of the Bulova name over a wide geographic area embracing several states. Since misappropriation and most other types of unfair competition are intimately connected with advertising, a large percentage of the cases are of this multistate variety. If the federal courts should attempt to apply state law to these cases, it would be far from easy to decide which state was to furnish the governing precedents. In the simpler cases it might be possible to ascertain the extent of the injury in each state and apply divergent local laws to segments of the proceedings. But such a course would be confusing at best and utterly unworkable in many instances. When such difficulties stand in the way of applying local law, perhaps the continued

44 Note, *The Choice of Law in Multistate Unfair Competition: A Legal-Industrial Enigma*, 60 Harv. L. Rev. 1315, 1317 (1947).

45 *Ibid.*

46 69 F. Supp. 543 (D. Mass. 1947), commented on in 60 Harv. L. Rev. 821 (1947).

use of federal common law provides the simplest and most equitable solution to the legal tangle.

Other disputes of an interstate character have also demonstrated the survival of national common law. Mr. Justice Brandeis who wrote the Erie Opinion was probably the first to recognize this fact when he spoke for the Supreme Court in *Hinderlider* v. *La Plata River and Cherry Creek Ditch Company*.[47] This suit was brought by a private irrigation company against the state engineer of Colorado. The state official had shut off the Company's water supply from the La Plata River in order to permit New Mexico to receive a part of the stream flow to which it was entitled by the terms of an interstate compact.[48] The Company claimed that its rights to preferred use of the water had been established by a decision of the Colorado courts made over thirty years before and that its rights could not be defeated by the compact. The highest court of Colorado had agreed with the irrigation company,[49] but the Supreme Court reversed this decision. Brandeis recognized that under the law of both Colorado and New Mexico the Company was entitled to appropriate the water even if such action left nothing for the users in New Mexico.[50] However, the Court held that the law governing apportionment of the waters of an interstate stream was federal common law. As the well settled federal rule was contrary to the law of both states, the claim of the irrigation company failed. Similar problems arise in suits between states.[51]

---

47 304 US 92 (1938).

48 Ratified by Colorado, Col. Sess. L. 1923, p. 696. Ratified by N. M. Sess. L. 1923, p. 13. Approved by Congress, 43 Stat. 796, 1925. Congressional consent to a compact does not make the compact a federal statute.

49 *La Plata River and Cherry Creek Ditch Co.* v. *Hinderlider*, 93 Col. 128, 25 P2d 187 (1933).

50 304 US 92, 98.

51 See note, 44 Col. L. Rev. 437 (1944). In suits between states, or between the United States and a state, the Supreme Court may also determine the ownership of land and minerals. In doing so, the Court makes a federal common law of real property. See *United States* v. *California*, 332 US 19,

Indeed the rule of " equitable apportionment " applied in the Hinderlider Case was developed by the Supreme Court in determining the rights of states to the waters of interstate streams.[52]

The unfair competition cases, particularly those of the multistate variety, and disputes relating to interstate streams present special problems which may be said to lie outside the area contemplated by *Erie* v. *Tompkins* policy. However, an expansion of national common law into a more general field of interstate legal activity would raise questions as to the modification of the policy. To date, no such expansion of federal common law has taken place, but two decisions require special notice because they point the way to such a possible expansion in the future. The first of them was decided by the First Circuit Court of Appeals in 1940; the second came from the Supreme Court more recently.

O'Brien v. *Western Union Telegraph Co.*[53] was a suit for libel. The plaintiff had been the object of a defamatory message transmitted by the defendant from Boston, Massachusetts, to Royal Oak, Michigan. In rejecting both Michigan and Massachusetts law, the Circuit Court of Appeals held that the Federal Communications Act contained provisions relating to the liability of telegraph companies and that since Congress had regulated this type of interstate communication, local law could not govern. Although the Communications Act did not contain any specific rules of substantive law relating to libel, it would seem that the comprehensive nature of the federal statute did provide

---

38 (1947). " Now that the question is here, we decide ... that California is not the owner of the three-mile marginal belt along its coast, and that the Federal Government rather than the state has paramount rights in and power over that belt, an incident to which is full dominion over the resources of the soil under that water area, including oil."

52 *New Jersey* v. *New York*, 283 US 336 (1931) ; *Kansas* v. *Colorado*, 206 US 46 (1907). See *Wyoming* v. *Colorado*, 259 US 419 (1922).

53 113 F2d 539 (CCA 1st 1940).

a basis for the application of federal law.[54] If the federal law of libel could not be ascertained by reading the Communications Act, it is at least possible to argue that such national common law is of the interstitial kind to be found in the areas of bankruptcy and employers' liability. However, this idea of federal occupancy of the field to the exclusion of state regulation has recently been carried much further by the Supreme Court. This occurred in the suit of a railway employee injured while off duty and riding on a free pass issued to him by the railroad.[55] The Company had sought to relieve itself from liability for injury in such cases by stipulating that pass-holders were not to hold the railroad accountable even where injuries were the result of company negligence. The accident in question occurred in Utah, and under state law, such stipulations exempting railroads from liability were inoperative.[56] From the circumstances of the case, it followed that the injured passenger should have recovered if Utah law were applicable. However, the Supreme Court, three justices dissenting, held that state law did not govern. The majority reasoned that the Hepburn Act of 1906 made it illegal for railroads to issue passes to public officials.[57] This legislation, said the Court, dealt with the entire pass question so that local law was inapplicable. The Court then proceeded to hold that as a matter of federal common law the railroad's stipulation denying liability was valid. This federal law was to be found in a case decided by the Supreme Court in 1904 wherein it had been held that railroads might excuse themselves from liability for injury to free passengers.[58] As the

---

54 Although the Federal Communications Act of 1934, 48 Stat. 1064, does not supply a federal definition of libel, sections 206-207 of the Act provide for liability for damages where private injury results from any unlawful act or omission.

55 *Francis* v. *Southern Pacific Co.*, 68 S. Ct. 611 (1948).

56 *Williams* v. *Oregon Short Line R. Co.*, 18 Utah 210, 54 P 991 (1898).

57 68 S. Ct. 611, 613.

58 *Northern Pacific R. Co.* v. *Adams*, 192 US 440 (1904).

minority pointed out, the federal statute was hardly of sufficient scope to be considered a complete declaration of policy with regard to railway passes.[59] In this view of the matter, *Erie* v. *Tompkins* should have been followed and Utah law applied. But the decision of the Supreme Court was otherwise, and if it is to be accepted as reliable law, it marks the boldest extension to date of federal common law into the general field of interstate commerce since the overruling of *Swift* v. *Tyson*. Whether this case will stand is a matter for the future to decide. In view of its dubious correctness and of the well reasoned dissent, it may be that the case will not be followed.

The areas of continuing national common law are certainly important, and at least one writer has characterized some of them as exceptions to the Erie Rule.[60] However, it would seem more accurate to consider them as manifestations of an entirely different principle and outside the purpose of the Erie Decision. The chief evil in an independent federal general common law was that it made justice depend on an extraneous factor—the court in which a case was tried. With the possible exception of the unfair competition and interstate commerce cases, present national common law does not carry this danger. It is well understood that in deciding constitutional questions state courts no less than national tribunals follow the decisions of the United States Supreme Court. When the federal government appears as a litigant, it would seem that it should be able to rely on federal law even in those rare instances where the suit is in a state court. And even where the administration of ordinary federal statutes is involved, the propriety of accepting federal decisional law hardly seems to be open to question.

Erie v. *Tompkins* was primarily designed to meet the problems raised by the federal diversity of citizenship jurisdiction.

59 The Hepburn Act, 34 Stat. 584 (1906), provides that free passes may only be issued to certain specified classes of persons, but it does not deal with railroad liability on such passes when issued.

60 See note 32, *supra*.

It is here that the only substantive questions presented to federal courts relate to local law, and it is in these cases that the need to prevent forum shopping arises. Over the vast field once comprehended by the Rule of *Swift* v. *Tyson,* the substantive law of the states now reigns supreme. It may be that federal machinery is still used by litigants who prefer the procedures of the federal courts, but there is no longer any substantial danger of evading state policy by electing to place the decision of law suits beyond the power of state judicial officers.

CHAPTER XII

IS DIVERSITY JURISDICTION
NECESSARY?

THE development of the Erie Rule has undoubtedly done much to bring order and harmony into federal-state judicial relations, but the present situation is not without its incongruities. Many suitors use all their ingenuity to avoid state courts in the belief that the national judiciary will treat them more favorably. But when they finally succeed in establishing the jurisdiction of the forum of their choice, it is only to discover that the federal judge is doing everything he can to find out how a state court would decide the case before him, and to give full effect to local law. Admittedly, the differences in substantive principles current during the Tyson Era have been replaced by differences between federal and state procedure, but where the outcome of a case is made to depend on these differences, the result is even less defensible than was the old conflict between national and local rules of substantive law. Before 1938 it could at least be argued that there was room for dispute as to whose substantive law was superior. One might occasionally be able to say that the outcome of a particular case had been more just because the rule containing the better substantive policy had been invoked. But procedure should be a mechanical aid to the securing of justice rather than a determinant of its content. If different procedures promote different substantive results it is probably because one of the competing methods of administration is defective. The remedy for such a deficiency is not to perpetuate the multiplicity of procedures but rather to settle on the best rule and make that one standard.

The real value of the Erie Rule is to be found in the lessened disparity between federal and state administered justice. If a greater identity of result is indeed a reality, we may ask whether there is any good reason to retain an arrangement which allows private citizens to choose between competing judicial systems. So long as diversity jurisdiction remains in its present form, such a choice will continue to be exercised. Some observers of our judicial scene have long been of the opinion that it is unnecessary and undesirable to permit this private selection of a forum. They began their agitation for the modification or abolition of the federal diversity jurisdiction many years before the decision of *Erie* v. *Tompkins*. If their arguments had any validity then, they must certainly be given increased consideration now.

A Monetary Restriction on Federal Jurisdiction

In view of the legislature's virtually complete power over the jurisdiction of federal courts, Congress was the appropriate recipient of proposals to modify or abolish the diversity jurisdiction exercised by United States Courts. Indeed, federal statutes have always restricted this jurisdiction to some degree. The chief limitation has been a financial one and has been designed to keep small claims out of the national courts.

The requirement that a case involve a minimum amount of money before it is eligible for consideration by a federal tribunal has already acted to reduce the number of cases in the national courts. There are many reported cases in which a litigant has sought to inflate his damages so as to meet the three thousand dollar prerequisite to entry into a federal court, and each of the instances in which a party has failed in this attempt is an example of a case kept out of reach of federal action. Conversely, it may be said that at least a portion of the litigation flowing through the state courts has been brought there because persons who would really prefer to have their rights decided by the federal judiciary know that they cannot meet the jurisdictional amount.

Yet it is not clear that our present three thousand dollar requirement is more of a barrier to litigation in the federal courts than the five hundred dollar jurisdictional amount was in the early days of the Republic. Unfortunately our knowledge of eighteenth and early nineteenth century price levels is scanty and almost entirely of the anecdotal variety.[1] But it is generally agreed that during the past one hundred and fifty years the price level has risen and more money has come into circulation.[2] Consequently, it would be a mistake to think that because three thousand is six times five hundred, it is six times as difficult to get a case into the federal courts than it once was. Whatever the long range effect of those changes which have actually been made in the size of the jurisdictional amount may have been, it is, of course, true that Congress can materially affect the flow of business to the federal courts by varying the size of the financial requirement. In fact, the prime reason for these changes has always been the hope that, by making it more difficult to bring a case into the national courts, those tribunals would be relieved of the flood of business which has resulted in the chronic congestion of federal court calendars.

Some opponents of diversity jurisdiction have urged that the jurisdictional amount be raised to $7500, $10,000, or even higher. Such a step would certainly exclude many of the cases which reach federal courts from consideration by federal authority. But there is a serious objection to the use of such tactics as a means of preserving state control over litigants and their cases: namely, that a monetary test for admission to federal protection is purely arbitrary and does not even pretend to get at the merits of the existing distribution of judicial business between national and local courts. It is probable that some statutory provision designed to keep small claims before state judiciaries, which are better equipped to handle them than are

1 See Bureau of Labor Statistics No. 499, *History of Wages in the United States from Colonial Times to 1928* (1929), pp. 1-25. Comparison of dollar values is made even more difficult by the tremendous changes which have taken place in the socio-economic conditions during the past one hundred and fifty years. Commodities which were staples at an earlier time are no longer important, and new products have come to be considered necessities. Therefore attempts to compare general price levels are of only limited usefulness. Thorp and Taylor, *Prices*, 6 Encyc. of Soc. Sciences 375, 380 (1937).

2 See Fisher, *The Purchasing Power of Money* (1920), Ch. XI.

the national courts, is wise. But once the jurisdictional amount is raised to the point where it affects other than petty cases, it gives the poor man and those who litigate with him a lesser measure of protection for their legal rights because they are denied the choice of forum permitted to other litigants. There is, for example, no reason to believe that a case brought by a small businessman on a two thousand dollar contract will necessarily involve legal problems of less concern to the nation as a whole than a suit on a larger transaction brought by one of our giant corporations. Yet the parties to the former dispute are forced to look to a state government for the enforcement of their rights while participants in the latter can decide whether they prefer to rely on state or federal authority for the enforcement of the law.

EARLY ATTACKS ON DIVERSITY JURISDICTION

During the sixty year period between the first serious attacks on the diversity jurisdiction of the national courts and the overruling of *Swift* v. *Tyson* in 1938, this important facet of federal judicial power was seldom discussed entirely on its own merits. This was largely due to the line of argument pursued by opponents of this jurisdiction who sought to capitalize on the obvious need for some reform in the judicial system designed to reduce the ever increasing burdens being placed on the federal courts.

In the 1880s, when the legal jam was at its worst, it took three years for an average case to reach the stage of final disposition after it had been placed on the docket of the Supreme Court;[3] and the lower federal courts were almost as hard pressed.[4] For the most part, this increase in the demands made upon our national judiciary was due to the phenomenal expan-

3 Taft, *Possible and Needed Reforms in the Administration of Justice in the Federal Courts*, 8 ABAJ 601, 602 (1922).

4 See McCrary, *Needs of the Federal Judiciary*, 13 Cent. L. J. 167, 168 (1881).

sion of commerce and industry immediately following the Civil War and to the concomitant rise in the number of business disputes. Whether this pressure was to be relieved by adding new judges and circuits to the federal judicial system or by restricting the jurisdiction of the federal courts, the existence of the log jam in our judicial machinery was very real. Indeed, it was so obvious that scarcely anyone could be found who did not recognize the need for some remedy.

One of the first lawyers of prominence to advocate abolition of diversity jurisdiction was William Meigs of Philadelphia who contributed a number of articles to leading legal journals over a period of some twenty-five or thirty years. In 1882, when still a comparatively young man, he contributed a piece to the American Law Register [5] detailing the overworked condition of the national courts and offering the discontinuance of federal activity in diversity cases as a cure for the situation. If we may judge from Meigs' entire attitude toward the relation between state and federal judiciaries as revealed in a number of his writings [6] as well as from the more specific evidence furnished by a careful reading of his original article, it seems clear that he actually thought that diversity jurisdiction was bad on grounds of fundamental principle. But he too wished to make use of this procedural argument because it might suceed without touching the basic antagonisms bound to be aroused by a frontal attack on diversity jurisdiction. The answer which Meigs received in the pages of the Washington Law Reporter for August, 1882, was telling and has lost none of its force with the passage of time.

5 Meigs, *The Relief of the Supreme Court of the United States*, 32 Am. L. Reg. 360 (1884).

6 Meigs was gravely concerned over the disruptive influences of *Swift v. Tyson* and its later extensions. In addition to his article cited in note 5, *supra*, see his pieces entitled *Decisions of the Federal Courts on Questions of State Law*, 45 Am. L. Rev. 47 (1911) ; *Shall the State Courts Adopt the Federal Doctrine of General Principles of Jurisprudence?*, 29 Cent. L. J. 465 (1889) ; *Decisions of the Federal Courts on Questions of State Law*, 8 So. L. Rev. 452 (n. s. 1882).

" The radical fault of this proposal is the same which has marked many other suggestions for the same purpose—viz., it is a proposal how not to do professional business, not how to do it." [7] The writer then proceeded to suggest that if the federal courts were overworked, the proper remedy was an increase in the personnel and facilities at the disposal of the national judicial system.

Congress has taken this means of improving the administration of justice in the federal courts on more than one occasion. In 1891 the Circuit Courts of Appeals Act [8] reorganized the federal judiciary. Prior to that date, the District and Circuit Courts had both acted as courts of original jurisdiction, and the latter had also been charged with duties of appellate review. Because of their double function, the Circuit Courts found it increasingly difficult to operate efficiently in the face of crowded dockets. Where the leisurely pace of business had once permitted them to manage an administratively cumbersome system, changed conditions made it impossible for them to do so. The remedy effected by the Act was the creation of new Circuit Courts of Appeals which assumed the appellate duties of the older Circuit Courts. Under this new system, the District and Circuit Courts were both able to devote their entire energy to pre-trial and trial work.[9] In addition, the Circuit Courts of Appeals could be depended upon to dispose of many of the cases which had previously kept the calendar of the Supreme Court so far in arrears. In 1925, when the Supreme Court was given power drastically to curtail the number of cases coming before it by an expanded use of certiorari, the Circuit Courts of

7 Editorial, *The Overburdened Federal Courts*, 12 Wash. L. Rep. 477 (1884).

8 26 Stat. 826 (1891).

9 The Circuit Courts were abolished in 1911 and their jurisdiction was assimilated to that of the District Courts, 36 Stat. 1167. Congress also provided for the transfer of judicial personnel from the expiring Circuit Courts to the District Courts, 37 Stat. 46 (1911).

Appeals were given authority to make final disposition of diversity cases,[10] and this type of litigation has not encroached upon the time of the Supreme Court except in so far as the Court itself has consented to hear such cases.

These statutory measures, together with periodic increases in the number of federal judges, have greatly relieved the pressure on the federal courts and have consequently reduced the strength of an argument against diversity jurisdiction because of the overcrowded condition of the federal dockets. But the national courts are still busy, and the old argument still finds an occasional champion. However, it is important to note that Congress has preferred to meet the problems of the federal judiciary by reorganizing that branch of government rather than by surrendering any of the national power to the states. Indeed, an act of 1940, far from disowning diversity jurisdiction, extended the principle so that citizens of Alaska, Hawaii, and the District of Columbia may now avail themselves of it.[11] In view of Congressional reluctance to curtail this type of federal jurisdiction in order to lighten the burdens of the national judiciary, it is apparent that any attempt to make a basic alteration in the present scheme of things must succeed on its intrinsic merits or not at all.

10 See Rule 35, Sec. 5, Revised Rules of Supreme Court, 266 US 653, 680 (1925).

11 54 Stat. 143. There are conflicting lower court decisions as to the constitutionality of this statute. It was upheld in *Glaeser* v. *Acacia Mut. Life Ass'n*, 55 F. Supp. 925 (D. C. Cal. 1944); *Winkler* v. *Daniels*, 43 F. Supp. 265 (D. C. Va. 1942). The statute was declared unconstitutional in *Behlert* v. *James Foundation of New York*, 60 F. Supp. 706 (D. C. N. Y. 1945); *McGarry* v. *City of Bethlehem*, 45 F. Supp. 385 (D. C. Pa. 1942). The disputed question is whether the word " states " in Art. III, Sec. 2 of the Constitution is to be interpreted literally or whether this word is sufficiently broad to include territories for purposes of diversity jurisdiction. For a general discussion see Dykes and Keeffe, *The 1940 Amendment to the Diversity of Citizenship Clause*, 21 Tul. L. Rev. 171 (1946).

LIMITED USEFULNESS OF THE HISTORICAL ARGUMENT
FOR DIVERSITY JURISDICTION

The general principle behind the exercise of diversity jurisdiction by the federal courts is not hard to find. Even the casual student of American history knows that interstate jealousies were rife in eighteenth century America and that state patriotism was much stronger than it is today. It may have been that sympathy for local people and hostility toward outsiders would lead local juries and judges to color justice with their emotional likes and dislikes and so to place the non resident litigant at a serious and altogether uncalled for disadvantage. To the extent that federal diversity jurisdiction was intended as a remedy for this local prejudice, it was an ingenious device whose wise use may have been responsible for minimizing some of the worst features of provincialism in some sections of the United States. By permitting each non resident litigant to appeal to federal authority—to a court which was as much his own as that of his adversary—it was hoped that each individual could decide whether the particular circumstances of his case called for this special protection or whether it was safe for him to submit to a local administration of justice.

On the other hand, it is at least possible that eighteenth century provincialism did not constitute an omnipresent barrier to the administration of impartial justice by local courts. One writer has found slight evidence to indicate that special protection of non residents may have been unnecessary even in the early days of the Republic. In his oft-cited article, Henry Friendly says that so far as he can see from an examination of available judicial reports of the period, non resident suitors do not appear to have been discriminated against by state courts because of their citizenship.[12] But Mr. Friendly freely admits that the records upon which he bases his speculation are frag-

12 Friendly, *The Historic Basis of Diversity Jurisdiction*, 41 Harv. L. Rev. 483 (1928).

mentary and cannot be trusted too far. They represent only cases heard by a few appellate tribunals and cover no more than a small part of the total litigation in any one state. Moreover, the subtle effects of bias do not always appear from the mere words of a judicial opinion. The printed reports are especially poor guides when the reader is one hundred and fifty years removed from the controversy and can have no knowledge of it or of its participants, except through the opinion of the judges whose bias the investigator wishes to test.

Whether the founding fathers were providing against a real danger may never be known to everyone's satisfaction. The records to support an incontrovertible judgment were never written down, or have long since disappeared. But whatever the ancient necessity for diversity jurisdiction may have been, the criticisms of this type of federal judicial power are much more recent than the era of Hamilton and Madison. The suspicion that national power has been used by private litigants for purposes detrimental to the public interest has grown in the generations since the Civil War. The modern judge must have a working knowledge of the body of law that he is to enforce. The more practice he has in ministering to the peculiar needs of his own jurisdiction, the more effective he becomes in enforcing his domestic body of law. If the federal judge must master state law in addition to the federal jurisprudence, his task becomes that much more difficult. Were common law the only concern of our courts, the difficulties would be serious enough, but it could properly be contended that skill in the use of precedent was an attribute of the judicial character useful in areas of federal and state law alike and might permit a judge to operate in both fields with a high degree of facility. But the present day administration of the law in the federal courts exhibits an additional problem. Much of a federal judge's work relates to the enforcement of highly technical statutes like the bankruptcy and anti-trust laws. It is often said that federal judges need all the time and practice they can get if they are to become adept in these fields. To divert their attention from these difficult tasks by forcing them to examine and administer state law is to make their already burdened positions well nigh intolerable. Moreover, it is probable that the administration of state law in the federal courts suffers just as much from this overburdening of the federal judicial personnel as does the enforcement of the federal law itself. For the judge who is unaccustomed to think in a context of local law may be guilty of serious errors that an experienced state judge would not commit. Nevertheless, if there are good reasons why litigants cannot get unbiased justice in a state court, it would seem to be necessary for federal diversity jurisdiction to continue despite the hardship to the federal courts. Consequently, it is on the basis of present day considerations that the fate of diversity jurisdiction must rest.

SOVEREIGNTY AS AN ARGUMENT FOR DIVERSITY JURIS-
DICTION: A DIPLOMATIC ANALOGY

Some years ago, Judge Parker of the Fourth Circuit made an interesting defense of the existing system.[13] He noted that in contemplation of law each of our forty-eight states is sovereign: each is an independent political entity with a government of its own. This is precisely the situation prevailing in the world at large with its many separate nations. Now, it is to be observed that independent nations maintain diplomatic relations with one another; each sovereign government has a state department or foreign ministry whose function it is to protect nationals who go abroad. If an American gets into trouble in Great Britain or France, a representative of the United States stands ready to aid him in order to see that he is treated fairly by the foreign authorities. However, when a Pennsylvanian finds himself in difficulty in Ohio, there is no official of his native state to whom he can turn for comfort and assistance. This void in the machinery of our federal system is filled by

13 Parker, *The Federal Jurisdiction and Recent Attacks upon It*, 18 ABAJ 433 (1932).

the federal courts. They stand ready to hear the Pennsylvanian's grievance and see that he is not injured by local bias.

From some points of view, Judge Parker's analogy is an attractive one. It is true that each of the member governments within a federal union enjoys some of the attributes of an independent country. Each of our states, for example, has its own body of law made by its own legislature, enforced by its own executive officers, and interpreted by its own courts. But it is not correct to say that in deciding diversity cases the federal courts perform the same function that consular officials undertake in foreign countries.

By way of illustration, let us suppose that Peter Smith of Philadelphia is currently in Paris seeing the sights. As he walks near the Arc de Triomphe, his mind is busy with thoughts of Napoleon, Clemenceau, and the beauties of the exhibitions at the Louvre. When he steps off the curb, Mr. Smith is hit and injured by a passing automobile. Peter is a stranger in Paris and goes to the American embassy for some advice. The vice consul with whom he talks listens to his story, suggests that Peter see a French lawyer and recommends one whose services should be satisfactory. This is likely to be the extent of the American State Department's participation in the affair. If Peter sues the driver of the French automobile, he will do so in accordance with French law in a French court, and his rights will be adjudged under the French Civil Code. It would be unheard of and utterly useless for him to suggest that French judges have a grudge against all foreigners and should not be allowed to decide his case. It would be equally out of order for him to expect an American court to take jurisdiction of his action merely because he is an American citizen while the defendant is a Frenchman. Yet this is precisely what might happen if Peter Smith had been injured on the streets of Columbus, Ohio, instead of Paris, France. He could successfully contend that as he is a citizen of Pennsylvania and the defendant is a citizen of Ohio, a federal district court and not an Ohio tribunal will decide his case.

Of course, it is not nearly as unfair to require that the resident of Columbus defend the suit in a federal court at Mr. Smith's option as it would be to compel the Parisian to submit to the jurisdiction of an American court. In the one instance, both litigants are Americans and the national judiciary is a branch of the government to which they owe a common allegiance; [14] in the other instance, the Frenchman would be deprived of all opportunity to be heard by a tribunal of his compatriots in a cause of action rightfully arising under French law within the territorial confines of France. But this difference is only one more evidence that it is not safe to compare the judicial organization persisting within the United States to the legal and diplomatic arrangements to be found in the realm of international relations.

CONTINUING LOCAL PREJUDICE AS AN ARGUMENT FOR DIVERSITY JURISDICTION

A more pressing problem than the one raised by Judge Parker is the question of local prejudice. Although it may serve

14 For an over strong emphasis on this point, See Parker, *The Federal Jurisdiction and Recent Attacks Upon It*, 18 ABAJ 433, 438 (1932). " But there is an argument based on principle which appeals to my mind more powerfully than any of these. When a citizen of the United States must go into a court in the United States to assert or defend his rights, he ought to have the right to go into a court which is as much his court as it is the court of his adversary. The judicial settlement of disputes appertains to the sovereign; and when I go into court I wish it to be my sovereign that exercises sovereign power. The federal court represents all of the people of the United States, and if I go into a federal court in New York, it is as much my court as it is the court of a citizen of that state. The judge is appointed by my President, is confirmed by my senate and is subject to have his actions called in question by the senators and representatives whom I vote for as well as by the senators and representatives who represent my adversary. If I go into a state court in New York, however, I am in a court which represents a sovereignty upon which I have no claim. The judge represents the people of New York, he does not represent me or the people of the state from which I come. Citizenship in the United States is both local and national. For matters involving the local citizenship the local courts are provided. For matters which involve citizens of different states, only the federal courts can furnish to both a tribunal of the sovereignty to which both owe allegiance and to which both look for protection."

little more than academic purpose to speculate about provincialism in early America, whether such localism continues to be a force in the United States of today is of the utmost importance. If the course of justice can still be affected by a favoritism shown neighbors and by an emotional dislike of outsiders, there is as much need of diversity jurisdiction in modern times as there was a century and a half ago.

An article of over thirty years ago in protesting the continuance of federal jurisdiction based on diversity of citizenship made the following observations on the changing character of the American scene:

" But ere long the forests began to fall before the axe of progress. The schoolhouse, the public press and facilities for intercourse multiplied; enterprise and commercial adventure pushed on; the advantages, soils and products of every section became the servitors of our people as a whole. The diffusion of general education, and the intimate acquaintance of the east and the west, the north and the south, abolished provincialism. War had its part in this. Now, local prejudice and jealousy, state attachments and interests, are anachronisms, so far as they may be thought to obstruct or control the administration of justice between individuals.[15]

Remarks of this kind have become common in recent years. We are constantly reminded that we use the same toothpaste, listen to the same radio programs, drive the same automobiles and read the same books wherever we live—Down East, on the Florida Coast, or by the Golden Gate. It is not easy to say just how much of an influence on our fundamental thought patterns this kind of standardization has had. The sharing of so much in the way of common experience must necessarily have made some impress on the shape of life throughout the entire United States. But it is obviously incorrect to suppose that modern

15 Collier, *A Plea Against Jurisdiction for Diversity of Citizenship*, 76 Cent. L. J. 263, 264 (1913).

technology and salesmanship have homogenized America until its many sections are indistinguishable one from the other.[16]

To single out only the most obvious example, the South is still a distinctive region with its peculiar tradition, its characteristic political outlook, its strong views on the race problem, and its earnest striving to overcome its economic backwardness. This last endeavor has produced a lengthy chain of litigation over the national freight rate structure [17] which may well represent a type of local bias at work. At the very least, we may be sure that it is a sectional conflict in which the states of one part of the country have been arrayed against the states in another region; a battle wherein each side has been swayed by considerations of local advantage rather than by a desire to promote the national welfare as a whole.

How far this sectional conflict spills over into the field of ordinary private litigation cannot readily be determined. It is not something which lends itself to easy measurement and on the basis of presently available information, must be attacked primarily through the uncertain channels of general impression. For example, it is common knowledge among members of the legal profession that juries are more likely to bring in substantial verdicts against defendants in personal injury cases when they believe that an insurance company will ultimately pay the judgment. We also know that there are certain types of cases where an attorney will ask to have a juror excused because of

16 Sectionalism in the United States is largely a product of the country's size and may never completely disappear. In fact Frederick Jackson Turner, writing in 1907, believed that sectionalism was increasing. See Turner, *Is Sectionalism in America Dying Away?* in *Sections in American History* (1932), p. 287.

17 For many years, the South has contended that railroad rate schedules were so arranged as to put Southern industry at a competitive disadvantage. For a discussion of the history of the struggle over freight rates see Tally, *The Supreme Court, The Interstate Commerce Commission and the Freight Rate Battle*, 25 N. C. L. Rev. 172 (1947); Scott and Stone, *Discrimination in Freight Rates: The South Wins A Battle*, 15 Tul. L. Rev. 335 (1941). See also Note, 31 Ia. L. Rev. 283 (1946).

his color, religion, education, or business background. These actions result from the belief that people may be swayed in their judgments by elements of unreasoned prejudice.

Professor Robert K. Carr has found that there is probably little difference between the biases of federal and state grand juries. In describing the difficulties encountered by the Civil Rights Section of the Department of Justice he writes: " Once it decides to prosecute a case, the CRS is faced with the initial difficulty of persuading a federal grand jury to indict the accused person or persons. A civil rights case, by its very nature is almost always one in which the victim enjoys little or no standing in his community. The Negro in the South, the Jehovah's Witness in New England, the Japanese-American in California, the labor organizer in almost any section of the country—these and similar individuals whose civil rights are most frequently in danger are usually members of weak and unpopular minorities. In taking the initiative to protect the rights of these people, the federal government, as an outside political agency, is relatively free from the deterring influence imposed by majority public opinion in the community where the violation has occurred. But in a criminal prosecution in such a case, even the federal government finds it necessary to conduct proceedings in the district where the offense was committed. It is seldom easier to obtain an indictment from a federal grand jury than it is to get a state grand jury to indict in a civil liberty case, since the personnel of these different agencies in any section of the country is apt to be similar. . . ." [18] Whether there is less danger of prejudice on the part of jurors in civil cases is an open question. Although there is little or no specific evidence of recent date tending to show that the section of the country from which a man comes is a consideration in the fairness of treatment which he receives from state courts, it must be admitted that there is at least a possibility of such bias just as there is a possibility of these other kinds of prejudice.

18 Carr, *Federal Protection of Civil Rights* (1947), pp. 133-134.

Since the reason for permitting federal jurisdiction in diversity cases was so clear, we may wonder why neither the Constitution nor the Judiciary Act of 1789 made the existence of local prejudice a condition precedent to the operation of federal authority. Perhaps it was because no one suspected that suitors might prefer national tribunals for reasons other than their freedom from bias. In these early days, there was not the slightest suggestion that the law to be applied in diversity cases was other than state law; any doubt on this point was intended to be removed by Section 34 of the Judiciary Act. This should have meant that local authority would be upheld in any event. The only difference was that where any person had reason to believe that local bias might warp the application of the law to his case, he could avoid this danger by calling on a federal court to act as the enforcement agency.

The views of those who oppose the continuance of federal jurisdiction based on diversity of citizenship do not rest on the assumption that local prejudice is never to be found. For the most part, they have been tremendously impressed with the inequities that have resulted from a dual enforcement of local law, and they wonder whether the damage done does not outweigh the supposed gain accruing from the system. As they see little hope of working a practical modification of present federal practice, they take the extreme position and favor the complete elimination of national jurisdiction in this field.

Although it is of only slight importance, one portion of the statute delimiting the original and removal jurisdiction of the United States District Courts does deal specifically with " local influence and prejudice ". In essence it provides in part as follows:

. . . where a suit is now pending, or may hereafter be brought, in any state court, in which there is a controversy between a citizen of the State in which the suit is brought and a citizen of another State, any defendant, being such citizen of another state, may remove such suit into the district court of the United States for the proper district, at any time before the

trial thereof, when it shall be made to appear to said district
court that from prejudice or local influence he will not be able
to obtain justice in such state court, or in any other state court
to which the said defendant may, under the laws of the State,
have the right, on account of such prejudice or local influence,
to remove said cause.[19]

This provision of the law was enacted immediately after the
Civil War and, as first conceived, was meant to apply only to
those states which had been members of the Confederacy. The
idea was that the people and governments of the South were
obviously resentful at the outcome of the War and feeling
against Yankees ran particularly high.[20] But in its final form,
all reference to " insurgent states " was omitted, and the legislation now stands as a general invitation to all non resident
suitors who may become victims of local influence or prejudice
to try their cases in federal courts. However, this provision of
the law does not dispense with the requirement that diversity
of citizenship be present in order to effect removal. As a result,
the total effect of this amendment to the statute is difficult to
see.

In recent years, however, there has been some sentiment in
favor of using this idea of " local influence or prejudice " as a
springboard for a genuine modification of federal diversity

19 14 Stat. 558 (1867).

20 For an early draft of the "local influence and prejudice" statute see
37 Con. Globe 1865 (1867).

"where a suit is now pending or may hereafter be brought in any
court of any State lately in insurrection in which there is a controversy
between a citizen of such State and a citizen of another State, and the
matter in dispute exceeds $500, exclusive of costs, such citizen of another
State, whether he be plaintiff or defendant, if he will make and file in
such State court an affidavit stating that he has reason to and does believe
that, from prejudice or local influence, he will not be able to obtain justice
in such State court, may, at any time before the final hearing or trial of
the suit, file a petition in such State court for the removal of the suit into
the next circuit court of the United Sates to be held in the district where
the suit is pending..."

jurisdiction.[21] The plan is simple and has much to recommend it. Were it adopted, there would no longer be any blanket national jurisdiction based on the accident of diverse citizenship. In its place, we would have a statute providing that non resident litigants could resort to the federal courts only on a showing that local sentiment was so hostile to them as to prevent their obtaining justice from state courts.

If this were the law, occasional instances of provincialism would be as fully provided for as they have always been. Cases like *Gelpcke* v. *Dubuque* and the host of other suits over railroad-aid bonds would still be litigated in the federal courts. The principals in litigations like the Black and White and Fairmont Coal cases,[22] whose only aim was to take advantage of disparate interpretations of substantive law, would have been compelled to content themselves with locally administered justice. This would also be the fate reserved for litigants whose only purpose in claiming federal protection is to take advantage of the differences in procedure which now constitute the chief variant in the administration of local law by state and federal courts.

Such a return to the relations originally intended between our state and federal courts now seems in order. Since the Supreme Court has announced its intention to respect the decisions of state tribunals, protection against local prejudice is, as indeed it always was, the only legitimate reason for entrusting non federal controversies to national courts. It seems only logical, then, that suitors wishing to claim federal protection for their rights be required to demonstrate that they are in need of such assistance. It is virtually certain that such a reform would drastically reduce the number of diversity suits, but whether there would be any substantial use of diversity juris-

21 Following the introduction of HR 4168, 79th Cong. 2nd. Sess. (1946), which would abolish diversity jurisdiction, the American Judicature Society took a poll of its officers and directors and announced the following results: for the bill — 26; against — 31; non-committal — 6; not voting — 42. See 30 J. Am. Jud. Soc. 169 *et seq.* (1947).

22 See Chs. IV, VI, *supra*.

diction under these new conditions cannot easily be determined. Experience with the current local prejudice statute indicates little because so long as the mere showing of differences in citizenship suffices to invoke the jurisdiction of federal courts, there is no inducement for litigants to attempt the difficult task of establishing local prejudice, or for courts to develop realistic tests for its recognition. However, it seems probable that of the several classes of litigant who might be disadvantaged by hostile sentiment, corporate suitors would find it most difficult to establish federal jurisdiction on this ground. Except in very unusual circumstances, popular resentment of big business is not so overt as to be susceptible of proof satisfactory to a court of law. Members of economic, religious, and racial minorities would likely find it easier to prove danger to their causes from discrimination, but all indications are that even they would have to rely on state courts in the overwhelming number of instances.

It is well known that labor unions have met with bitter opposition and, at the present time, these organizations encounter more strenuous resistance in some localities than in others. But in their classic study of the labor injunction, Frankfurter and Greene were of the opinion that no appreciable difference in labor's treatment of federal and state judiciaries could be observed.[23] Moreover, the Strawbridge Rule which denies the existence of diversity unless all plaintiffs in a suit are of a citizenship different from all defendants makes it impossible for many unions, especially the larger ones, to invoke the federal diversity jurisdiction whether or not they are the victims of local prejudice. For a time after the Coronado Case decided that unions could be sued as legal entities in their own names,[24] it was thought that rules applicable to corporations might make

[23] See Frankfurter and Greene, *The Labor Injunction* (1930), pp. 5-17. It appears that the section of the country in which the suit takes place is more important than whether the court is state or federal.

[24] *United Mine Workers* v. *Coronado Coal Co.*, 259 US 344 (1922).

labor organizations citizens of their home states only, but the federal courts have continued to look to the citizenship of individual members.[25]

Persons who have reason to fear prejudice because of their race or religion might be thought to be the principal beneficiaries of federal protection against hostile local sentiment. But what evidence there is seems to indicate that mere assertions of membership in an unpopular minority are insufficient to establish local prejudice.[26] Yet it has been abundantly demonstrated that such prejudice exists and is often strong. For example, it is known that in many Southern communities a Negro does not dare to sue a white man except in those unusual circumstances where he is able to secure a white " patron " to support his interests.[27] But this type of community pressure operates on a prospective litigant before he ever comes into court and is just as strong in discouraging Negroes to bring civil suits into federal courts as into state courts.

Indeed the social pressure which has induced minority groups to relinquish some of their rights under the threat of local reprisal probably goes far to explain why the famous cases wherein the Supreme Court has reversed state decisions which deprive Negroes and other racial minorities of their rights have almost always been criminal prosecutions.[28] In a similar con-

---

25 *Levering & Garrigues Co.* v. *Morrin*, 61 F 2d 115 (CCA 2nd. 1932) ; *Washington Cleaning and Dyeing Co.* v. *Cleaners, Dyers & Pressers Union*, Local No. 17920, 34 F 2d 897 (CCA 8th 1929) ; Ex Parte Edelstein 30 F 2d 636 (CCA 2nd 1929).

26 *Gibson* v. *Mississippi*, 162 US 565 (1896) ; *State* v. *Bobb*, 138 Me. 242, 25 A2d 229 (1942) ; *Cooper* v. *State*, 64 Md. 40, 20 A 986 (1885) ; *Fitzgerald* v. *Allman*, 82 NC 492 (1880). See *Williams* v. *Mississippi*, 170 US 213 (1898).

27 See Dollard, *Caste and Class in a Southern Town* (1937), pp. 127, 261, 291.

28 In such cases the person who runs the risk of discrimination is a defendant who has been forced into court by the action of law enforcement officers. He does not have the opportunity to decide whether or not he shall submit his rights to judicial determination. The only significant types of

nection it is also interesting to note that a federal statute passed soon after the close of the Civil War permits persons who cannot secure justice in state courts to remove either criminal or civil suits to federal courts.[29] This statute has been little used, but the few reported instances of its use fail to disclose any examples of its employment in civil cases. Nevertheless, it seems likely that a small percentage of the cases now reaching federal courts by the diversity route do represent bona fide attempts to escape local prejudice. In order to protect the participants in such litigations it would be necessary for Congress to supply a broad statutory definition of local prejudice. The courts might then be induced to find that in specific situations there really is danger of miscarriage of justice due to hostile local sentiment.

---

cases of a non criminal nature wherein the Supreme Court has protected the civil rights of minority groups are to be found in the fields of the suffrage and the alien land laws. In the former instance the cases are usually pressed by organizations representing minority interests rather than by individual suitors. The land law cases are analogous to criminal prosecutions because they customarily arise out of attempts to deprive members of minority groups of their holdings and so do not represent situations wherein the persons discriminated against can decide whether or not to sue. See *Oyama* v. *California*, 68 S. Ct. 269 (1948)—especially the dissent of Justices Murphy and Rutledge.

[29] 18 Stat. 471 (1875).

PART V

CONCURRENT JURISDICTION

Introductory Note

In the preceding parts of this study, we have been concerned with the frictions arising out of the existence of separate systems of federal and state courts. Of course, competition between judiciaries has never been the avowed object of either national or state governments, but the course of events has produced such rivalry and has made it necessary for courts and legislatures to find ways to minimize the competition.

There is, however, a more positive side to our judicial federalism. It is often possible for national and state governments to take advantage of the increased judicial facilities resulting from the existence of separate systems of federal and state courts, and, by cooperation in law enforcement, to produce an improved brand of judicial service for the people of the entire country. The problems of intergovernmental law enforcement are many and an exhaustive study of them is beyond the scope of the present work. However, any analysis of our dual judicial system would be incomplete without a recognition of the problems and opportunities presented by the exercise of concurrent jurisdiction by federal and state courts. The following analysis is offered in the hope that it may lead the reader to an understanding of some of the basic problems raised by concurrent jurisdiction. If this part of the study raises more questions than it answers, it is because the subject has received all too little attention. It is hoped that the few remarks possible here will at least serve to clarify the nature of some of the problems.

CHAPTER XIII

PRESENT PROBLEMS AND HISTORIC CONCEPTS

In most cases courts apply the law of their own jurisdiction. As integral parts of the governments to which they belong the enforcement of domestic law is their plain duty. Moreover, as a practical matter, legal disputes are likely to be taken to tribunals near a party's residence or place of business, thus making the relevance of domestic law highly probable. There are, however, a large number of situations wherein good sense suggests that it is desirable for courts to look to the laws of a jurisdiction other than their own. Although they present by no means the only opportunities for the enforcement of foreign law, disputes arising from the flow of international trade give courts their most frequent occasions for its application. By their very nature such cases arise out of transactions partly located in each of two or more separate countries. Almost all the world's judicial systems deal with such cases and so give some effect to the laws of foreign countries. Because of its federal structure, the United States spawns an unusually large number of these " international " situations. The national government and all of the states are distinct though partial sovereigns. Consequently, there are at least forty-nine separate jurisdictions in the United States, each of them regarding the others as foreign jurisdictions for purposes of the conflict of laws. However, contact between these jurisdictions is closer and more continuous than the contact that foreign countries experience with one another because governments within the United States constitute part of the same country. It follows that cooperative enforcement of law across state lines and in the federal-state sphere is of special interest to both nation and states. Wherever called for by its conflict of laws rules, every American jurisdiction applies law emanating from other governments within the United States. If each of the states and the federal government were related to one another in precisely the same way as independent foreign countries, these conflicts rules, perhaps supplemented by treaties, would provide the only means for the intersovereignal enforcement of law. But the peculiar needs of our federalism have called forth constitutional and statutory provisions which either supplement or modify the ordinary conflict of laws principles. The resulting body of American jurisprudence is a combination of judicial and legislative ingredients designed to cope with two distinct problems: 1. The interstate enforcement of law, and 2. The federal-state enforcement of law.

INTERACTION OF " FULL FAITH AND CREDIT " AND CONFLICT OF LAWS RULES

Generally speaking, state courts determine whether they shall give effect to the law of sister states by applying their conflict of laws rules. But they must also follow the Federal Constitution which provides that: " Full Faith and Credit shall be given in each State to the public Acts, Records, and Judicial Proceedings of every other State. . . . " [1] In 1789 this " full faith and credit " clause was probably indispensable insurance of the orderly enforcement of law within the country. The exaggerated tendencies of the states toward independence of action under the Articles of Confederation made it likely that they would not respect the laws of other governments within the federation unless compelled to do so by fundamental law. Now that the conflict of laws has advanced from its comparatively undeveloped condition to an important place in American jurisprudence, it may be that the constitutional provision imposes approximately the same duty on state judiciaries that they now assume toward foreign law in general. However, the full faith

---

1 U. S. Constit., Art. IV, Sec. 1.

and credit clause continues to be important because it places the interstate enforcement of law on a firm basis by making it constitutionally impossible for the states to refuse respect to the legal creations of other members of the federalism.

Nevertheless, it should be remembered that the Constitution does not require a state to enforce the laws of sister states under all circumstances. The primary duty of state judicial systems is still to administer the law of their own jurisdiction, and the public acts, records, and judicial proceedings of another state replace the law of the forum only in a limited number of situations. In deciding what these situations are to be, the state courts are bound partly by decisions of the United States Supreme Court interpreting the Constitution and partly by their own conflict of laws rules. For example, it is settled that whereas states may occasionally refuse to enforce the law of a foreign country because it violates local conceptions of good morals and sound public policy,[2] they may not refuse to apply the law of a sister state on this public policy ground.[3] On the other hand, it is a general rule in the conflict of laws that a court will not enforce the penal laws of a foreign jurisdiction,[4] and application of this rule to the penal laws of sister states is not prevented by the full faith and credit clause.[5]

The full faith and credit clause and conflict of laws rules reduce many of the problems incident to the large number of political and judicial boundaries within the United States. If courts did not give effect to the laws of sister states, the protection of state created rights and the enforcement of state created duties would be restricted to the home jurisdiction. As a result, administration of the law would become in a measure

2 Goodrich, *Conflicts* (1938), p. 20.

3 *Fauntleroy* v. *Lum*, 210 US 230 (1908).

4 Goodrich, *supra*, note 2. See *Prigg* v. *Pennsylvania*, 16 Pet. 539, 615 (1842).

5 3 Beale, *Conflicts*, 1639, 1647 (1935). See *Huntington* v. *Attrill*, 146 US 657 (1892).

uncertain. Non residents wishing to secure their rights under state law would have to travel to or remain in the state of their creation so that they might obtain judicial enforcement of them. In almost all cases such a procedure would be inconvenient, and in many it would be impossible.

Under the present system one might almost say that there is a pooling of judicial personnel and facilities with the result that in appropriate circumstances a state may rely on its law being enforced by the judicial officers of a sister jurisdiction. However, it should be noted that such cooperative law enforcement is not, except in a very general way, the result of a preconceived plan. It is known that continuous intercourse among the people of the several states produces conflict of laws situations. But what these are to be in specific instances is left to the sequence and content of disputes in the general stream of litigation.

Problems partly similar to, but in many respects distinct from the interstate enforcement of law are presented by federal-state judicial relations. The full faith and credit clause, for example, speaks only of states. From a mere reading of the Constitution, then, it would seem possible to infer that even though federal courts are likely to encounter " public Acts, Records, and Judicial Proceedings " of a state in much the same way that state courts meet them, it is not incumbent upon federal courts to accord full faith and credit. However, the Judiciary Act of 1789 provides in part: " . . . That the records and judicial proceedings of the courts of any state, shall be proved or admitted in any other court within the United States . . . " [6] and then goes on to detail the procedure by which this shall be done. The words " any court *within the United States*" are broad enough to include both state and federal courts and seem to indicate a Congressional purpose to introduce at least some of the principles of full faith and credit into the relations between the judicial arms of federal and state governments.

6 1 Stat. 122 (1790).

Indeed, the Supreme Court has held that federal courts are bound to give full faith and credit to the records and judicial proceedings of the states.[7]

To a degree, federal court enforcement of state law is similar to local court enforcement of law emanating from a sister state. We have seen that the Rules of Decision Act directs federal tribunals to employ the laws of the states as rules of decision in cases where they apply. Since the demise of *Swift* v. *Tyson*, it cannot be said that the Rules of Decision Act refer to any specific laws or types of law. On the contrary, the Congressional enactment seeks to obtain the enforcement of whatever local laws happen to be relevant to the settlement of disputes brought to the federal judiciary. The existence of specific constitutional and statutory sanction for federal jurisdiction based on diversity of citizenship does, however, make it clear that federal courts are to have more opportunities to enforce local laws of many kinds more frequently than they otherwise would.

Federal Enforcement of State Law in Order to Protect National Interest

In two special areas statute does indicate the nature of national enforcement of local law with more particularity. The first of these enactments originated in South Carolina's Nullification Movement when that state sought to prevent the collection of customs duties by making it a crime for federal officers to collect taxes under the tariff laws of the United States. In order to meet this challenge to national authority Congress passed legislation making it possible for federal revenue officers indicted for crimes because of acts done while enforcing the federal revenue laws to remove their cases from state to federal courts.[8] When convictions are had in such removed cases, they are convictions for the violation of state criminal laws and the

---

7 *Huron Holding Co.* v. *Lincoln Mine Operating Co.*, 312 US 183 (1941), rehearing denied 313 US 598 (1941).

8 4 Stat. 632, 633-34 (1833).

offenders are punished as they would be if their cases had not been taken out of the local courts. The second statute was enacted following the Civil War and permits litigants to remove either civil or criminal cases to federal courts if they cannot receive protection for their civil rights from the local judiciaries.[9] However, the civil rights legislation and the statute dealing with officers of the United States Government are both concerned with possible local interference with the administration of federal law, in the one instance of revenue laws, in the other, provisions of the Constitution. Accordingly, it may be said that in these instances federal administration of state law is only collateral to the achievement of a national purpose. Furthermore, the federal courts do not act in cooperation with the states, but rather in order to obviate present or potential subversion of national law by local authorities.

STATE COURT ENFORCEMENT OF RIGHTS CREATED UNDER FEDERAL STATUTES

Some acts of Congress expressly provide that rights created by them may be enforced in either state or federal courts. Present day laws of this type, unlike the laws just mentioned, do not result from distrust between central and local governments. Instead they are attempts to increase the judicial personnel and facilities available for the enforcement of a limited number of federally created rights. Although these statutes are few in number, especially when measured against the total body of national legislation, they present both an opportunity and a question. The opportunity is for a better administration of federal law by intergovernmental cooperation; the question relates to the desirability of a dual judicial system wherein both nation and states may be increasingly led to duplicate one another's activities.

Between 1794 and 1815 Congress enacted a number of laws calling for state courts to exercise concurrent jurisdiction with

9 18 Stat. 471 (1875).

federal tribunals over suits by the federal government and its officers to collect certain fines, penalties, and forfeitures exacted as punishments for violations of particular statutes.[10] Many of these laws provided for state jurisdiction only where the nearest federal courthouse was more than fifty miles distant from the place where trial might be had and were clearly designed to supplement available federal resources for law enforcement. For their part, the states seem to have been quite willing to discharge the duties laid upon them by these laws even though the increased judicial business necessarily raised the cost of maintaining local courts and added to the work of local judges. However, beginning in 1815 there was a marked change in the attitude of the states. Deepening sectional antagonisms throughout the country made some of the laws unpopular in individual states and made local courts less sympathetic with their enforcement. In addition, administrative burdens gladly assumed in the beginning began to grow onerous as the number of cases arising under the federal statutes increased. A consequence of this growing disinclination to exercise concurrent jurisdiction was a series of state court decisions announcing that it was constitutionally impossible for local judiciaries to entertain suits for the enforcement of rights created by the criminal laws of the United States.[11] It was said that courts could not enforce the penal laws of a foreign sovereign and that since each of the states and the federal government were sovereign, offenders against national criminal law must be punished in national courts. As a result of this state resistance, Congress, although it did not systematically repeal existing legislation, discontinued the practice of expressly authorizing state courts to exercise concurrent jurisdiction in the administration of federal law.

10 See Warren, *Federal Criminal Laws and State Courts*, 38 Harv. L. Rev. 545, 552 *et seq.* (1925).

11 Warren, *op. cit., supra*, note 10, p. 577 *et seq.*

Of course, it should be remembered that state courts continued to enforce rights created by federal statute whenever they were willing to do so provided only that the law in question did not confer exclusive jurisdiction on the federal courts. This was strikingly illustrated in *Claflin* v. *Houseman* [12] decided by the Supreme Court in 1876. The suit was brought in a New York court to secure the return of money paid to a creditor within four months of a bankruptcy. The right to recover depended entirely on a provision of the national bankruptcy law. Moreover, that statute conferred exclusive jurisdiction over proceedings in bankruptcy on federal courts. However, *Claflin* v. *Houseman* was not really a suit in bankruptcy but merely a proceeding auxiliary thereto. The New York courts, both trial and appellate, rendered judgment for the plaintiff, thereby giving effect to the provision of the federal bankruptcy statute. The defendant argued that since the right in dispute existed under an act of Congress, state courts were inherently lacking in power to enforce it. The United States Supreme Court affirmed the New York decision and its opinion emphasized that the states and the federal government formed part of a single nation. It followed that state courts were not barred from enforcing federally created rights unless forbidden to do so by express provision or by necessary implication from federal statute.

Helpful as this kind of voluntary state cooperation might be, it was not always enough to insure the efficient administration of federal law. Just as in the days before 1815, Congress might deem it especially desirable that rights created under particular statutes be regularly protected by local judiciaries. Congress could count on such state cooperation only if it could confer concurrent jurisdiction over suits arising under named federal statutes and require state courts to exercise that jurisdiction. Where federal courts did not provide adequate facilities because of their distance from the scene of prospective litigation or

12 93 US 130 (1876).

because of their overcrowded dockets, reliance on state judicial officers offered a promising means of increasing the resources available for administration of federal law.

During the latter part of the nineteenth century, Congress once more began to experiment with legislation authorizing state courts to take jurisdiction concurrent with inferior national tribunals in certain prescribed instances. By a series of laws relating to individual tribes and their reservations, Congress empowered state courts to take a hand in the supervision of Indian lands and to determine the heirs eligible to inherit " allotted " lands.[13] In western states where reservation Indians were to be found in large numbers, the activities of state courts in these matters assumed some importance. Indeed, this was and still is especially evident in states like Oklahoma where oil has been discovered on Indian lands and where the management of " allotted " holdings has been complicated by a desire to exploit the petroleum resources. Moreover, much of the work done by the courts of Oklahoma and other states is particularly useful because it lies in the field of probate. Federal district courts exercise no jurisdiction in probate and if required to do so in areas where there are Indian reservations, they would have to establish special machinery in order to deal with problems of inheritance of Indian lands.

The cooperativeness exhibited by local courts in sharing the burdens placed upon them by federal Indian laws was a gratifying example of amicable federal-state relations. State judicial officers recognized that in a sense they were acting as agents of the national government,[14] but they were not inclined to offer this as an argument for declining jurisdiction. The result was that the Congressional provision for concurrent federal and state jurisdiction was a working reality within this one field but that the legal questions raised by state courts at a much earlier date

13 Cohen, *Handbook of Federal Indian Law* (1942), pp. 118-119.

14 See *Marcy* v. *Board of Com'rs. of Seminole County*, 45 Okl. 1, 7, 144 P. 611, 613 (1914).

went temporarily unanswered. Indeed, whether Congress had the power to compel local courts to enforce rights created by and solely dependent on federal statute could not be known for certain until a state should once more refuse to enforce such rights. This did not happen until after the passage of the Federal Employers' Liability Act in 1908.[15]

In the cases to which it applied, the statute removed the "fellow servant" rule [16] thereby making it much easier for workmen injured in the course of their employment to succeed in actions brought against their employers. An additional feature of the law was a provision to the effect that state courts were to exercise concurrent jurisdiction over suits arising under the act and that no cases begun in local courts could be removed to federal courts. Here was the strongest possible reliance on local judicial machinery short of leaving the administration of the law completely in state hands. A case brought in the Superior Court of Connecticut raised the question of federal power. On appeal to the highest court of the state, it was held that Congress could not force the Connecticut judiciary to entertain employees' suits where the sole ground for the actions was the Federal Employers' Liability Act.

The case, *Mondou* v. *New York, New Haven, & Hartford R. Co.*,[17] was an action brought by an injured railroad worker. In the particular circumstances of his case, Mondou was not entitled to compensation for his injury under Connecticut law. That state followed the "fellow servant" rule,[18] and it appeared that Mondou's injury had been caused by the negligence of

15 35 Stat. 65 (1908).

16 At common law an injured employee could not recover from his employer unless the injury was due to the fault of the latter. If the negligence of a "fellow servant" (employee) was responsible for the accident, the employer was not liable.

17 82 Conn. 373 (1909), following *Hoxie* v. *New York, N. H. & H. R. Co.*, 82 Conn. 352 (1909), decided on the same day.

18 See *Hoxie* v. *New York, N. H. & H. R. Co.*, 82 Conn. 352, 355 (1909).

another worker. The Court reasoned that Congress could not force a state tribunal to grant a remedy where local law emphatically denied the existence of one. Enforcement of the Federal Employers' Liability Act was said to contravene the public policy of the state. It followed that if the workman was to secure his rights under the federal statute, he must do so in a federal court. However, the United States Supreme Court reversed this decision [19] and pointed out that in the words of the Constitution, laws of Congress are " the supreme law of the land ". In cases where it applied, the Federal Employers' Liability Act was law in all the states and its public policy became a part of the public policy of Connecticut.

If there had been doubt of the Congressional power to require local courts to take concurrent jurisdiction with federal tribunals in ordinary civil cases arising under federal statutes, the Mondou case made the existence of such a power clear. But the decision could not provide an answer to all the questions raised by the nearly one hundred year old state refusal to enforce " penal " laws of the United States. At the time, such a problem was not of pressing interest. However, several statutes of which the Emergency Price Control Act in force during World War II and the Fair Labor Standards Act are notable examples, have brought this question to the fore. Laws such as these provide that private persons injured as a result of violations of the particular statute may sue the violator and recover two or three times the amount of their damages plus attorneys' fees. Although the government does not receive the money paid by unsuccessful defendants in these suits, the laws are intentionally punitive in character. Are such laws penal, and do provisions calling for the exercise of concurrent jurisdiction by state and federal courts compel local judiciaries to participate in their enforcement?

Most states have readily accepted the duties assigned to their courts by these Congressional enactments and have offered no

19 Second Employers' Liability Cases, 223 US 1 (1912).

opportunity for a decision of the question. However, in 1947, the case of *Testa* v. *Katt* [20] reached the Supreme Court from Rhode Island. This was a private suit under the treble damages provision of the Price Control Act.[21] It was brought to recover three times the amount of an overcharge on a used automobile. The highest court of Rhode Island, relying on one of its own precedents,[22] held that the provision of the act was penal and for that reason could not be enforced in a court of the state despite the express direction of the law that state courts were to exercise concurrent jurisdiction in its enforcement.[23]

In giving effect to federal statutes containing extraordinary damage provisions, state courts have usually declined to classify them as penal [24] and so have avoided the necessity for determining whether they could or would enforce the penal laws of another jurisdiction. But in *Testa* v. *Katt* the Supreme Court speaking through Mr. Justice Black said:

" For the purpose of this case, we assume, without deciding, that Sec. 205(e) is a penal statute in the ' public international,' ' private international ', or any other sense. So far as the question of whether the Rhode Island courts properly declined to try this action, it makes no difference into which of these categories the Rhode Island court chose to place the statute which Congress had passed. For we cannot accept the basic premise on which the Rhode Island Supreme Court held that it has no more obligation to enforce a valid penal law

20 330 US 386 (1947).

21 56 Stat. 34 (1942), as amended 58 Stat. 632, 640 (1944).

22 *Robinson* v. *Norato*, 71 R. I. 256, 43 A2d 467 (1945).

23 *Testa* v. *Katt*, 71 R. I. 472, 47 A2d 312 (1946).

24 Note, *Utilization of State Courts to Enforce Federal Penal and Criminal Statutes*, 60 Harv. L. Rev. 966 (1947). See Hatton, *State Court Jurisdiction of Federal Rights of Action—Emergency Price Control Act*, 40 Ill. L. Rev. 355, 364-368 (1946). Rhode Island was one of the states to hold the extraordinary damages provision of the Fair Labor Standards Act non penal and to enforce it. *Newman* v. *George A. Fuller Co.*, 72 R. I. 113, 48 A2d 345 (1946).

of the United States than it has to enforce a penal law of another state or a foreign country. Such a broad assumption flies in the face of the fact that the States of the Union constitute a nation. It disregards the purpose or the effect of Article VI of the Constitution." [25]

The Testa Decision makes it clear that the national government has a special claim on the states in matters of law enforcement. It would seem that, with a few possible exceptions, Congress may now require local judicial systems to take jurisdiction of cases arising under federal statutes of all kinds.[26] An expanded use of concurrent jurisdiction opens up large possibilities for the more effective administration of federal law. However, any extensive imposition of new burdens on state courts would raise serious questions of practice and policy.

The statutes which now call upon state courts to exercise jurisdiction concurrent with national courts create new rights. The relevant provision of the Fair Labor Standards Act, for example, permits actions for wrongfully withheld back wages [27] which would be meaningless if it were not for other provisions of the same act. Such laws necessarily result in an increase of the amount of judicial work. To the extent that state courts administer these federal statutes, the national judiciary is relieved of the increasing burden, but it is also true that the number of cases to be dealt with by the state judiciaries grows by the very process of unburdening the national system. Local courts are maintained by the states and as the volume of their business expands, the cost of operating them also mounts. The more federal business the state judiciaries are called upon to handle, the more significant this financial burden will become.

25 330 US 386, 389.

26 Jurisdiction in admiralty is exercised exclusively by the federal courts and it has been held that state courts inherently lack the power to exercise such jurisdiction. *Southern Pacific Co.* v. *Jensen*, 244 US 205 (1917). However, the Jensen doctrine is strictly limited to the admiralty field. See *Standard Dredging Corporation* v. *Murphy*, 319 US 306 (1943).

27 52 Stat. 1060, 1069 (1938).

At the present time, the federal government makes no contribution to the upkeep of state court systems. However, any further expansion of national reliance on state machinery may raise the question of federal aid in meeting the expense. Assuming the desirability of state enforcement of certain federal laws, it would seem that the national government might find it worth while to carry part of the financial burden. The most likely alternative would involve an expansion of the present federal court system at a cost probably greater than that of payment for federal work done by local courts. Indeed, United States District Courts are nowhere as numerous as organs of the various state systems and it is probable that no foreseeable growth in federal judicial business would justify a degree of expansion which would make United States courts as fully accessible to all of the people as local tribunals.

Even more important to our judicial federalism than the problems of finance is the advisability of concurrent jurisdiction. The comparatively few causes of action now maintainable in either federal or state courts by virtue of express statutory provision include types of cases where the practice has real advantages. Suits for wrongfully withheld wages under the Fair Labor Standards Act and actions under the Federal Employers' Liability Act are both types of litigation wherein persons of modest means seek to enforce claims against employers whose financial resources are often extensive. In these cases the burdens of litigation are more serious for the claimants than for their adversaries, and the geographical accessibility of judicial machinery weighs more heavily in the scales of justice than is normally the case.

A general broadening of the area wherein federally created rights might be enforced in either local or national courts would raise a deeper issue. If the time were ever to come when national and state judiciaries spent a substantial portion of their energies in enforcing the same laws, it would be appropriate to ask whether a wasteful and confusing duplication of effort did not exist. It might then be desirable to plan for the consolidation of federal and state courts into a single judicial system. The decision in *Testa* v. *Katt* makes it clear that there is no constitutional obstacle to an overdevelopment of concurrent jurisdiction.[28] However, it is Congress which decides when and in how many instances it shall require state courts to entertain suits for the assertion of rights created by federal statute. Legislative action may some day make the question a pressing one, but for the present it seems likely that, when due allowance is made for the expansion of our country and the increased tempo of all governmental activity, Congress relies far less on concurrent state enforcement of its statutes than it was wont to do prior to 1815. Consequently, the danger, if any there be, lies in the future rather than in the present.

28 using *McCulloch* v. *Maryland*, 4 Wheat. 316 (1819) as an analogy, the courts might decide that an unreasonable expansion of federal reliance on state courts would place an undue burden on instrumentalities of state government. However, such an approach would be difficult because the courts must decide individual cases as they arise and it is unlikely that any single case or statute would of itself produce an unreasonable burden.

PART VI

CONCLUSION

AN APPRAISAL

So long as our dual judicial system continues to operate, there will probably be a certain amount of friction in the area where federal and state jurisdictions meet. It is unlikely that any scheme for the allotment of judicial tasks among our present judiciaries can insure anywhere near a complete segregation of questions relating to local and national law and thereby avoid the need for coordinating the day-by-day administration of justice in all our courts. It may be, however, that advantages flowing from the present system outweigh the difficulties inherent in the existing structure of our judicial establishment, and if this be so, there is good reason to preserve the main features of our dual court system, even though we recognize its limitations. But before we can either justify or condemn the existing structure, there are two questions that should be answered: 1. Does the federal structure of the United States require or make it advisable that substantially independent systems of national and state courts exist, and 2. If the present system is to continue, what should be the division of jurisdiction between federal and state judiciaries?

Is a Dual Judiciary Necessary or Advisable?

The propriety of having state courts has not been seriously challenged during the entire period from Independence to the present day. The states had their judiciaries before the adoption of the Constitution and it seems to have been taken for granted that local courts would continue to function after the new form of government was adopted. On the other hand, an extensive network of federal courts might never have been developed. The Constitution mentions only the Supreme Court by name and leaves the creation of inferior tribunals to the discretion of Congress. But one of the first enactments of the national legislature established lower federal courts and they have continued to grow in number and importance throughout our history. Indeed steady expansion has characterized both federal and state judicial systems during the past century and a half. As a growing population and an ever more complex social fabric have produced more disputes requiring judicial settlement, the courts of nation and states alike have come to be busier and busier.

However, justification for separate federal and state courts is not to be found in the mere size of the judicial load. Were volume of business the sole consideration, it would be more appropriate to increase the personnel and facilities available to a single judiciary. If it is desirable to maintain both federal and state courts, it must be that the work done by each judiciary presents its own peculiar problems and that judges unfamiliar with them are not likely to function effectively. It is, of course, true that any competent person with adequate training in the ways of Anglo-American law can find and eventually master the substantive and procedural rules in force in any jurisdiction within the United States. But learning takes time and the crowded condition of modern court calendars makes sureness and speed an indispensable element in the administration of justice. Because they are constantly applying the laws of their own jurisdiction, judges are familiar with them and, although continual checking of domestic precedents and statutes is made necessary by the complexity and vastness of modern law, it seems reasonable to expect courts to enforce the law of their own jurisdiction authoritatively and efficiently. It is less reasonable to expect courts to deal satisfactorily with the laws of another jurisdiction.

In the United States there are, not counting the Territories and Dependencies, forty-nine different jurisdictions, forty-eight state, and one federal. So long as these jurisdictions have the power to legislate for themselves, and so long as the courts in all of them continue to elaborate their own bodies of common law, it is obvious that a single judicial system, whether it belonged to the nation or to the states, would have to face the confusion attendant upon its attempts to master and enforce divergent principles of law. Such an arrangement could hardly be satisfactory. Consequently, it is submitted that the federal structure of the United States makes a dual judicial system highly desirable.

Nor is the need for effective legal administration the only reason for the existence of separate federal and state courts. The provisions for appeal to the Supreme Court in cases involving federal law contained in the Constitution and the first Judiciary Act demonstrate an early recognition that some insurance against frustration of federal policy by misinterpretation in local courts is necessary. The need for state control over the content of local law is equally as great. Our experience with the Tyson Rule gave ample evidence that independent federal interpretation of local common law and statutes could have a seriously upsetting effect. Of course, the worst effects of *Swift* v. *Tyson* have disappeared since its reversal in 1938, but in spite of the Supreme Court's declaration that the federal judiciary's obligation to follow local precedents is a constitutional one and perhaps because of it, the need for state courts which have authority to make final determinations in matters of local law remains undiminished. Moreover, it is a commonplace that judicial interpretation is often a creative part of the law-making process, and not merely a reiteration of predetermined legislative policy.

How Should Jurisdiction Be Divided Between Federal and State Courts?

In order to receive the benefits of a dual judicial system, it is necessary that federal and state courts occupy themselves primarily with the interpretation and enforcement of law emanating from the government to which they belong. When Congress made it possible for the lower federal courts to take original cognizance of cases arising under the Constitution and laws of the United States, it took a long step toward establishing a satisfactory division of judicial labor between the judiciaries within our federal system. However, there are still a number of obstacles to a symmetrical allotment of judicial jurisdiction between nation and states. Some of them can be justified as necessary or convenient exceptions to the general rule that in a federal system questions of national importance should be handled by the central government whereas matters of primarily local significance should be dealt with by the states. But other incongruities in our present jurisdictional arrangement are more difficult to defend.

The Constitution itself makes it incumbent on the states and their courts to enforce federal law when it provides that the Federal Constitution, laws, and treaties shall be the supreme law of the land. But as we have seen, the Supremacy Clause does not result in a general enforcement of local rights created by national statute or common law. So far as this constitutional provision prevents state nullification of national policies it is a necessary safeguard against the undercutting of the central government, but it does not seriously divert the attention of state courts from the enforcement of local law.

The exercise of concurrent jurisdiction pursuant to acts of Congress like the Federal Employers' Liability Act, the Fair Labor Standards Act, and the Emergency Price Control Act raise more perplexing questions. In so far as state courts are required to enforce rights accruing under these laws, they must administer law with whose principles they may be less familiar than they are with enactments of their own local legislatures. Indeed the same courts which hear cases arising under the FLSA and the Employers' Liability Act are often called upon to administer their own state labor laws and workmen's compensation statutes. When asked to operate in all of these related fields where the problems calling for judicial attention are similar, but where the substantive rules of law and remedies provided may diverge, it may well be that opportunities for confusion and mistaken administration of the law can result. When federal courts are not readily accessible, there is good reason to ask state judiciaries to assume additional burdens because the practical result of an alternative course would be to deny the protection of the law to many persons with just claims. But it should be recognized that state court enforcement of federally created rights is advisable only where litigants may not reasonably be expected to make use of the federal courts. If one may judge from the character of the statutory rights now enforceable in both federal and state courts, it would seem that Congress has impliedly recognized the special nature and limited usefulness of concurrent jurisdiction.

The only serious difficulty with our present division of judicial labor between nation and states is to be found in the exercise of diversity jurisdiction by the federal courts. So long as it is possible for any person, provided only that his dispute involve three thousand dollars or more, to bring virtually any question of state law into a national court for decision, it is inevitable that a certain amount of wasteful and confusing competition between our various judicial systems should exist. Story did not think of independent federal judgment as a promoter of rivalry, but despite his earnest hope for uniformity in federal and state common law, disagreement and friction was the product of *Swift* v. *Tyson*. It is true that the worst features of the Tyson Rule have been swept away by *Erie* v. *Tompkins,* but no judicial decision can keep questions of state law in local courts as long as diversity jurisdiction remains in its present form and litigants see, or think they see advantages to be had by shopping for a forum. Undoubtedly, there is need to protect a limited number of suitors against the local prejudice which forms the only reasonable justification for diversity jurisdiction. However, the needs of this group, in so far as the federal courts may possibly afford them a haven from hostile local sentiment, could be served by a much more narrowly drawn diversity statute that would apply specifically to the situations needing attention. Such a drastic curtailment of the diversity jurisdiction would have two beneficial results: 1. It would make the reason for resort to federal authority clear, and 2. It would make it unnecessary for federal judges to enforce unfamiliar state law except in those few instances where local authorities cannot or will not protect the rights of individual citizens.

Any student of our dual judiciary is early brought to realize that the mere existence of more than one set of courts creates problems. Even when the system functions smoothly, it is necessary to mark out the boundaries to be observed by federal and state judiciaries and to perfect a set of rules whereby conflict and confusion can be kept at a minimum in the border areas where federal and state jurisdiction meet. But these are problems to be faced in all phases of national-state relations. Of course, the high degree of initiative left in the hands of the private litigant makes the problems of judicial federalism more difficult to attack, but the tools are at hand. The constitutional grant of extensive judicial power to the United States makes it unlikely that state courts can exercise jurisdiction beyond the bounds of local law without at least the tacit consent of the national government. The present willingness of our federal courts to apply local law as interpreted by local courts does much to simplify intergovernmental judicial relations. The rest is up to Congress which, by regulating the jurisdiction of the federal courts can restrict the operations of our federal judiciary to areas of genuine national concern.

SELECTED BIBLIOGRAPHY

The reference materials that I have used are cited at the appropriate places in the notes. The following is meant only as a partial list of those books which I have found especially helpful as background reading.

Adams, Henry. *History of the United States During the Administrations of Thomas Jefferson and James Madison.* Houghton Mifflin Company. Boston, 1909.

Anderson, William. *American Government* (3rd ed.). Henry Holt & Company. New York, 1946.

Beard, Charles A. *An Economic Interpretation of the Constitution of the United States.* The Macmillan Company. New York, 1913.

Bureau of Labor Statistics No. 499. *History of Wages in the United States from Colonial Times to 1928.* 1929.

Cardozo, Benjamin N. *Nature of the Judicial Process.* Yale University Press. New Haven, 1922.

Carr, Robert K. *Federal Protection of Civil Rights.* Cornell University Press. Ithaca, N. Y., 1947.

Clark, Dan E. *The West in American History.* Thomas Y. Crowell Company. New York, 1937.

Commager, Henry S. *Documents of American History* (4th ed.). F. S. Crofts & Company. New York, 1948.

Cook, Walter W. *The Logical and Legal Bases of the Conflict of Laws.* Harvard University Press. Cambridge, 1942.

Dollard, John. *Caste and Class in a Southern Town.* Yale University Press. New Haven, 1937.

Fisher, Irving. *The Purchasing Power of Money.* The Macmillan Company. New York, 1920.

Frankfurter, Felix and Greene, Nathan. *The Labor Injunction.* The Macmillan Company. New York, 1930.

Frankfurter, Felix and Landis, James M. *The Business of the Supreme Court.* The Macmillan Company. New York, 1928.

Hafen, Leroy R. and Rister, Carl C. *Western America.* Prentice-Hall. New York, 1941.

Hamilton, Alexander, Madison, James and Jay, John. *The Federalist.*

Henderson, Gerard C. *The Position of Foreign Corporations in American Constitutional Law.* Harvard University Press. Cambridge, 1918.

Holdsworth, William S. *History of English Law.* Methuen & Company. London, 1924.

Holt, George C. *The Concurrent Jurisdiction of Federal and State Courts.* 1888.

Myers, Gustavus. *History of the Supreme Court of the United States.* C. H. Knox & Company. Chicago, 1912.

Oppenheimer, Heinrich. *The Constitution of the German Republic.* Stevens and Company. London, 1923.

Pepper, George W. *The Borderland of Federal and State Decisions.* 1889.

Pound, Roscoe. *The Spirit of the Common Law.* Marshall Jones & Company. Boston, 1925.

Prentiss, Hervey P. *Timothy Pickering as Leader of New England Federalism, 1800-1815.* Salem, Mass., 1934.

Quiett, Glen C. *They Built the West.* D. Appleton-Century Company. New York, 1934.

Story, William W. *Life and Letters of Joseph Story.* C. C. Little & J. Brown Company. Boston, 1851.

Turner, Frederick J. *Significance of Sections in American History.* Henry Holt & Company. New York, 1932.

Warren, Charles. *The Supreme Court and Sovereign States.* Princeton University Press. Princeton, 1924.

Warren, Charles. *The Supreme Court in United States History* (rev. ed.). Little, Brown & Company. Boston, 1947.

TABLE OF CASES

INDEX